INTERNATIONAL MIGRATION AND RURAL AREAS

Studies in Migration and Diaspora

Series Editor:
Anne J. Kershen, Queen Mary College, University of London, UK

Studies in Migration and Diaspora is a series designed to showcase the interdisciplinary and multidisciplinary nature of research in this important field. Volumes in the series cover local, national and global issues and engage with both historical and contemporary events. The books will appeal to scholars, students and all those engaged in the study of migration and diaspora. Amongst the topics covered are minority ethnic relations, transnational movements and the cultural, social and political implications of moving from 'over there', to 'over here'.

Also in the series:

Migrant Women Transforming Citizenship
Life-stories From Britain and Germany
Umut Erel
ISBN 978-0-7546-7494-8

Polish Migration to the UK in the 'New' European Union
After 2004
Kathy Burrell
ISBN 978-0-7546 7387-3

Gendering Migration
Masculinity, Femininity and Ethnicity in Post-War Britain
Edited by Louise Ryan and Wendy Webster
ISBN 978-0-7546-7178-7

Contemporary British Identity
English Language, Migrants and Public Discourse
Christina Julios
ISBN 978-0-7546-7158-9

Migration and Domestic Work
A European Perspective on a Global Theme
Edited by Helma Lutz
ISBN 978-0-7546-4790-4

International Migration and Rural Areas
Cross-National Comparative Perspectives

Edited by

BIRGIT JENTSCH
Ionad Nàiseanta na h-Imrich
(National Centre for Migration Studies), Scotland

MYRIAM SIMARD
Institut National de la Recherche Scientifique, Canada

ASHGATE

Published by
Ashgate Publishing Limited
Wey Court East
Union Road
Farnham
Surrey, GU9 7PT
England

Ashgate Publishing Company
Suite 420
101 Cherry Street
Burlington
VT 05401-4405
USA

www.ashgate.com

British Library Cataloguing in Publication Data
International migration and rural areas : cross-national
  comparative perspectives. -- (Studies in migration and
  diaspora)
  1. Emigration and immigration--Social aspects.
  2. Emigration and immigration--Economic aspects.
  3. Sociology, Rural. 4. Rural conditions--Case studies.
  5. Manpower policy, Rural--Case studies.
  I. Series II. Jentsch, Birgit. III. Simard, Myriam
  305.9'06912'091734-dc22

Library of Congress Cataloging-in-Publication Data
Jentsch, Birgit.
  International migration and rural areas : cross-national comparative perspectives / by
Birgit Jentsch and Myriam Simard.
    p. cm. -- (Studies in migration and diaspora)
  Includes index.
  ISBN 978-0-7546-7484-9
  1. Urban-rural migration--Case studies. 2. Rural development--Case studies. I. Simard,
Myriam - II. Title.

  HB1956.J46 2009
  307.2'6--dc22

                                                                    2009016683
ISBN   9780754674849 (hbk)
ISBN   9780754697879 (ebk)

Mixed Sources
Product group from well-managed
forests and other controlled sources
www.fsc.org Cert no. SGS-COC-2482
© 1996 Forest Stewardship Council

Printed and bound in Great Britain by
TJ International Ltd, Padstow, Cornwall

Contents

To Philip – B.J.

List of Figures and Tables

Figures

Tables

Notes on Contributors

Liam Coakley is a social and cultural geographer, with a particular interest in the geographies of everyday environments. He is currently employed as an assistant lecturer in the Department of Geography, Mary Immaculate College, at the University of Limerick, Ireland. Liam has also been employed in the Department of Geography, University College Cork, Ireland and the Department of Geography, University of Otago, New Zealand. Over the past number of years, he has researched issues of identity and difference in Ireland. His special interests include the experiences of immigrant communities. Liam has authored a number of papers/reports on the experience of immigration to Ireland and has published/presented them in a variety of appropriate fora.

Mike Danson is Professor of Scottish and Regional Economics, and Associate Dean of Research at the University of the West of Scotland, as well as Treasurer of the British Academy of Social Sciences. He has a strong academic and applied interest in regional and rural economic development and, in the last 5 years, has been editor of 5 books, had 20 refereed articles published, contributed 20 chapters in books and presented nearly 50 conference papers. Mike also has a wide range of expertise and experience in regeneration analysis and evaluation, including a secondment to Future Skills Scotland to explore research and policy issues regarding 'employability'. He is well known across Europe and has organised over 60 national and international conferences since 1980 across the continent, including several meetings around employment and demographic change. Mike is a member of the Economic and Social Cohesion Advisory Group of the West of Scotland European Partnership and has acted as advisor to the European Commission, UN Economic Commission for Europe, WHO, various Scottish, UK and local governments and development agencies on such issues as regional policy, demographic and population change, the Scotch Whisky industry, land reform, poverty and inclusion, regional development agencies, the Gaelic economy, employability, ageing and volunteering. He was commissioned to undertake the first ever research for the Scottish Parliament and research for the first ever independent debate in the Parliament, he delivered the first ever paper at a cross-party conference in Holyrood, and has presented research on Whisky to the House of Commons, and on volunteering to underpin the Volunteering Strategy for Scotland.

Irina Ivakhnyuk is a Senior Researcher and Deputy-Director of the Population Department at the Faculty of Economics, Moscow State Lomonosov University. She is a Demography graduate of Moscow State Lomonosov University and was awarded her Doctoral (Candidate of Science/PhD) Degree in Population Economics at the Russian Academy of Sciences in 1981. In 2008 she successfully defended her post-doctoral Population Economics Degree, with its focus on the Eurasian migration system, and is now a Doctor of Science and full Professor. Irina specialises on international migration studies, including migration trends, migration and development, migration and security, and migration management. She is a lecturer on the course 'World Labour Markets and International Labour Migration: the Space for Russia' for Master students at the Faculty of Economics of her University. She has been an invited guest lecturer to a number of overseas institutions on migration issues in the CIS region. Irina is the Executive Secretary of the scientific series 'International Migration of Population: Russia and the Contemporary World'. She performs as an expert on migration at the Council of Europe, the International Organization of Migration (IOM), the UN Population Division, the UN Population Fund (UNFPA), the Organization for Security and Co-operation in Europe (OSCE). Irina is the author of more than 90 publications.

Leif Jensen is Professor of Rural Sociology and Demography at The Pennsylvania State University (USA), where he served as Director of the Population Research Institute from 2003 to 2006. He received a Ph.D. in Sociology from the University of Wisconsin – Madison in 1987. On the faculty at Penn State since 1989, his research and teaching interests are found within social stratification and poverty, demography, and international development. Beginning with his doctoral dissertation research, Jensen has had a stream of research projects and publications on immigration to the United States. This work has examined immigrant poverty and use of social welfare programs; the circumstances of the children of immigrants (the second generation); the impact of enclave economies on the economic status of immigrants; and immigrant underemployment. More recently he has focused on immigrants in small cities and towns, and rural areas of the United States. This research has explored Dominican-origin immigrants in Reading, Pennsylvania; the educational and employment aspirations of teenagers in families of migrant farm workers; and the causes, nature and consequences of new rural immigrant settlements.

Birgit Jentsch is Senior Researcher at *Ionad Nàiseanta na h-Imrich* (INI) (National Centre for Migration Studies) on the Isle of Skye in Scotland. She obtained her PhD in Social Policy from the University of Edinburgh (UK) in 1997. She has been a principal researcher on a wide range of policy and practice relevant research projects at Scottish, European and global level. Before joining INI in 2004 as senior researcher, Birgit held the posts of research fellow and deputy manager of a global research project (co-ordinated by the University of Aberdeen) exploring access to health services of the poorest rural and urban women in developing countries. Prior to this, she researched on and co-ordinated a European Commission funded cross-national project on rural development, comparing the situation of seven EU countries. Her most recent activities have focused on research with immigrants and receiving communities in mainly rural and remote areas of Scotland.

Charalambos Kasimis is Professor of Rural Sociology at the Department of Agricultural Economics and Rural Development, University of Athens. He .holds a BSc in Economics, an MPhil in Industrial Sociology and a PhD in Rural Sociology from the University of Bradford (UK). He served as a member of staff at the Department of Economics of the University of Patras between 1986–2003 while for the period 1995–2000 he was the Director of the Institute of Urban and Rural Sociology of the National Centre for Social Research of Greece. Additionally, he has co-edited a special issue of the journal *Sociologia Ruralis* entitled: *Rural Greece: Fragile Structures and New Realities* (1997). His research interests have focused on questions of rural transformation and development in Greece and the Balkans and more particularly on family farming, employment and rural community change. Migration and, more particularly, migration to rural regions has become one of his research priorities in the past years.

Piaras Mac Éinrí is a Lecturer in Geography (migration studies) at the Department of Geography in University College Cork and was Director from 1997–2003 of the inter-disciplinary Irish Centre for Migration Studies focusing on Irish and comparative international migration research. He is an advisor to the Dublin-based NGO, the Immigrant Council of Ireland, and was a member from 2003–2005 of the National Consultative Committee on Racism and Interculturalism. He has lectured and published extensively in the fields of Irish and comparative migration studies, with a particular interest in immigration and integration issues. He is programme director of an MA programme in contemporary migration and diaspora studies at Cork.

Myriam Simard holds the post of research professor at the National Institute of Scientific Research (*Institut National de la Recherche Scientifique*) of the University of Quebec (INRS – Urbanisation, Culture et Société). Trained in anthropology and sociology, her principal research field comprises immigration outside urban centres. She has studied, over an 18-year period, diverse immigration populations in Quebec: immigrant agricultural entrepreneurs and their families; seasonal migrant workers in agriculture; locally established youth from immigrant families; and immigrants who worked as medical professionals and their families in remote rural areas.

She is particularly well recognised for her expertise in rural immigration. Her studies have adopted a diachronic and inter-generational perspective, examining especially integration processes of parents as well as youth with an immigration background; their contributions to rural and regional development; factors which attract immigrants to and keep them in the region; work and migration practices; cultural reconstitution; and transnational links. She spent one year in 2004 on a sabbatical stay in France and Scotland, comparing the transformation of the rurality with the arrival of new populations. She has published extensively in these fields, including the following relevant cross-national study, which compares the situation of new rural populations in Québec, France and United Kingdom,

'Nouvelles populations rurales et conflits au Québec: regards croisés avec la France et le Royaume-Uni', *Géographie, Économie, Société*, Vol. 9, No. 2 (avril-juin 2007), Lavoisier, France, 187–213.

Tse-Chuan Yang is a Research Associate in Spatial Social Science in the Social Science Research Institute at The Pennsylvania State University (USA). He received his Ph.D. in Rural Sociology and Demography from Penn State in 2008. His research focuses on rural health, health disparities, demography, and social inequality. His dissertation research explored rural-urban differences in mortality in the United States, and shed new light on the paradoxically lower mortality rates in rural areas. Drawing on his methodological expertise in spatial statistics and hierarchical modelling, he is involved in several projects examining the dynamics of poverty in developing countries; the impacts of neighbourhood environment on education and health; and spatially varying effects of rapid climate change on health.

Acknowledgements

Both editors would like to express their sincere thanks to The British Academy for awarding a grant which allowed all contributors to gather at *Ionad Nàiseanta na h-Imrich* (INI – the National Centre for Migration Studies) and discuss the book project.

The meeting proved enormously helpful for the preparation of the individual chapters and strengthening the book's overall coherence.

We acknowledge and thank Annette Kerr of INI for her contributions to the preparation of the typescript. Birgit is grateful to Sabhal Mòr Ostaig and the University of the Highlands and Islands Millennium Institute (UHI) for approving and sponsoring sabbatical leave, which allowed her the time and opportunity to co-edit this book.

On a personal note, Birgit and Myriam are grateful to their partners, Graeme and Raymond, for their never failing support and patience throughout this project.

Series Editor's Preface
International Migration and Rural Areas

The first decade of the 21st century has been one in which the movement of people around the globe has continued at a pace. *The World Migration Report 2008*,[1] issued by the IOM, calculates the figure of global migrants to stand at over 214 million people – economic migrants, asylum seekers and refugees, seasonal workers and retirees all heading for new destinations. Traditionally it has been urban centres, particularly major cities and industrial areas, which have attracted immigrants and provided the first points of settlement. Glasgow, London, Madrid, New York and Paris have all played host to outsiders who cluster in the poorer areas of the city, often moving into the homes – and economic activities – vacated by earlier migrants who have moved on. However, settlement patterns have taken on a fresh dimension, as recently, new arrivals have shown a tendency to locate in rural, as opposed to urban, areas. For those concerned with the welfare of new immigrants and the impact of immigration on the receiving society, this phenomenon brings with it a range of needs, problems and benefits, which often differ from those that occur in a metropolitan environment.

One would assume that an automatic outcome of this development would be published research and analysis that identifies the implications of this trend. Yet, as the editors of this ground breaking volume note, whilst there has been, and continues to be, an ever increasing number of works on urban immigration, little or nothing has appeared which addresses current rural immigration. In putting together this book Birgit Jentsch and Myriam Simard buck the trend and provide readers with a 'cross-national perspective' of 21st century rural migration presented by leading academics from North America, Southern and Western Europe and Russia.

As the contributions in the volume highlight, the major factors which emerge from rural immigration not only echo those which arise from urban settlement, in addition they illuminate those which are peculiar to small communities often distant from large conurbations. A prime concern of all receiving countries, irrespective of migrant spatial location, is the integration process of newcomers; integration defined and analysed in the context of the economic, social, cultural and political. In a rural environment, one unused to the cultural and linguistic differences of the outsider, the integration process is more complex, as the chapters in this book illustrate. For whilst the physician in rural Ottawa may have positively merged with the host society and thus be encouraged to remain, inadequate social services, poor housing and language training in rural Cork, inhibited integration and discouraged long-term settlement.

---

1 www.iom.int accessed 10 April 2009.

All the contributions to this volume highlight the barriers and misconceptions that surround contemporary rural immigration; pressure on health, housing and education resources, competition for jobs, lowering of wage rates and lack of social interaction. However the reader is shown a positive side. In many cases migrant incomers to rural communities revitalise areas that were deteriorating due to indigene emigration. Eastern Europeans in Greece, Hispanics in America and immigrants from former Soviet Republics in Russia are all recorded as having put life back into dying rural neighbourhoods.

International Migration and Rural Areas is a book which makes a contribution that goes far beyond the topography of its title. It demands that those who study migration should not be hide bound by geographic boundaries, rather they should, at the very least, evaluate the variations in migration and settlement that occur between the urban and the rural. From such findings, it is to be hoped that practices and policies that regulate and provide for the movement of people locally, nationally and internationally, take account of all the spatial aspects of the migrant experience.

Anne J. Kershen
Queen Mary University of London
Spring 2009

Chapter 1

Introduction: Key Issues in Contemporary Rural Immigration

Myriam Simard and Birgit Jentsch

A distinguishing feature of immigration since the era of industrialization up to the late 20th century has been its urban orientation. Since immigrants settled mainly in metropolitan areas, research focused primarily on the characteristics of these urban immigrants, the integration challenges and opportunities they encountered, as well as the strategies they employed to overcome difficulties. In the 1990s, migration researchers developed an interest in the role of locality in migration processes, and the argument was advanced that much closer attention must be paid to the 'city as context' (Brettell 1999). Terms such as 'global city' and 'gateway city' have been used to focus analyses on the connections between cities and their migrant populations.

However, a relatively new feature in European migration is the significant and growing impact it has had on peripheral and rural areas. Immigrants have been employed in the labour intensive agricultural sector. In addition, the expansion of other non-agricultural activities like tourism and provisions for leisure and recreation have resulted in demands for types of labour not available from the locally established population (Kasimis and Papadopoulos 1999). In Southern Europe, there has been a relatively steady stream of migrants to rural areas since the 1990s, in part connected with the comparatively large, labour-intensive agricultural sector there (Kasimis 2005). In the same decade in Eastern Europe, net migration from ex-USSR states to Russian rural areas amounted to more than two million (out of a total of six million) (Ivakhnyuk). In some Northern European countries, such as Ireland and Scotland, rural areas have particularly benefited from the 2004 EU enlargement. The subsequent inflow of immigrants have turned Ireland and Scotland into countries of immigration, when their history has been very much characterised by emigration. Increasing evidence suggests that the majority of migrant workers from the 2004 accession states[1] have found employment in

---

1   In May 2004, European Union membership was extended to include the ten countries of Cyprus, Czech Republic, Estonia, Hungary, Latvia, Lithuania, Malta, Poland, Slovakia and Slovenia. While nationals from Cyprus and Malta have had full free movement rights and have been able to work throughout the EU, transitional measures were put in place to restrict movements by nationals from the other eight (Accession 8 or A8) countries. For the first two years, only Ireland, Sweden and the UK granted full access to their labour markets

rural areas rather than the traditional migration centres. High proportions have registered in the more peripheral parts, for example the Highlands and Islands, and lower proportions than expected have been attracted to London and the common destination cities within Scotland – Edinburgh, Glasgow and Dundee (Danson and Jentsch). Some Scottish rural NHS Boards reported that they were dealing with 800 to 1,000 new migrants each month (Watt and McGaughey 2006).

Similarly, in the USA, recent evidence indicates that immigrants are increasingly arriving in small cities and their peripheral towns, as well as in rural areas. For example, over the 1990s, the number of Hispanics (who make up the vast majority of immigrants in rural areas) more than doubled in the non-metro parts of 20 states, mostly in the South and Midwest (Jensen and Yang). In Canada, immigrants' urban orientation is still dominant. In 2006 nearly two thirds (62.9 per cent) of the immigrant population settled mainly in three metropolitan areas, namely Toronto (Ontario), Vancouver (British-Colombia) and Montreal (Quebec) (Simard).[2] However, some changes have emerged, particularly highlighted with the last population census in 2006, which counted 628,295 immigrants in predominantly rural regions in Canada, mainly in agriculture, transformation and services (Beshiri et al. 2009, 2004, 2002). Since the 1990s, immigrants seem indeed to have moved increasingly to small urban and rural communities, mainly prompted by policies and programmes which were developed at different levels (federal, provincial and municipal), and which have supported the regionalisation of immigrants (Carter et al. 2008; CIC 2001). Yet, this trend has differed in strength by province. Some provinces have clearly benefited more than others, with British Columbia, Yukon Territory, Ontario and Alberta being the main gainers in the last decade. In fact, it appears that not only in Canada, but globally, national immigration programmes have increasingly aimed to include smaller regions, which had been neglected as possible destinations by new immigrants (Akbari 2008).

Despite these developments, recent academic literature in Europe has paid scant attention to immigration to rural areas, although a growing number of policy and practice oriented research reports emerged in the UK and Ireland following EU enlargement in 2004 and the associated marked increase in rural immigration in these two countries. In North America, only few books have covered rural populations or industries, but are now either dated (for example, Goldfarb 1981; Friedland and Nelkin 1971), or focused on particular aspects of rural immigration, such as the US guestworker programme, which has often provided agricultural workers. An established body of literature on the US does exist, focusing on the presence of migrant workers in rural California. However, the literature on

---

to these new EU citizens. In May 2006, Finland, Greece, Portugal and Spain lifted all restrictions, followed by Italy in July 2006, and the Netherlands in May 2007.

2   Toronto and Vancouver can be compared with some large cities in the USA, such as Miami (Florida) and Los Angeles (California) in terms of their proportion of inhabitants born abroad. In all these cases, immigrants constitute over one third of the total population of these cities (Chui et al. 2007).

the recent movement of immigrant groups to other rural areas is only gradually evolving (Jensen and Yang). The situation in Canada is similar. Historical and ethnographic studies have been conducted on ethnic communities settling in rural provinces, particularly in west Canada, but there are still very few contemporary studies which concern themselves with immigrants' and rural communities' experiences.[3]

Why is immigration to rural areas an important topic worthy of academic investigation, and in need of policy and practice development? A more balanced geographical distribution of immigrants can benefit immigrants themselves, as well as their urban and rural host communities and their new country as a whole. Too often, immigrants in metropolitan areas have found themselves segregated, in poor quality and expensive housing, and suffering from high unemployment and poverty rates as large cities have been struggling with the burden of absorption. By contrast, for decades, rural and remote areas have been afflicted by depopulation trends, mainly due to the exodus of young people to urban areas, low birth rates and an ageing population. Maintaining an adequate population base has become a challenge in many places (Wulff et al. 2008; Reimer 2007). As the chapters in this book illustrate, such trends seem to be shared by the vast majority of rural communities in the developed world.

Analysts have recognised that immigration cannot be the single solution to repopulation, but could contribute an important component to a healthier demographic, economic and socio-cultural profile in rural areas. Certainly in the context of wider local and regional development strategies it holds considerable promise. A larger population can help to overcome a shortage of labour, increase local tax revenues and support the sustainability of public and private services in rural communities. It is also likely to produce active citizens and engaged community members, such as entrepreneurs and volunteers (Hall Aitken and INI 2007; Simard 1994). This can result in a virtuous cycle where well-serviced rural areas may be attractive to a number of groups, those who once out-migrated as well as internal in-migrants and immigrants (Jentsch 2006). However, with the lack of research evidence on rural immigration issues – such as the nature, causes and effects of such migration – it has been difficult to formulate policies and practices which can support rural immigrants and the receiving communities. The development of theories and concepts, which would help to understand this new reality, has been hampered for the same reason.

Barriers to Rural Immigration

Given the potential immigration has for rural areas, it is important to recognise and address obstacles to the attraction and retention of immigrants to rural areas. Internationally, there have generally been strong positive correlations between

---

3   A recent compilation of articles (Reimer 2007) seems to constitute the first comprehensive synthesis on the matter, covering all of Canada.

the size of cities and the growth of their foreign born populations, as well as the retention of these populations (Burstein 2007). Barriers to an increase in immigration to rural areas, which have been identified by several authors, include immigrants' perception of a lack of opportunities and services in rural areas to an extent which in many cases does not reflect reality (Rose and Desmarais 2007). Possible misperceptions of rural areas can be linked to the fact that such places are at a distance from the centres of economic and political power, resulting in a deficiency of accurate information available to immigrants (Reimer 2007).

At the same time, many rural (and especially remote) areas do tend to have limited labour markets, with employment that is less diverse, yields less competitive salaries, and offers fewer career advancement opportunities than tends to be the case in larger centres. Even if a person found a suitable post, such a situation can also pose problems for their partner's search for appropriate employment. Other barriers frequently mentioned in the literature refer to the fact that there is often a mismatch between rural immigrants' qualifications and the needs of the local economy, a lack of a reliable public transport system, and a shortage of affordable, good quality accommodation.

Long distances and low population density certainly impact on the extent and range of social, cultural and institutional services. Such services tend to be less available in rural areas than in cities. Since lifestyle and family concerns (including good quality educational facilities) have been shown to be very important to immigrants, a deficiency in public (and private) services can often undermine the selection of rural communities as a destination by immigrants (Wulff et al. 2008). In addition, rural areas tend to lack large immigrant communities when this condition has been identified as significant in attracting new immigrants (Akbari 2008). Related to this, social network structures are weaker, but such networks seem crucial to the long term retention of immigrants. They can provide knowledge of, as well as confidence and support in, a destination (Green and Hardill 2003). Furthermore, locally established community members may not welcome immigrants, as they may perceive them as competitors for local jobs, even when there is in fact an unmet demand for labour. Related barriers, of which there is informal evidence, include locally established people's concerns for the protection of local values to an extent which may stimulate and strengthen exclusion, racism and discrimination (Reimer et al. 2007; Dey and Jentsch 2001). These barriers are critical as research on rural immigration has demonstrated the importance immigrants attach to 'social connectedness', that is to social interactions between immigrants and the locally established population (Wulff et al. 2008), to overcome, for instance, their social and cultural isolation when they first arrive.

Given the challenges rural areas face when depopulation could mean the disappearance of a community, it is tempting to adopt a solely instrumental approach when promoting rural immigration. However, as Burstein (2007) has argued in the Canadian context, instead of highlighting economic benefits and self-interests, it is possible to focus on diversity as a good in itself. This has particular relevance for countries which regard diversity as one of their core values. Where countries have 'branded' themselves in this way, that is where their national citizenship and immigration programmes clearly reflect this value, it is only consistent to argue for regional policies that promote racial, ethnic, religious and cultural diversity.

Aims and Objectives of the Book

In order to contribute towards bridging the research gap on the relationship between immigrants and rural localities of settlement in the contemporary context, this book is underpinned by two main aims. One is broadly concerned with immigrants' and receiving communities' experiences, and the other with conceptual development, especially of the concept of integration and its meaning in rural contexts. As to the former, we wish to examine the causes and nature of immigration to rural areas. We also aim to analyse the consequences and challenges of immigration for rural communities, and conversely, the impact of rural localities of settlement on immigrants' engagement with economic, social, and cultural processes. These analyses include identifying those factors in rural localities which attract international migrants, and which support them in integration processes, as well as those factors which affect the opposite. Regarding the latter aim, the different uses of the term integration will be examined in the various geographical, socio-economic, cultural and political contexts covered in this book. This will allow us to show the complexity and variability of this concept, including the multiple factors of structural and circumstantial nature which affect integration processes. Throughout, the particularities of rural immigration experiences are to be explored and highlighted in this book.

A cross-national approach is adopted, which refers to studies of rural immigration from a range of geographical and political contexts in the Euro-Atlantic region. The book also benefits from the contributions of a multidisciplinary team of authors. The fact that it brings together complementary bodies of literature in different languages, especially French and English, has further enriched the analysis. The book examines experiences in North America (Canada and the USA), Southern Europe (with a focus on Greece) Northern Europe (Ireland and Scotland) and Eastern Europe (Russia). Hence, it draws on the wide-ranging experiences of established receiving countries in North America, as well as of European countries, which have only recently become (again) countries of immigration.

Russia bisects the European and Eurasian migration system. After 70 years of strict immigration restrictions under the Soviet period, it has since 1992 received rural and urban immigrants of diverse backgrounds and characteristics. Significant groups of immigrants to the Russian Federation include ethnic Russian and Russian speaking people from other Soviet republics. Moreover, especially in Russia's Far East, Chinese citizens have become a dominant rural migrant group (Ivakhnyuk). Greece – as well as other Southern European countries – have recorded a significant immigration increase in urban and rural areas since the 1980s. The majority of Greece's foreign population has come from Albania,

Bulgaria and Romania (Kasimis). Scotland and Ireland are traditionally sending states but have particularly benefited from urban and rural immigration following EU enlargement in 2004, with Poles having constituted by far the largest national grouping in both countries (Coakley and Mac Éinrí; Danson and Jentsch). Canada and the USA are traditional receiving states in the New World, the majority of rural immigrants having come from Latin America for the USA (Jensen and Yang) and from a mix of European and more recently non European countries for Canada (Simard). The two countries are also considered to have had considerable experiences with immigrants' integration – a key concern of this book.

A cross-national comparison of immigration in a rural context can provide us with different angles from which to examine immigrants' and receiving communities' experiences. The various national (and sub-national) contexts will therefore facilitate an analysis of the relationship between place of settlement, migrants' profiles and their experiences. These contexts will also help us to reflect what integration means for rural areas.

Cross-National Comparisons – Some Methodological Issues

Rural immigration is a relatively new subject area of investigation with no easily comparable datasets or bodies of literature, and with significant differences in the nature, causes and consequences of immigration in the different countries and regions covered in this book. While a common framework of issues was developed in the preparation phase of the book, which was to be covered by all chapters, it was not considered helpful to offer chapters with uniform structures, or to give the identified issues equal importance in all chapters. Too rigid an approach would have compromised contributors' ability to cover the contemporary and key concerns in their respective country or regions. It would also have constrained the ability to benefit from the different disciplinary backgrounds of the authors, and the different perspectives they were able to take on similar issues, resulting in deeper insights.

Even with the different scopes of the chapters, common and overlapping themes and issues have emerged, which have lent themselves usefully to cross-national as well as intra-national comparisons. Such themes include the reasons for migration to rural areas; the profiles of immigrants in those spaces; their experiences and integration processes in rural host communities; and the impacts of immigrants on rural communities. We found that while chapters differed in their foci, they were often able to usefully complement each other. For example, while most chapters focus on immigrants in basic skilled employment, the Canadian contribution concentrates on immigrants in professional posts and related issues of retention. Some commonalities still exist between this and the other chapters, since many professionals have spent some time in basic skilled employment to bridge the period until their qualifications are recognised. Equally important, the Canadian chapter identifies retention issues for immigrant health professionals in this traditional immigration country. The insights gained here will also be relevant to those new settlement countries which are currently aiming to address the lack of progression opportunities for their professionally qualified immigrants with the hope of retaining them.

Concerning more specific methodological issues, a cross-national approach involving new settlement countries is particularly hampered by a lack of evidence. For example, although a good number of studies have emerged in recent years in Ireland and Scotland, they have been specifically commissioned, often with a remit reflecting the specific interests of the commissioning body rather than a desire to advance immigration research more generally. In addition, given the short time spans in which such studies are usually required to be completed, they may not have very robust methodologies. Especially as evidence gaps are being filled, there will be much scope for future, fruitful comparisons, perhaps in particular between countries that have similar immigrant groups and are dealing with similar issues.

Other main challenges in cross-national (rural) social research consist of the lack of equivalence of concepts and of meanings, as well as cross-cultural variability. The former comprises issues of translation from one language to another, and the false assumption that there can be a one-to-one correspondence between words or concepts in different languages (Lupri 2008; Hantrais 1995). Lupri (2008) observes that the problem increases when concepts are abstract (for example, as with 'democracy' or 'peace'). However, noteworthy challenges can also occur with concrete terms. In our case, this applies to a concept which is fundamental to rural research – 'rurality'. It could be argued that some measure of equivalence exists in that any national definition will revolve around two key variables – distance and density. Rural communities are relatively distant from each other and from major urban centres. They also have lower population density across and within communities (Bollman et al. 2007; Reimer 2007; Jentsch and Shucksmith 2004). Attempts have been made by international organizations to offer global definitions of rural areas, which go beyond these variables. According to the OECD (1994), regions are predominantly rural if more than 50 per cent of the population of the region is living in rural communities, which are defined as having a density of less than 150 persons per square kilometre. However, national definitions of rural areas still differ widely. For example, 'rural' can relate to a population of less than 50,000 in the US (Jensen and Yang), but of less than 10,000 in Québec (Canada) (Simard), and less than 3,000 in Scotland (Danson and Jentsch). Due to these varying definitions, 'rurality' in this book needed to be defined by each individual chapter.

The implications of this for the interpretation of findings do not seem too different from single-country studies. Rural communities, even within one country, differ enormously, for example, in terms of size, remoteness and economic base, and all these different factors will have an impact on community members' experiences. Some of the key differences in experiences we can reasonably anticipate on the basis of population size alone includes the fact that larger rural populations are likely to enjoy a greater level of service provision, as such provision is more easily sustainable in this context than in small, remote communities. For immigrants, there may be an increased chance of meeting people with a similar national, ethnic, language or cultural background. A situation of the latter kind has been described in the US context, with the Hispanic immigrant population clustering spatially in rural areas (Jensen and Yang). This may in part be attributed to the fact that 'rural areas' in the US can include relatively large populations compared to other countries. In addition, it needs to be understood that immigrants of Hispanic background constitute by far the largest group of immigrants to the US. The dominant size of this ethnic group allows more easily for spatial clustering than is the case with very diverse immigrant populations. This indicates that an important aspect in cross-national research in general is to interpret findings in the relevant context, of which the definition of 'rural areas' is but one aspect.

Another challenge in this cross-national study consisted of the great variety of terms employed to refer to the people who migrate and settle in a different (part of a) country, including immigrants, migrants, in-migrants, newcomers, incomers, new rural residents and new community members. In Europe, the term 'migrants' is frequently used to refer to international as well as internal migrants. In North America, it is more common to refer to international migrants as 'immigrants', and to internal migrants as 'migrants'. The double meaning of the European term 'migrant' can clearly cause confusion in studies comparing European with North American countries, and will always need to be examined in its context. There are also cultural issues here, reflecting the fact that different concepts are underpinned by cultural values, and cannot simply be translated from one language into another. We are reminded that in rural communities, who is 'local' and who is regarded as an 'incomer' can be sensitive questions. In fact, the use of the term 'incomer' in the UK can be value loaded in a rural context, and suggest negative connotations. It may refer to an implicitly accepted hierarchy headed by those who have been in a community the longest. By contrast, 'new community members' tends to be the chosen term when the emphasis is on a person being an equal member of a community (even if they have newly arrived). In order to refer to these groups 'correctly' in a scientific sense, research would have to establish if there is a consensus on such issues at community level, or would need to determine who considers themselves to be local or established, and who as an incomer or visitor. In most cases, this will be an impractical task.

There are also challenges with the terminology which serves to describe the population which has already stayed in rural areas for a long time, sometimes for several generations, and which is to be contrasted with new community members. A range of terms have appeared that are not only imprecise, but also ambiguous in a global context. These terms include native, indigenous, and local. Of course, in the contemporary situation with increasing mobility, it has become progressively rare for adults to not have moved from the locality of their birth (if this condition is a requirement for being considered 'local'), so that it is questionable how relevant or meaningful these references are. Concerning the terms native and indigenous, they may in a European context relate to people whose families have stayed in an area for a long time. However, in North America (and especially Canada), they tend to refer to the population of Aboriginal ancestry. Without having completely resolved the questions of terminology, we have attempted in this book to exclude those terms that could lead to confusion in an international context, and to use as much as possible a common vocabulary to facilitate comparisons. We have thus opted for terms such as 'long-term established' or 'locally established' to describe those people who have stayed in a locality for a long time, but accept that these terms also lack precision.

Another key concept of the book is that of immigrant 'integration'. One of the advantages of the concept is its potential to accommodate both the rights (such as access to services and the labour market) and responsibilities (such as respect for a core set of values) of individuals and communities. This applies at least in cases where integration is conceived of as a two-way process, requiring changes from communities as well as the individual. It may be for this reason that it is considered a key concept by intergovernmental agencies, such as the International Organization for Migration (IOM) (IOM 2006).

However, there is no clear, and certainly no globally relevant definition of integration, as this widely used term lacks precision and criteria for operationalisation and measurement (Gibney and Hansen 2005). This has resulted in a situation where integration appears to be used as a catch-all concept, referring to both, processes and objectives of inclusionary strategies. The concept has been described as little more than a default term, given that there is no less-contentious alternative (Geddes 2001). The international literature, which makes reference to the concept, appears to offer little to properly grasp it, especially in a rural context. Definitions are vague, or appear incomplete, lacking clarity and rigour. Often, they confine themselves to economic integration, and neglect obvious other dimensions (such as social, cultural, political and legal). Comprehensive discussions of the complexity of integration processes and outcomes have thus remained rare (IOM 2006; Simard 1994). There are also approaches which appear normative in that they prescribe what aspects and types of integration should be desirable for immigrants, and which do not examine sufficiently the structural constraints and the relationship with wider inequalities and power relations which affect integration.

The flexibility of the term is reflected in the different chapters of this book. While integration has become an important issue in all the countries covered, the reasons for this encompass a wide range of concerns, including national and cultural security, immigrants' well-being, and the sustainability of rural communities. The foci of national and sub-national policies relating to integration vary accordingly. This demonstrates the importance of understanding the context of different notions of 'integration'. Especially if twinned with rural development concerns, the goal policies often seem to share is the long-term retention of immigrants. However, this goal can be confined to certain ethnic groups, and be contingent on certain characteristics (for example, language skills) and expected behaviour on the basis of immigrants' (assumed) cultural backgrounds.

Given the different meanings the concept may represent – inter and intra-nationally – it seems important to bring together its different aspects and contexts in the concluding chapter. Our aim is to work towards a more comprehensive understanding of the concept of integration and its relevance for rural areas. Drawing on a range of national and sub-national situations, we wish to consider 'integration' in more depth, from more perspectives and in more contexts than a single-country study would have allowed us to do. The concluding chapter demonstrates that integration definitions are shaped to a considerable extent by country-specific situations, such as the prevailing legal statuses of a country's immigrants, and labour market conditions. We cannot claim that the resulting account is 'complete'. Rather, it seems to constitute a reasonable basis for further development.

There are thus clear benefits of the cross-national approach despite all its challenges. We have been able to empirically examine some conceptual ideas in different settings, especially related to the concept of integration, and could consider answers to key questions which have guided the book on the basis of different experiences at national and sub-national levels. Such key questions included the following.

- Has recent rural immigration led to the integration of the new immigrants and their families in their settlement countries? What kind of integration?
- What factors may have facilitated, and what factors possibly undermined immigrants' integration?
- What type of employment have immigrants experienced? Have they been able to access good quality jobs, or are they rather confined to sectors which are characterised by low pay and low status?
- Are immigrants mainly seen as useful for addressing labour shortages, or are the welfare concerns of immigrants and their families also addressed?
- What opportunities does the host country offer for the construction of a new rural, multi-ethnic society?
- What can be done to support the new rural immigrants so that they are likely to stay long-term?

Introducing the Chapters

The two North American chapters present the situation of immigrants and rural communities in countries which have a long tradition of immigration, but for whom relatively high numbers of rural immigrants is also a rather new phenomenon. The second chapter (Jensen and Yang) provides a general overview of where immigrants (especially of Hispanic origin) are going in the USA, and reasons behind their choices of destination; it analyses immigrants' characteristics and how they are faring. Moreover, it assesses immigrants' possible impacts on rural localities to date, which includes their ability to revitalize rural communities which have experienced sharp declines in their population. Given the demographic challenges many localities in the countryside have to deal with, it has been recognised as important to strengthen the capacity of rural communities to attract and retain immigrant populations.

The third chapter, the Canadian contribution (Simard), focuses on this theme of retention, concentrating on well qualified immigrants. This social group tends to have been neglected in the literature in general, and in the rural context in particular. The chapter examines issues of attraction and retention of a specific group of highly skilled immigrants, namely health professionals, in rural Quebec. The discussion takes place in a policy context in which public authorities have tried to address the geographical maldistribution of general practitioners so as to correct the accessibility to health services for remote populations. Through the adoption of a comprehensive and diachronic perspective, many important factors were identified as influencing the staying or leaving decisions of those immigrants. Professional, socio-cultural and community, family, personal, financial and environmental factors were analysed. Policy and practice recommendations include suggestions by the physicians of how to improve the retention of medical professionals in rural areas.

Chapter 4 considers the situation of new settlement countries in Southern Europe with a particular focus on Greece (Kasimis). The chapter provides insights into immigrants' situation and their impact on rural areas in countries with very different features from those in Northern Europe. These include a relatively large agricultural sector, an extensive informal economy, mass illegal immigration, and a number of recent regularisation programmes. In contrast to Ireland's and Scotland's low unemployment rates (under 5 per cent), Greece's unemployment rate is relatively high (over 8 per cent) (CIA 2008). Yet, Greece has an exceptionally large immigrant population (about 10 per cent of the total population) (Baldwin-Edwards 2002a).

While the recent immigrants from EU accession states to Ireland and Scotland often have professional qualifications and high levels of skills, they still tend to be employed in basic skilled jobs in labour intensive industries, such as agriculture and food processing. Moreover, with mass immigration being a new phenomenon in Ireland and Scotland, the needs of immigrants are still being examined, and ways explored how they can be met. Some important provisions, such as English language classes, have been put in place, but concerns have remained about the quantity and quality of available services. Chapter 5 on Ireland (Coakley and Mac Éinrí) shows particular interest in the different aspects of immigrants' integration, and the support provided for them by governmental and non-governmental organisations. The sixth chapter concentrates on labour market issues in Scotland (Danson and Jentsch). While the authors accept the general research findings in the UK that migrants are usually filling positions which locally established workers are not prepared to take up under the employment conditions offered, the chapter examines possible indirect processes of exclusion. It first of all explores factors which seem to prevent some social groups (for example, women with caring obligations, established minority ethnic groups) from accessing employment, and second, the degree to which some workers (including immigrants) remain excluded from the primary labour market.

Chapter 7 turns to Eastern Europe, and examines the specific situation of Russia's immigrants (Ivakhnyuk). The chapter constitutes one of the first attempts to describe and analyse the experiences of immigrants in rural areas of this country. Immigrants' possible impacts on economic, demographic, and social developments of rural areas in Russia are examined, and those factors explored, which may facilitate or undermine immigrants' integration in rural communities.

Chapter 8 concludes and looks in more detail at the factors which shape immigrants' employment, social and community life experiences across the different countries covered in this book. The chapter's particular focus is on issues of integration.

While interesting insights can be gained by examining *inter*national variability in cross-national research, there is also, of course, much to learn from *intra*national variability, such as regional differences. The two studies on Russia and Greece have been designed to highlight regional differences within these countries, while the Canadian research has an explicit and comprehensive rural-urban component. All other chapters refer occasionally to rural-urban or regional differences within each country, and draw sometimes on international comparisons. Clearly, there is no standard rural reality. Important differentiators, such as geographies, local economies, policies, histories (also with respect to immigration), and attitudes and perceptions surrounding immigration, are discussed and analysed in all chapters.

From this outline of the chapters, it will have become clear that the book's focus is on contemporary immigration, rather than historical accounts. However, many contemporary immigration issues experienced in particular countries or communities have obvious roots in historical experiences. The individual chapters offer therefore a brief account of the history of immigration in each country covered as part of important contextual information.

References

Anderson, B., Ruhs, M., Rogaly, B. and Spencer, S. (2006), *Fair enough? Central and East European migrants in low-wage employment in the UK* (COMPAS/ Sussex Centre for Migration Research: University of Oxford/University of Sussex).

Akbari, A. (2008), 'Introduction: Regionalization of Immigration in Host Nations of Western World', *International Migration and Integration*, 9:4, 341–44.

Baldwin-Edwards, M. (2002a), 'Southern European Labour Markets and Immigration: A Structural and Functional Analysis', *Mediterranean Migration Observatory* [Working Paper No. 5].

Baldwin-Edwards, M. (2002b), 'Immigration and the Welfare State: A European Challenge to US Mythology', *Mediterranean Migration Observatory* [Working Paper No. 4].

Beshiri, R. and He, J. (2009), 'Immigrants in Rural Canada: 2006', *Rural and Small Town Canada Analysis Bulletin*, 8:2, 1–28. (Ottawa: Statistics Canada, Catalogue no.21-006-XIE). <http://www.statcan.gc.ca/english/freepub/21-006 XIE/free.htm>.

Beshiri, R. (2004), 'Immigrants in rural Canada: 2001 update', *Rural and Small Town Canada Analysis Bulletin*, 5:4, 1–27. <http://www.statcan.ca/english/freepub/21-006-XIE/21-006-XIE2004004.pdf>.

Beshiri, R. and Alfred, E. (2002), 'Immigrants in rural Canada', *Rural and Small Town Canada Analysis Bulletin*, 4:2, 1–20. <http://www.statcan.ca/english/freepub/21-006-XIE/21-006-XIE2002002.pdf>.

Bollman, R.D., Beshiri, R. and Clemenson, H. (2007), 'Immigrants to Rural Canada', *Our Diverse Cities*, Summer, 3, 9–15.

Brettell, C. (1999), 'The City as Context: Approaches to Immigrants and Cities', *Proceedings Metropolis International Workshop*, Lisbon, 18–29 September, Luso-American Development Foundation.

Burstein, M. (2007), 'Promoting the Presence of Visible Minority Groups across Canada', *Our Diverse Cities*, Summer, 3, 42–6.

Carter, T., Morrish, M. and Amoyaw, B. (2008), 'Attracting immigrants to smaller urban and rural communities: Lessons learned from the Manitoba provincial nominee program', *Journal of International Migration and Integration*, 9:2, 161–83.

Central Intelligence Agency (CIA) (2008), The World Factbook. Updated 4 December.

Chui, T., Tran, K. and Maheux, H. (2007), *Immigration au Canada : un portrait de la population née à l'étranger, Recensement de 2006* (Ontario: Ottawa).

Citoyenneté et Immigration Canada [CIC] (2001), *Vers une répartition géographique mieux équilibrée des immigrants*, Recherche et examen stratégiques, Ministre des Travaux publics et Services gouvernementaux du Canada, Canada.

Collins, J. (2007), 'Immigrants in Regional and Rural Australia', *Our Diverse Cities*, Summer, 3, 36–41.

Dey, I. and Jentsch, B. (2000/2001), 'Rural Youth in Scotland: The Policy Agenda', *Youth and Policy*, Winter, 11–24.

Favell, A. (2005), 'Assimilation/integration', in Gibney and Hansen, (eds).

Friedland, W.H. and Nelkin, D. (1971), *Migrant Agriculture Workers in America's Northeast* (New York: Holt, Rinehart and Winston).

Friedman, M. (2002), *Capitalism and Freedom* (Chicago: Chicago University Press), 8–21.

Geddes, A. (2001), *Ethnic Minorities in the Labour Market: Comparative Policy Approaches (Western Europe)* Report commissioned by the Ethnic Minorities Labour Market Project of the Performance and Innovation Unit (London: Cabinet Office).

Gibney, M.J. and Hansen, R. (eds) (2005), *Immigration and Asylum: From 1900 to the Present* (Santa Barbara, CA: ABC-Clio).

Goldfarb, R.L. (1981), *A Caste in Despair: Migrant Farm Workers* (Ames: Iowa State University Press).

Green, A.E. and Hardill, I. (2003), 'Rural Labour Markets, Skills and Training. Final Report', *Institute of Employment Research, University of Warwick*. <http://www.defra.gov.uk/rural/pdfs/research/rural_labour_markets.pdf>, accessed 12 September 2008.

Hall Aitken and Ionad Nàiseanta na h-Imrich (INI) (2007), *Outer Hebrides Migration Study. Final Report*. <http://www.cne-siar.gov.uk/factfile/population/documents/OHMSStudy.pdf>, accessed 12 February 2009.

Hantrais, L. (1995), 'Social Research Update. Comparative Research Methods', University of Surrey: Guildford. <http://sru.soc.surrey.ac.uk/SRU13.html>, accessed 27 January 2009.

Holzmann, R. and Münz, R. (2004), *Challenges and Opportunities of International Migration for the EU, Its Member States, Neighboring Countries and Regions: A Policy Note*. Social Protection Discussion Paper Series, No. 0411, Social Protection Unit, Human Development Network (Washington: The World Bank).

International Labour Office [ILO] (2003), *Decent work in agriculture*, Background paper, International Workers' Symposium on Decent Work in Agriculture, International Labour Organization, Bureau for Workers' Activities, Geneva, September 2003, 15–18.

IOM (2006), *IOM Policy Brief. Integration in Today's World*. IOM: Geneva. <http://www.iom.ch/jahia/webdav/site/myjahiasite/shared/shared/mainsite/policy_and_research/policy_documents/policy_brief_1.pdf>, accessed 9 February 2009.

Jentsch, B. (2006), 'Youth Migration from Rural Areas: Moral Principles to Support Youth and Rural Communities in Policy Debates', *Sociologia Ruralis*, 46: 3.

Kasimis, C. and Papadopoulos, A.G. (eds) (1999), *Local Responses to Global Integration* (Aldershot: Ashgate).

Kasimis, C. (2005), *Migrants in the Rural Economies of Greece and Southern Europe*, Migration Information Source (Washington DC: Migration Policy Institute).<http://www.migrationinformation.org>, accessed 16 February 2009.

Kayser, B. (1990), *La renaissance rurale. Sociologie des campagnes du monde occidental* (Paris: Armand Colin), 316.

Kayser, B. (1993), *Naissance de nouvelles campagnes* (France: Éditions de l'Aube).

Kirat, T. and Torre, A. (ed.) (2007), No. spécial sur les 'Conflits d'usages et dynamiques spatiales: les antagonismes dans l'occupation des espaces périurbains et ruraux (II)', *Géographie, Économie, Société*, 9:2.

Kirat, T. and Torre, A. (eds) (2007), No. spécial sur les 'Conflits d'usages et dynamiques spatiales: les antagonismes dans l'occupation des espaces périurbains et ruraux (I)', *Géographie, Économie, Société*, 8:3.

Lebaube, A. (1988), *L'emploi en miettes* (Paris: Hachette) 258.

Luginbühl, Y. (dir.) (2007), *Nouvelles urbanités, nouvelles ruralités en Europe* (Bruxelles: P.I.E. Peter Lang).

Lollier, J-C., Prigent, L. and Thouément, H (dir.) (2005), *Les nouveaux facteurs d'attractivité dans le jeu de la mondialisation* (Presses Universitaires de Rennes) 226.

Lupri, E. (2008), 'Theoretical and methodological problems in cross-national research', *Sociologia Ruralis*, 9:2, 99–113.

Mauthner, N., McKee, L. and Strell, M. (2001), *Work and Family Life in Rural Communities* (York: Joseph Rowntree Foundation).

Organisation for Economic Co-operation and Development (OECD) (1994), *Creating rural indicators for shaping territorial policy* (Paris: OECD).

Perrier-Cornet, P. (dir.) (2002), *Repenser les campagnes* (Éditions de l'Aube et Datar).

Phillips, T. (2008), *Speech at the Confederation of British Industry (CBI) Migration Summit*, London, 28 October 2008. <http://www.equalityhumanrights.com/en/newsandcomment/speeches/Pages/CBIMigrationSummit.aspx> accessed 21 January 2009.

Pugh, R. (2007), *New Migrants and Minorities: Understanding Difference and Discrimination in Rural Areas*. Paper distributed at the conference *International Migration and Rural Areas: Global Perspectives*, 11–12 October 2007, Isle of Skye, Scotland.

Reimer, B. (ed.) (2007), 'Rural communities', *Our Diverse Cities*, Summer, 3.

Reimer, B., Burns, M. and Gareau, P. (2007), 'Ethnic and Cultural Diversity in Rural Canada: Its Relationship to Immigration', *Our Diverse Cities*, Summer, 3, 30–35.

Rose, M.M. and Desmarais, J. (2007), 'Directions to Consider in Favour of the Regionalization of Immigration', *Our Diverse Cities* Summer, 3, 52–8.

Rosenberg, S. (1989), 'De la segmentation à la flexibilité', *Travail et société*, 14: 4, 387–438.

Ruhs, M. (2006), 'Greasing the wheels of the flexible labour market: East European labour immigration in the UK' (Oxford: COMPAS), Working Paper 06-38.

Simard, M. (2007), 'Nouvelles populations rurales et conflits au Québec: regards croisés avec la France et le Royaume-Uni', *Géographie, Économie, Société* No. spécial sur Conflits d'usages et dynamiques spatiales: les antagonismes dans l'occupation des espaces périurbains et ruraux (dir. T. Kirat et A. Torre, CNRS et INRA), 9:2, 187–213.

Simard M., avec la collaboration Mimeault, I. (1997), 'La main-d'oeuvre agricole saisonnière transportée quotidiennement de la région de Montréal: profil socio-économique et insertion professionnelle', *Cahier de recherche de l'INRS-Culture et Société*, 182. <http://www.ucs.inrs.ca/default.asp?p=rr>.

Simard, M. (1994), *Les entrepreneurs agricoles immigrants européens: insertion dans la société rurale québécoise*, Gouvernement du Québec, ministère des Affaires internationales, de l'Immigration et des Communautés culturelles (MAIICC), collection *Études et recherches*, 11, 154.

Tremblay, D. (1994), 'Chômage, flexibilité et précarité d'emploi: aspects sociaux', *Traité des problèmes sociaux, Québec, Institut Québécois de Recherche sur la Culture*, 623–52.

Wallerstein, I. (2008), 'The Demise of Neoliberal Globalization', *Yale Global Online*, <http://yaleglobal.yale.edu/display.article?id=10299>, accessed 20 January 2009.

Watt, P. and McGaughey, F. (eds) (2006), *How Public Authorities Provide Services to Minority Ethnic Groups, Northern Ireland, Republic of Ireland, Scotland. Emerging findings discussion paper.* <http://www.nccri.ie/pdf/Service_Provision_Report.pdf>, accessed 17 February 2009.

Wulff, M., Carter, T., Vineberg, R. and Ward, S. (2008), 'Special Issue: Attracting New Arrivals to Smaller Cities and Rural Communities: Findings from Australia, Canada and New Zealand'. Introduction by special guest editor, *International Migration and Integration*, 9:119–24.

Chapter 2

Taken by Surprise: New Immigrants in the Rural United States[1]

Leif Jensen and Tse-Chuan Yang

Introduction

That the United States (US) is a nation of immigrants is beyond question. The history of the country is marked by great waves of immigration, first from Northern and Western Europe, then Southern and Eastern Europe, and, since the mid-1960s, from Latin America, Asia and elsewhere in the global South. These successive waves have generated predictable concerns among previous arrivals about the social and economic impact of immigration, even as prevailing evidence points toward repeated patterns of successful labor market adaptation and incorporation into mainstream social institutions. For over a century, immigrants to the US have settled overwhelmingly in the country's largest urban areas. While this remains true today, a new phenomenon has caught many by surprise. Evidence suggests immigrants are deconcentrating away from large urban centers into small cities and towns at their periphery, and into rural areas. Some new arrivals are bypassing traditional gateway cities altogether and moving directly to less urban locales. This rise in immigration to rural areas is occurring in all regions of the country and often in places that are unaccustomed to immigration and unprepared.

This chapter describes and analyzes new immigrants to the rural US, and places this new phenomenon in social, economic and policy contexts. The chapter describes where immigrants are going and why, what their characteristics are, how they are faring, and what their impacts on rural localities seem to have been thus far. The chapter argues that rural and small-town areas constitute crucibles within which the dynamics and social tensions of immigration are intensified and in plain view. While 1,000 new immigrants in a metropolitan area may hardly be felt, in

1　This research was conducted as part of The Pennsylvania State University Agricultural Experiment Station Multi-State Research Project NE1029. Computational support was provided by the Population Research Institute, Penn State, which has core support from the US National Institute on Child Health and Human Development (R24 HD041025-06). The material presented in this chapter draws significantly on a 2006 report by the lead author titled, 'New Immmigrant Settlements in Rural Areas: Problems, Prospects, and Policies,' *Reports on Rural America* 1: 3. (Carsey Institute, The University of New Hampshire, USA) <http://carseyinstitute.unh.edu/documents/Report_Immigration.pdf>.

smaller places a given absolute increase can quickly stress local resources needed to provide health care, education, housing, police protection and other basic services. Social strains owing to linguistic, religious, and other cultural differences are also often magnified when immigrants move into small communities. The chapter will also pay special attention to the relevant policy discourse. In particular, a spotlight is thrown on the mounting tension between the Federal government where jurisdiction over immigration policy resides, and municipalities scrambling to cope.

By way of overview, we begin by placing this new rural immigration within the broader context of US immigration history. We then draw on the research literature to describe the dispersion of immigrants away from urban and toward rural areas, and illustrate new settlement patterns through county-level maps. We pay special attention to the industrial structure of settlement areas to provide insight into the underlying causes of these streams. Based on analysis of US Census Bureau data, we then provide a demographic portrait of new immigrants to rural areas. Finally, we consider the impact of immigrants on rural communities, and investigate policy implications in the concluding section.

A Brief History of US Immigration

In his historical account of immigration to the US, Oscar Handlin (1951, 3) begins, 'once I thought to write a history of the immigrants in America. Then I discovered that the immigrants *were* American history.' Beginning with the first flows of colonists to the New World during the 17th Century and continuing up to about 1820, the colonies and the young US began to be populated by immigrants arriving from Great Britain and elsewhere in Northern and Western Europe. Hazardous transatlantic travel and limited economic opportunity meant that the flows during this period were comparatively modest. Nonetheless, as in later periods, popular worries about negative cultural and economic impacts of new immigrants were voiced by those already settled. Culturally, derision and distrust were often directed toward newcomers with new languages or religions, and who often settled in ethnic enclaves (Jones 1960). Economically, popular outcry drew attention to the poverty and pauperism among immigrants. Indeed, new arrivals during this period were often quite destitute. Many arrived as a result of European countries purging their own relief rolls by facilitating the emigration of the poor (Jones 1960; Stephenson 1926). Immigrants tended to settle residentially with co-ethnics and often in destitute circumstances. These enclaves—spatially obvious to those outside—perhaps contributed to anti-immigrant sentiment. Concerns about poverty, social service use, and spatial concentration among immigrants continue to be heard in both rural and urban America. In sum, immigration during this earliest period was numerically modest but was, in microcosm, typical of US immigration history generally. It was halting, it was characterized by distrust of newcomers who were culturally different, and immigrants were often poor and spatially concentrated in co-ethnic enclaves in both urban areas and the countryside.

The first great wave of immigration to the US began around 1820 and lasted until about 1900. Absolute inflows were significant, numbering some 2.6 million during the decade of the 1850s alone (Jensen 1989). That the entire US population in 1850 was only 23 million underscores the tremendous size of this wave of immigration in relative terms. Labor displacement and population growth in Europe, improved transatlantic transportation and communication with the US, and economic expansion and labor recruitment in the US were all at play (Vialet 2002; Jensen 1989; Portes and Bach 1985; Davis 1974; Stephenson 1926; Mayo-Smith 1890).

This first wave of immigration was comprised principally of those arriving from Northern and Western Europe. By and large they were economically successful, readily acquired English, and blended into the emerging society. Immigration policy at this time was largely pro-immigration in nature. The Homestead Act of 1862 made agricultural land in the Midwest, the Plains and beyond available to immigrants as well as the native born (Vialet 2002). The settlement of Norwegians, Swedes and other northern Europeans in these regions still bears its mark today. Ironically, it is some of these same communities in the Midwest and Plains that are today suffering population and economic decline and which might be rejuvenated by a new stream of immigration from abroad.

The second great wave of immigration to the US (1860–1930) overlapped with the first. What distinguishes it is the striking shift away from northwestern European origin countries, to countries in Southern and Eastern Europe (Jensen 1989). In terms of appearance, religion, and other ways, they differed noticeably which made it difficult to immediately assimilate into the predominantly Anglo-Saxon majority. They were arriving to a more urban and industrial country, and were far more likely to settle in the city, often in ethnic enclaves near places of work. Despite evidence that second wave immigrants proved to be economically successful (Lieberson 1980), perceptions of negative social and economic consequences were strong. With respect to policy, the late 19th and early 20th centuries were an era in which restrictive immigration laws began to be implemented.[2] Most notably, the Immigration and Nationality Acts of 1921 and 1924 gave rise to the National Origin Quota System, which invoked strict limits on immigration, and set country of origin quotas that greatly restricted future immigration to those from Northern and Western Europe.

The National Origin Quota System contributed to a sudden decline in the flow of immigrants to the US, and the Great Depression further reduced the

---

2   The Chinese Exclusion Act of 1882 quickly halted Chinese labor. In 1891 Congress sought to restrict the entry of 'classes' of immigrants, notably paupers and those deemed likely to become a public charge. The Immigration Act of 1917 institutionalized literacy as a criterion of entry, doubled the head tax on new arrivals and extended the exclusion of Chinese immigrants to other Asian nations as well (Jones 1960).

motivation and ability to leave Europe. As a result, the period 1930–1965 was one of highly limited immigration. Labor shortages during World War II gave rise to some easing of restrictions and pro-immigration efforts. Notably, the Bracero Program actively recruited Mexican labor into US agriculture (Samora et al. 1971). However, the Immigration and Nationality Act of 1952, passed despite a presidential veto, maintained the quota system which President Truman regarded as blatantly discriminatory.

The third great wave of immigration (1965–present) was caused in large part by 1965 legislation that dismantled the National Origin Quota System and replaced it with a far more equitable worldwide distribution of visas. By raising the overall numerical ceiling on immigration, equalizing flows by country, and stressing family reunification as a criterion for legal entry, the 1965 legislation served to dramatically increase migration flows and changed the country of origin composition toward Asian and Latin American nations. Like the second wave of immigration, there was a shift toward less developed and poorer countries of origin, and toward immigrant groups who themselves were often culturally and phenotypically distinct. And like the second wave, it spawned popular discontent and policy debate that continue. While today's debate focuses largely on the problem of undocumented immigration, it continues to pit those pointing to the virtues of immigration and the rights of immigrants—whether documented or not—as human beings, against those who look to new immigrants flows with trepidation and, for some, suspicion and disdain.

In recent decades there have been additional pieces of immigration legislation. Notably, the Immigration Reform and Control Act [IRCA] of 1986 imposed penalties on those employing undocumented workers,[3] and featured an amnesty program that ultimately legalized 2.7 million undocumented immigrants (Martin and Midgley 2003). For the rural US, a key component of the legalization program was the Special Agricultural Worker program [SAW] which accounted for some 40 percent of all those legalized. An unintended consequence was that these agricultural workers, now legalized, became footloose and free to move to other regions and sectors of the economy (Kandel and Cromartie 2004). They did so, and left behind unmet demand for agricultural labor and thus a magnet for new undocumented immigrants in subsequent years. This had implications both for the rural communities the amnestees were leaving, and the communities where they settled, many of which also were rural.[4]

---

3   In part due to the ubiquity of false documents, it is widely acknowledged that employer sanctions were minimally effective in curtailing undocumented immigration. By the same token, to the extent that sanctions were on the minds of employers, there is evidence that there was discrimination against foreign-born individuals whose documents were in fact legitimate (for example, legal temporary workers) (LeMay 2004).

4   Other relevant pieces of legislation include the Immigration Act of 1990 which raised the limit on legal immigration to 675,000 per year. The Personal Responsibility and Work Opportunity Reconciliation Act [PRWORA] of 1996 had an impact on immigrants

New Immigrant Settlements in the Rural US

Many early immigrants settled in rural areas to eke out a living in farming and related areas, however it is fair to say that since the later 1800s mass immigration to the US has been a principally urban phenomenon. While this remains true today (Singer 2004), there is evidence the immigrant groups are also settling in small town and rural US as well. The purpose of this section is to describe these new settlement patterns. Here we rely on the definition of 'rural' most commonly used by researchers, to wit, people and places outside of metropolitan areas, and use the terms rural and non-metropolitan (non-metro) interchangeably.[5]

Recent Evidence of Dispersion to Rural Areas

Because the vast majority of immigrants in rural areas are from Mexico and other Latin American countries, it is worth reviewing the settlement patterns of Hispanics. William Kandel and John Cromartie analyzed data from the 1980, 1990, and 2000 US decennial censuses to determine the extent of the dispersion of Hispanics to new destination areas in the non-metro US (Kandel and Cromartie 2003). To motivate their study, they note that, first, over the 1990s the number of Hispanics more than doubled in the non-metro portions of fully 20 states, mostly in the South and Midwest. Second, the number of non-metro counties in which Hispanics comprised ten or more percent of the population increased from 230 to 316. Third, Hispanic population increases in more than 100 rural counties averted what otherwise would have been declines in county population; they demographically revitalized these places. Fourth, while rural Hispanics traditionally were concentrated in the Southwest of the US, fully half of them reside elsewhere. Finally, while only five percent of the non-metro population was Hispanic in 1990, they accounted for

---

by severely tightening restrictions on immigrant receipt of Public Assistance. The Illegal Immigration Reform and Immigrant Responsibility Act of 1996 provided increased border patrol and increased penalties for fraudulent documentation, among other things. The USA Patriot Act of 2001 expanded the definition of inadmissibility to include endorsement of terrorist activity and called for increased border security. Finally the Homeland Security Act of 2002 broke up the Immigration and Naturalization Service (formerly in the Department of Justice) and moved it to the new Department of Homeland Security (the Bureau of Citizenship and Immigration Services now handles immigration and naturalization services).

   5   A metropolitan (metro) area is a county containing one or more urbanized areas with a population of 50,000 or more, plus surrounding counties tied economically to the central county via commuting patterns. As of 2003, there were 3,142 counties in the US, 2,052 (65 percent) of which were non-metro and accounted for 17.3 percent of the total population. It should be noted that metro counties can have people living in very small towns or the open country (what one might call rural), while non-metropolitan counties can have people living in the downtowns of small cities of up to 50,000 (what casual observers might call urban).

over one-quarter of the non-metro population growth over the decade. The point is, Hispanics, many of whom are immigrants and recent immigrants in particular, moved to new parts of rural US over the 1990s.

With regard to spatial integration, Kandel and Cromartie (2003) found that there was increasing residential integration between Hispanics and non-Hispanic whites in non-metro areas when measured at the county level. This reflects their spread throughout rural areas during the 1990s. Interestingly, however, they found decreasing integration between Hispanics and whites when measured at the sub-county level. So while Hispanics are diffusing to rural counties, they are clustering spatially within them.

Focusing on the foreign-born population and the movement of recent arrivals to emerging rural settlements, Daniel T. Lichter and Kenneth M. Johnson (2005) provide an in-depth analysis of county-level data from the 1990 and 2000 US Censuses. In part, they seek to assess the so-called 'balkanization hypothesis' (Frey 1996) which holds that new immigrants are displacing native workers, who then leave to find work in places where competition from foreign-born workers is less. Lichter and Johnson (2005) find that 297 counties, or nearly ten percent of all counties, had foreign-born populations that were five or more percent of total population for the first time in 2000. Importantly, they note that many of these counties are at the peripheries of traditional settlement areas with already high concentrations of foreign-born individuals. However, they document a geographic scattering of new immigrant destinations in the Midwest, Southeast and elsewhere in the rural US In many counties, especially in the heartland, these immigrant increases over the 1990s prevented or reduced population losses. Calling the balkanization idea into question, they document a *decline* at the county level in spatial segregation of the native-born and the recently arrived foreign-born over the 1990s.

Mapping New Immigrant Settlements

Where are new immigrants to rural areas moving, and what are these places like? In this section we use mapping to identify counties around the US that have experienced sizable inflows of recent immigrants. County-level data were drawn from the 1990 and 2000 US Census of Population and Housing. The key variable driving this analysis is the change between 1990 and 2000 in the number of recent immigrants (foreign-born individuals excluding those born abroad of US American parents and regardless of citizenship, who arrived in the US to stay after 1965). Recognizing that a given absolute change can have very different effects depending on whether the population of a county is large or small, we divide the change in the recent immigrant population by the county's 1990 total population and multiply by 100 to obtain a measure of relative change. A value of 5.0 for this variable can be interpreted as the increase in the recent immigrant population as a percentage of the 1990 population.

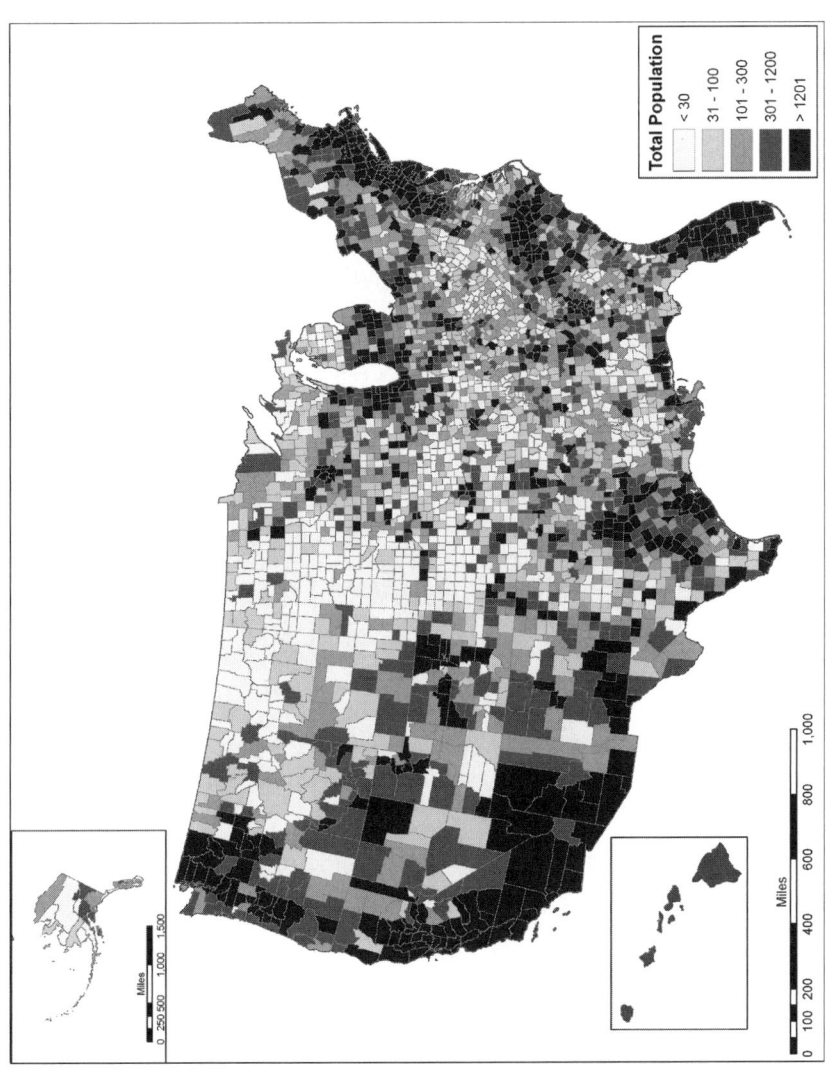

Figure 2.1 Total post-1990 foreign-born population in all USA counties, 2000

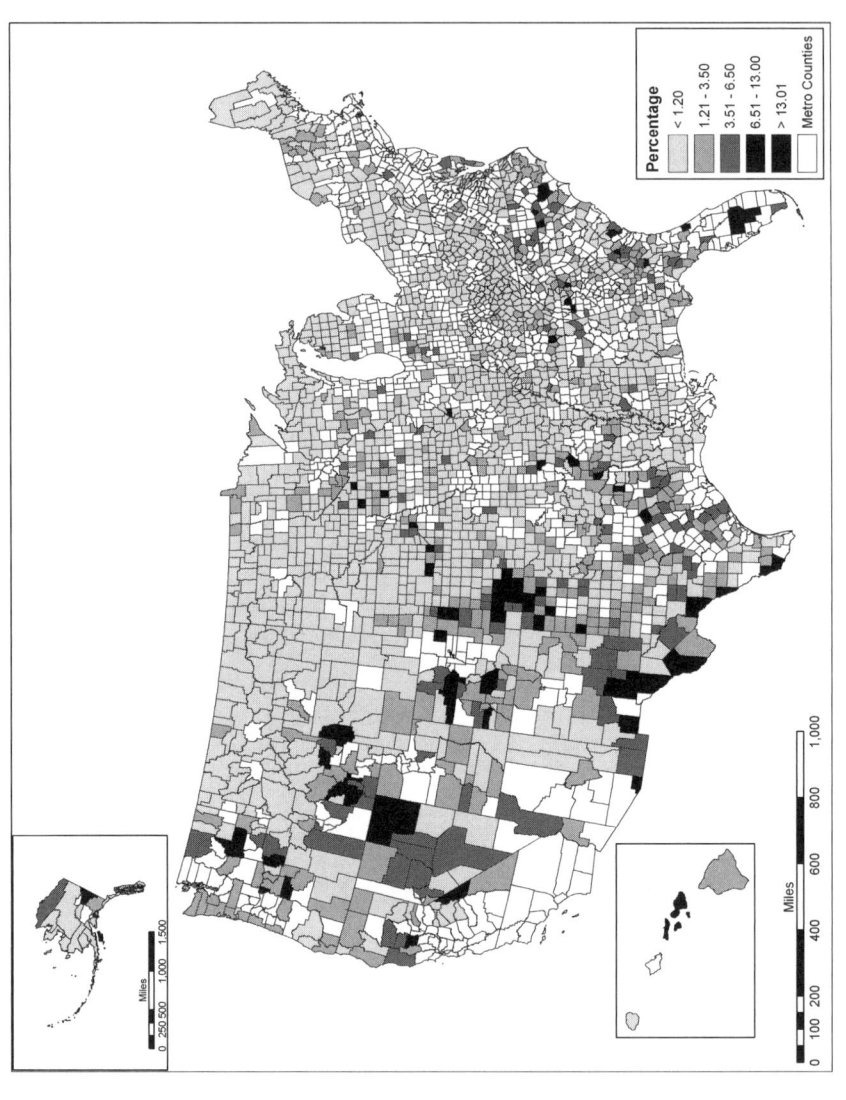

Figure 2.2   New immigrant population change in the USA non-metro counties

As a point of departure it is important to indicate where recent immigrants are, and where they are not.

Figure 2.1 shows the absolute size of the recent immigrant population in counties as of 2000, with darker shades indicating places with the greatest numbers. Recent immigrants continue to live in traditional destinations, such as the Boston to Washington urbanized corridor, south Florida, the metropolitan areas and border region of Texas, Chicago, and urban California.

Figure 2.2 shows the relative change of the recent immigrant population between 1990 and 2000 (again, as a percentage of total 1990 population) among all non-metro counties in the US. First, that large swaths of the map are shaded simply reflects the fact that two-thirds of all counties and the vast majority of all US land area is non-metropolitan. The map also suggests that every region of the country has some non-metro areas that have experienced at least moderate inflows of recent immigrants. A brief review by region is instructive.

The Northeast

While there are no non-metro counties in the northeast that have experienced extremely high inflows, modest flows are seen in northern tier of Vermont and New Hampshire, in places between New York City and Albany, NY, and in eastern Pennsylvania. In Monroe County, Pennsylvania, for example, the recent immigrant population more than doubled, from 2,259 to 5,805. Monroe County is sometimes referred to by locals as the sixth borough of Manhattan as more and more residents are commuting the 80 miles or so to New York City. Although there are certainly rural counties and communities in the Northeast that have been destinations for recent immigrants, the majority of the action is elsewhere.

The Southeast

Proceeding south, a belt of non-metro counties with high immigrant influx is seen traversing east-west across North Carolina. Places like Duplin County, North Carolina features a website offering a Spanish version, and boasts a rural charm and agricultural heritage but with 'urban access.' Its recent immigrant population increased nearly ten-fold over the 1990s (from roughly 500 to 5,000), and only 11 percent of its current total foreign-born population are citizens. This percentage is low because a high proportion are recent arrivals, and the process of obtaining US citizenship is extremely complicated and can take years. Other counties in this swath share a relatively low percentage Hispanic which is very roughly half the size of the African American population. Their industrial structure is dominated by manufacturing, including poultry, pork, vegetable and other food processing, as well as lumber processing and furniture manufacturing. In this region it is important to consider relations between recently arriving Latinos and the sizable African American population. In one study of a small North Carolina town whose economic base is in textiles, furniture manufacturing, mobile home assembly and meat processing, Altha Cravey (1997) pointed to a highly stratified and racialized local division of labor that newly arrived immigrants are, by virtue of their own economic vulnerabilities, only adding to and reinforcing. Lumber and its processing into molding and other wood products is also common further south in Georgia, where carpet manufacturing also attracts many recent immigrants. Finally, a cluster of non-metro counties in southern interior Florida [FL]—many of which are highly agricultural—is noteworthy. Hendry County, FL for example, 'Citrus Capital of Florida,' has 23 percent of its workforce employed in agriculture. About 40 percent of Hendry's population is Hispanic, and its recent immigration population grew from about 3,200 to about 8,100 over the decade.

The Heartland

Vast swaths of the Midwest are non-metropolitan, and the map indicates pockets here and there where recent immigrants are flowing in substantial numbers, at least relative to the base population. Almost without exception, these counties also are home to sizable meatpacking or other food processing concerns. An example is Cass County, Illinois [IL], home of a large Cargill hog processing plant employing some 2,300 workers according one local official. While only 8.5 percent of Cass County's population is Hispanic, the recent immigrant population grew some 25 times, from 41 to 1049 over the 1990s. A pallet plant and a hardwood drying company also provide local employment. There are numerous examples of counties in Minnesota, Nebraska, Kansas and elsewhere in the heartland where agri-business corporations such as Swift, Conagra, Tony Downs Foods, and IBP have opened massive plants that have attracted thousands of immigrant workers. To take just one example, Finney County, Kansas is home of Garden City, site of an Iowa Beef Processors, Inc. [IBP] plant that emerged in the early 1990s (see Gouveia and Stull 1995). Its recent foreign-born population increased nearly three fold over the 1990s to 9006, this increase being nearly 18 percent of the 1990 population. It is important to stress that over the years, work in the meatpacking industry has become de-skilled with the manufacturing process being fragmented into highly specific and monotonous tasks. The result is an arduous, grueling, and hazardous job (Stull, et al. 1995).

Arkansas, East Texas, and the Rio Grande

A line of counties receiving large numbers of recent immigrants flows south from Arkansas and arcs west into east Texas. Again here, meat processing is a driving force. For example, Yell County, Arkansas is 13 percent Hispanic with an economy featuring poultry, hog and beef processing and 32 percent of its labor force in manufacturing. Its recent immigrant population grew twelve-fold. A string of non-metro counties along the border of Texas and Mexico, and stretching into New Mexico and Arizona also have experienced rapid increases in their recent immigrant populations. Given their proximity to Mexico and roots as former territories of Mexico, they are overwhelmingly Hispanic. The economies across these border counties are somewhat diverse, but are typically dominated either by agriculture and other extractive industries (mining), or services.

Mountain States and the West Coast

A distinctive feature of many of the non-metro counties in the west that are attracting recent immigrants is their tourism-based economies that capitalize on natural amenities. Examples include Summit County and Eagle County, Colorado, home to the Breckenridge, and Vail ski areas, respectively. In both cases the leading industry of employment is recreation services (that is arts, entertainment, recreation, accommodation, and food services), followed by construction which, no doubt, also is related to the growth of tourism in the area. In addition to skiing, these localities are capitalizing on their natural beauty, fishing and other outdoor recreation to build economies that are attracting recent immigrants. Other counties in the west attract recent immigrants due to the strength of their agricultural sectors. These can be found in California, Oregon, and Idaho, and Washington. Products include vegetables, potatoes, and apples.

To summarize, recent immigrants have been moving to rural areas of all regions of the US. The cluster of industries may differ across these regions, whether it is meatpacking, agriculture, manufacturing, construction, or recreation and tourism. But they share in common an industrial base that features ample demand for immigrant labor. The work involved tends to be low-skilled, low-paying and labor intensive, and the working conditions—notably in meatpacking—are often quite harsh. Next we briefly review who these new arrivals are, which then sets up a discussion of their impact.

Recent Immigrants to the Rural US: Socioeconomic and Demographic Characteristics

Here we describe recent immigrants in rural areas of the US through an analysis of multiple years of data from a nationally representative household survey conducted by the US Census Bureau, the Current Population Survey.[6] We compare

---

6   This demographic portrait of recent immigrants in the rural and urban US is based on original analysis of data from the March Current Population Survey [CPS] that appears in Jensen (2006). The CPS is a nationally representative survey of approximately 50,000 US households and the individuals residing within them conducted by the US Census Bureau on behalf of the Bureau of Labor Statistics. To increase the cases available for analysis, we pooled data from the 1996–2003 CPS surveys and used the outgoing rotation groups, such that any given sampled household is incorporated in this analysis only once. Data are weighted by the March supplement weight for a given year. We used the CPS rather than public use micro data files of the Census 2000 because this set of surveys includes

the recent immigrant population (those who are foreign-born who arrived since 1965), and the very recent immigrant population (those arriving since 1990), to the native-born population (including those born abroad of native-born parents). In the following description, we highlight differences between immigrants residing in non-metro versus metro areas.

Age Composition

We begin this demographic portrait by considering the age distribution of natives, recent immigrants, and very recent immigrants. There are considerable age differences. Compared to natives, the foreign-born themselves are more likely to be non-elderly adults, rather than children or elders. For example, about 12 percent of natives are aged 65 or more, which compares to only 3.2 percent of the foreign born who arrived since 1990. And while 28.2 percent of the native-born are under age 18, only 11.0 and 19.8 percent of post-1965 and post-1990 arrivals, respectively, are children. Compared to the metro foreign-born population, proportionately more of the non-metro foreign-born population are children, and proportionately fewer are elderly. In other words, non-metro immigrants are somewhat younger. This stands in direct contrast to the residential pattern for natives, where there is a greater prevalence of elders in the countryside compared to the metro US. While proportionately fewer of the foreign-born population overall are children, it should be borne in mind that these age distributions do not count as immigrants the native-born children of the foreign born, that is, the second generation. Clearly their social and economic circumstances and trajectories have tremendous implications for the future impact of immigration to the US. This is all the more so to the extent that immigrant fertility is high. Indeed, Johnson and Lichter (2008, 16) note that 'Hispanic natural increase is a significant demographic component of population growth in both metro and non-metro areas, and its relative impact on rural population growth is increasing.'

Race/Ethnic Composition

As noted, the mid-1960s saw the beginning of a new wave of immigration to the US that has been marked by a dramatic shift toward Asian and Latin American countries of origin. As a result, the nativity differences in race-ethnic profiles are stark. The vast majority of the native population is non-Hispanic white, while immigrants are far more likely to be Mexican, Other Hispanic, and Other (largely Asian). About three-quarters of natives are white, which compares to only about one in five recent immigrants.

While the same general pattern holds for recent immigrants in the non-metro US, that is, they are far less likely to be non-Hispanic White than their native

---

key indicators not included on the census long form (for example, those needed to define underemployment).

counterparts, and more likely Asian and Hispanic, there are some important differences. Most notably, rural immigrants are far more likely to be of Mexican origin. Almost half (48 percent) of all post-1965 immigrants living in the non-metro US are Mexican, which compares to only about 25 percent in metro areas overall. By contrast, urban locales are more likely to have recent immigrants who are of Asian or African decent.

Marital Status

Marital status is a clear factor in individual and family well-being, and marriage promotion has been part of the anti-poverty political discourse in the US in recent years. We find that recent immigrants residing in non-metro areas are somewhat advantaged in terms of their marital status. About three-quarters of adult recent immigrants in non-metro areas are married, which compares to less than 70 percent among recent immigrants generally, and about 64 percent of their counterparts in central cities. Being younger, new immigrant adults, recent arrivals in particular, are more likely to be never married. However, recent immigrants in non-metro areas are much less likely than their counterparts elsewhere to have never been married, and the prevalence of divorce or separation among them is also quite low.

Educational Attainment

As a fundamental indicator of human capital, educational attainment is critical for success in the labor market. We consider three educational categories, less than high school, high school and some college, and four-year college graduate or more. With respect to differences between natives and immigrants overall, there is a bifurcated distribution of education among immigrants. That is, compared to natives, immigrants are more likely to be very poorly educated, and very well educated. This pattern is consistent with the legal immigration preference categories that continue to stress both family reunification as well as superior labor market skills. Regarding residential differences in educational attainment, immigrants in rural areas are at a distinct disadvantage. About half of all recent immigrant adults in non-metro areas have not completed high school, which compares to about one-third of all recent immigrants. Recent immigrants are also less likely than their counterparts elsewhere to have completed college (though their college completion is higher than that of rural natives).[7]

---

7   While recent immigrants to rural areas are less well educated, this does not necessarily mean they are unskilled. In a study of workers in Marshalltown, Iowa, Baker and Hotek (2003) find that the Hispanic workforce has a wide range of skills, often with years of experience, in the domains of communications (for example, telecommunications), construction (for example, carpentry), industrial service (for example, vehicle repair), and manufacturing (for example, assembly). While less well educated, immigrant workers often

Employment Status

Recent immigrants, particularly those in residing in non-metro areas, are more likely than their native counterparts to be employed. Reflecting a greater attachment to the labor force and economic need for work, almost two-thirds (65.0 percent) of the foreign-born population who arrived since 1965 and who are residing in non-metro areas are employed (either full- or part-time) which compares to 61.5 percent among those arriving since 1990 and 56.4 percent among non-metro natives.

Employment in Agriculture

Overall, the percentage of population employed in agricultural industries is quite low in the US. Only about two percent of the native-born are employed in agriculture, though given their prominence in the pool of farm workers, recent immigrants—regardless of where they live—are well more than twice as likely than natives to be so employed. Of course, rural residence and farming are not synonymous, nonetheless the prevalence of agricultural work is far greater the in non-metro US, and here recent immigrants are strikingly more likely to be employed in agriculture than their native counterparts. Almost 14 percent of recent immigrant workers in non-metro areas are in agriculture, which compares to just over 5 percent of native-born non-metro workers. Brought to national attention vividly through the 1960s documentary *Harvest of Shame*, the plight of farmworkers—notably manifest in poverty, poor health and nutrition, and unsafe working conditions (for example, exposure to herbicides and pesticides)—has never been adequately addressed or ameliorated (Martin and Martin 1994).

Underemployment

Simply being in the labor force does not guarantee success; employment adequacy also is important. A useful concept in this regard is underemployment.[8] Nationally, about 12.1 percent of native workers are underemployed, which compared to

---

deploy a pool of human capital through their labor force participations that can revitalize rural economies.

8   As defined here, the underemployed include (1) the unemployed – those not working but looking for work, (2) discouraged workers – those out of a job and not looking for work, but who would like a job if they thought they could find one, (3) involuntary part-time workers – those working part-time only because their employer(s) cannot provide full-time hours, and (4) the working poor – those whose wages (adjusted for weeks and hours worked) are insufficient to bring them significantly above poverty. All other workers are considered adequately employed (see Jensen and Slack 2003). While underemployment by occupational mismatch – being overeducated for one's occupation – has been proposed as an underemployment category (Hauser 1974), it is seldom used in research on US underemployment due to perceived measurement shortcomings specified by Clogg (1979). Nonetheless, future research on US immigration would benefit from such a focus.

19.2 percent of post-1965 foreign-born individuals, and 22.6 percent of those who arrived since 1990. The rates for recent immigrants in non-metro areas are quite a bit higher. Outside of the metropolitan areas of the US, 24.1 of post-1965 immigrants and 28.6 percent of those who arrived since 1990 are underemployed. To be sure, immigrants represent a pool of cheap labor. As such, much of their disadvantage in underemployment prevalence can be traced to high rates of 'working poverty.'

Poverty Status

The official poverty measure in the US is absolute, and defines as poor those families whose annual income is less than three times the cost of a minimally acceptable diet. Thresholds are defined separately based on family size, number of children present, and other indicators of need. Apart from rising with the inflation rate, the official definition has remained largely unchanged since developed during the 1960s. We find that both recent and very recent immigrant groups have a higher poverty rates than their native-born counterparts. This immigrant disadvantage is even starker in rural areas. Using 150 percent of the poverty threshold as a measure of near poverty, we find that the near poverty rate among very recent immigrants (those arriving since 1990) was 48.2 percent among those residing in non-metro areas, which compares to only 39.3 percent among all recent immigrants.

Food Stamp Receipt

Immigrant use of means-tested public assistance programs has long been controversial. At issue is not so much the admission of the poor per se, than those apt to burden prevailing social welfare systems. An important program is Food Stamps, which gives qualified low-income families 'money' that can be used for the purchase of food. Using the prevalence of food stamp receipt as an indicator, we find that the rate of receipt in the entire population does not differ tremendously across nativity and residence categories. However, when restricting attention to the near poor, the prevalence of receipt is decidedly lower among recent immigrants than natives, a finding that is consistent with other studies (e.g., Jensen 1989) and reflects more than anything else an aversion to state assistance. About 31 percent of near-poor natives are in households receiving Food Stamps which compares to 20 percent of post-1965 and 18 percent of post-1990 arrivals, respectively. The rate is even lower among recent immigrants living in rural areas (about 15 percent). In short, recent immigrants may be poor, but they are less likely to receive this form of means-tested assistance. Both facts are most pronounced in the countryside.

Home Ownership

Living in a home that is owned (outright or with a mortgage) carries near iconic distinction in the American psyche as an indicator of economic status. For immigrants, in particular, it is a clear marker of social and economic integration within localities. Not surprisingly given their more limited economic means and years of residence within the US, recent immigrants are less likely than natives to own their own home. However, like rural residents generally, recent and very recent immigrants residing in non-metro areas are more likely than those elsewhere to live in an owned-home. Fully 38.0 percent of post-1990 immigrants in non-metro areas do so.

Health Status

The Current Population Survey includes a subjective health item indicating whether individuals are in excellent, very good, fair or poor health. Given their more youthful age structure, very recent immigrants are more likely to report excellent health. However, few significant residential differences in this regard were seen. Where recent immigrants show a clear disadvantage relative to natives is with respect to access to health insurance. While over 80 percent of natives live in households with some form of health insurance, only 62.7 percent of post-1965 arrivals, and 56.2 percent of post-1990 foreign-born individuals are in households with any health insurance. By roughly seven percentage points, recent immigrants in non-metro immigrants are *less* disadvantaged in this regard compared to those in central cities. Because the United States lacks socialized health care, not having health insurance is quite problematic and often results in terribly inadequate access to primary and acute health care.

In summary, the picture that has emerged is a recent immigrant population in rural US differs in some important ways from recent immigrants living in metro areas. They are more likely to be Hispanic (and of Mexican origin in particular), they are less well-educated, they are poorer but less prone to receive means-tested assistance (that is Food Stamps), they are more likely to be married, more likely to be working but also more likely underemployed, more likely to own their own home, and they may be in better health and more likely to have access to health insurance.[9]

9　This portrait of where new immigrants to rural areas are going and who they are is consistent with the findings of Kandel and Cromartie (2003). They report that rural places with the most rapid Hispanic growth had economies that were dominated by meat processing, furniture and textile manufacturing, or recreation and tourism industries. New arrivals themselves were also younger, more likely to be male, more likely to be married with children than non-Hispanic whites, more recently arrived, and they were less proficient in English, less well educated, but more likely to be working than their Hispanic counterparts elsewhere in the rural US.

Assessing the Impact

The movement of recent immigrants to small cities at the periphery of traditional gateway destinations, and rural and small-town US has caught many by surprise. As a result, while the research community has accomplished much in terms of describing the magnitude and broad contours of the phenomenon, less systematic research has rigorously assessed its impact. In this section we review the emerging evidence.

An initial question is whether the impact of immigration is stronger in rural areas. Indeed, the new immigration to rural areas magnifies longstanding concerns. Flows to places like New York City may hardly be felt. Traditional gateways are used to accommodating cultural difference, often have pre-existing ethnic enclaves that new arrivals can rely on to build a new life and, while frequently stressed, have social service and other infrastructures in place to provide for those in need. Not so in rural areas. Because of small base populations, any sizable immigration flow may be profoundly felt. Folks arriving speaking only their native languages, and being noticeably different in appearance and culture, can spark fear, hostility, and indignation in native populations that, in many places, have been established for many generations. Even modest inflows can quickly exhaust prevailing housing stocks, tax local school systems ill-equipped to handle low-income and non-English-speaking students, and stress public and faith-based social service systems. In short, rural communities where new immigrants are increasingly settling are crucibles, where the social and economic tensions posed by immigration are greatly intensified. At the same time, however, the potential benefit to rural communities needs to be kept in sight. New arrivals often bring vitality, determination, diligence, and other assets that can breathe new life into towns that might otherwise be failing. They work, they consume, and they volunteer in local sports and community organizations. They bring new cuisines, music, and cultural practices that can make rural communities vibrant and exciting. The metaphor of the crucible is apt here as well. Like the 'smelting pot' or 'cauldron' it connotes the ongoing process of blending new peoples to form a new rural and urban places (Martin and Midgely 2003:35).

Does Immigration Cause Rural Poverty?

In *The New Rural Poverty*, Martin, Fix and Taylor (2006) tackle the provocative question of whether immigration increases poverty in rural areas. At issue is whether there is a circular relationship, a 'vicious circle' in their terms, between three key characteristics of rural communities: farm employment, immigration and poverty. Elsewhere the authors describe a four-phase process of immigrant integration to agricultural areas that has implications for poverty (Taylor, Martin, and Fix 1997; Martin and Taylor 2003). First, solo male workers act as pioneers to take seasonal farm jobs, remitting much of their income and otherwise costing localities little and being statistically invisible. Second, some seasonal workers successfully exit seasonal work to take more full-time work in agricultural and other industries, creating unmet demand of agricultural labor and thus additional immigration. Third, families of solo males join them, and their presence—particularly that of their children—begins to be felt and noticed locally as poverty and demand for services increases. Fourth, new immigrants become more integrated and politically active, calling for action to address the chronic and deep poverty they face.

Martin et al. (2006) empirically confirm this nexus of farm employment, immigration and poverty. Through an analysis of 66 California towns, they found that between 1990 and 2000, a 100-person increase in the foreign-born population was associated with a 59-person increase in farm employment, and that a 100-person increase in farm employment was associated with a 186-person increase in the foreign-born population and a 176-person increase in the poverty population. What they did *not* find was a a an effect of foreign-born population on poverty that was independent of its effect on farm employment. That is, in their analysis of these 66 agricultural towns, immigration increased poverty only indirectly through its effect on farm employment. Their 1990 data *did*, however, indicate a direct immigration to poverty link suggesting that immigration did increase poverty above and beyond what would be expected given their presence in farming—a relatively high-poverty industrial sector.

The inevitable question is whether such results for a highly agricultural area of California, an area well-known for the presence of Hispanic (mostly Mexican-origin) workers in the farm labor force, holds for the country as a whole. Analyzing 1970, 1980 and 1990 data from a random sample of rural and urban census tracts, Martin and Taylor (2003) do confirm a circular relationship between farm employment and immigration, with one reinforcing the other. Interestingly, they find that in 1980 farm employment *reduced* poverty, but by 1990 the relationship had reversed. In that year 'a 100-person increase in farm employment was associated with an 85-person *increase* in poverty' (Martin, Fix, and Taylor 2006:24, emphasis in original).

Hence, there does appear to be an interconnection between farm employment, immigration and poverty. To the extent that areas apt to be most significantly impacted by this dynamic are located in rural areas, any discussion of the new immigration to rural and small town US needs to be informed by this research. At a minimum, farm and agricultural labor policy needs to recognize the impact of farm labor on prevailing poverty rates in localities, and be coordinated with policies regarding rural development and social service provision at the local level. At the same time, it will be important to reach beyond farm employment or even agriculture, which even in the rural US are not the industries where a majority of immigrant workers are found.

Inferring Impact from the Changing Characteristics of Settlement Locations

Here we statistically describe rural counties that have experienced significant inflows of recent immigrants.

Table 2.1 provides assorted economic and demographic data for non-metro counties subdivided into thirds according to the growth in their recent immigrant populations relative to the total 1990 county population. We show characteristics of counties as they were in 1990, before the change in recent immigrant population, as well as the relative (percentage) change over the ensuing decade.

First, with respect to industrial structure, counties with relatively high influxes of recent immigrants (for convenience referred to here as high-growth counties) had somewhat lower employment in agriculture and other extractive industries, and registered less decline in agricultural employment over the decade. Otherwise, high-growth non-metro counties had somewhat more employment in construction in 1990, less than average in manufacturing (and the decline in manufacturing over the decade was greatest), and slightly more in services.[10]

Table 2.1 also shows that high-growth non-metro counties had the lowest rates of Public Assistance receipt in 1990, as was still the case in 2000 (not shown). Of course, receipt rates declined sharply over the 1990s owing to both a drastic change in the US social welfare system in 1996 as well as a strong economy, but these declines were least in non-metro counties with the highest inflows of recent immigrants. A similar story can be said of poverty. High-growth non-metro counties had lower poverty rates in 1990, but the decline in poverty over the decade was least.[11] Likewise, the percentage of the population without a high school degree was lowest in high growth places, but the decline least over the decade. Finally, results for age structure suggest that high-growth non-metro counties had somewhat more prime aged adults (aged 18–64) and fewer elders in 1990. Perhaps reflecting the rejuvenating effect that immigrants and their children have, the overall declines in percentages under age 18 over the decade were least in high-growth non-metro counties. Taken together, these results suggest that recent immigrants to rural areas are moving to places that are comparatively vibrant economically, but their presence can be seen in unfavorable trends in poverty and other such indicators.

---

10   The result for manufacturing is intriguing. We know that an important draw for new arrivals in non-metro counties experiencing the most explosive growth is in meatpacking and other food processing categorized as manufacturing. That the overall percentage employed in manufacturing was somewhat lower and declined more precipitously in high growth counties may reflect the infusion of immigrant labor into a manufacturing sector that is employing a declining number of native workers.

11   The implication is that new immigrants are moving to places with better economic prospects and lower poverty rates. Given that recent arrivals are more likely to be poor, their influx to new destinations necessarily places upward pressure on local poverty rates over time. It is important to bear in mind, however, that this movement is likely to increase the economic status of migrants themselves. Indeed, Crowley, Lichter and Qian (2006) show that the dispersal over the 1990s of Mexican workers (immigrants especially) away from the Southwest resulted in lower measured poverty rates among this group.

Table 2.1   Characteristics of non-metropolitan counties by change in recent immigrant population*

	Agriculture/extraction		Construction		Manufacturing		Services		Public Assistance	
	1990	Change	1990	Change	1990	Change	1990	Change	1990	Change
Low growth	15.3	-27.9	6.4	12.5	17.3	-11.2	42.6	23.7	9.7	-60.6
Medium growth	12.0	-29.2	6.5	14.7	19.6	-11.5	42.6	23.5	9.4	-60.3
High growth	12.6	-27.1	7.1	14.1	17.3	-13.4	43.5	23.0	8.3	-51.3
Total	13.3	-28.0	6.7	13.8	18.0	-12.0	42.9	23.4	9.2	-59.2

	Poverty rate		Less than high school		Age less than 18		Age 18–64		Age 65 +	
	1990	Change	1990	Change	1990	Change	1990	Change	1990	Change
Low growth	19.8	-17.7	33.2	-26.7	27.1	-7.3	55.9	3.8	16.7	0.7
Medium growth	18.2	-17.0	32.1	-27.2	27.0	-6.5	56.6	3.7	16.2	-1.1
High growth	17.4	-12.6	31.6	-22.0	27.2	-5.1	57.4	3.0	15.4	-2.3
Total	18.5	-15.9	32.3	-25.3	27.1	-6.3	56.7	3.5	16.1	-0.8

* All cell entries are percentages. 'Growth' refers to absolute change in recent immigrant population in counties relative to 1990 total population. "Change" refers to the relative (percentage) change, 1990–2000, in the percentages for each characteristic.

Source: 1990 and 2000 U.S. Censuses of Population and Housing, summary files.

Summary, Discussion, and Policy Implications

In recent decades a new chapter in US immigration history appears to be emerging. Ample ethnographic and demographic evidence suggests that immigrants are deconcentrating, and that while the vast majority of the foreign-born still live in the nation's cities, much smaller places in the rural US are seeing dramatic increases in their populations of recent immigrants. And they are found all over the country.

There is some reason to be concerned about the implications of these trends for the rural communities involved. After all, compared to their urban counterparts, recent immigrants in rural areas tend to be poorer and less well educated. But it appears also that they carry some comparative advantages in that they are more likely to be working (if also more likely underemployed), less likely to use means-tested welfare programs, more likely to be married, and more likely to own their own homes. They also are more likely to be Hispanic (and more specifically of Mexican-origin), and thus are bound by a common non-English language. Understandably, the reaction among natives populations to these influxes have been mixed with some locals reacting negatively out of concern for presumed negative social and economic impacts, some reacting positively and viewing these newcomers as a source of much needed revitalization, and a large number being more ambivalent. Whether indeed the new arrivals are a bane or a blessing for the rural US depends on some blend of reality and perception. But one thing is certain, and that is that rapid increases in immigrant populations are apt to be more acutely felt in rural than urban areas.

In recent years the US Congress has been in the midst of a heated debate over legislation that would address the problem of illegal or undocumented immigration to the US. This issue is as complex as it is contentious in part because it places various interests (for example, labor versus business) and values (for example, humanitarianism versus respect for the rule of law) against one another. It is noteworthy that the key issues of conflict—employer sanctions, border security and, especially, amnesty for undocumented workers—are the same as those that fueled debate over the 1986 immigration reform (that is The Immigration Reform and Control Act [IRCA]), which itself was the result of a protracted and acrimonious legislative debate.

National level immigration policy needs to be highly attentive to real and potential impacts on localities. It is, after all, the communities in which immigrants settle that contend day to day with the pressures that necessarily accompany rapid increases in immigrant populations. To reiterate, the smaller size of rural places and often more limited resources and social service infrastructures make them especially vulnerable to the negative externalities of immigrant inflows. Today the US is wrestling with the question of whether to provide amnesty to millions of immigrants who are living and working in the country illegally. If amnesty is offered, governments at all levels need to be prepared for the possibility that legalized workers become footloose, and move to new destinations while also leaving behind a vacuum in the labor force. Employers are not likely to substantially improve pay and working conditions to retain them, if they expect that new pools of undocumented labor may well be right behind them. The impact on rural communities in this regard would warrant special scrutiny.

This contradiction, that in the US immigration policy is set and administered at the national (Federal) level, but the impact (positive and negative) of immigration is most acutely felt at the state and local level, has become painfully obvious in many small rural and urban communities in recent years. A flagrant example is the case if Hazleton, Pennsylvania. A very small and erstwhile coal mining city embedded in an otherwise rural setting, Hazleton has a very long history as a destination for new immigrant groups (for example, Italians). During the 1990s the Hispanic population, many of whom are immigrants and their children, grew rapidly. While social services were stressed and some natives grumbled, the city's mayor initially defended the immigrant community, recalling the heritage of the town and highlighting the positive impact on the local economy. But things changed. Reacting to documented instances of violent crime and other problems linked to the influx of undocumented immigrants, in July 2006 the city enacted, under the mayor's leadership, the *Illegal Immigration Relief Act Ordinance.* The ordinance declares that 'illegal immigration leads to higher crime rates, contributes to overcrowded classrooms and failing schools, subjects our hospitals to fiscal hardship and legal residents to substandard quality of care, contributes to other burdens on public services, increasing their cost and diminishing their availability to lawful residents, and destroys our neighborhoods and diminishes our overall quality of life.' It revokes or denies business permits to businesses found to employ undocumented workers, fines landlords 'not less than $1,000' for renting to illegal immigrants, and makes English the official language of the city (all forms, signage, and so on, will be in English only). The ordinance sparked an immediate national reaction because of its boldness and severity, and because it underscored the frustration of one small locality that perceived inadequacies in federal immigration law. While Hazleton spawned the enactment of similar laws in many other localities around the US, their enforcement has been held up by resulting litigation.

The story of Hazleton and numerous case studies suggest that communities differ in their receptivity to new arrivals. Marshalltown, Iowa, a meatpacking town with an exploding Hispanic (largely immigrant) population, had a local leadership that decided to embrace new arrivals. Town leaders took proactive steps—including a study tour of the Mexican community where many new immigrants originated— so that they could better understand the newcomers and help orient the community to their arrival (Grey and Woodrick 2005). In Lexington, Nebraska, citizens organized forums, organized community seminars on cultural sensitivity, and established volunteer groups in anticipation of the opening of a new meatpacking plant there (Gouveia and Stull 2007). On the other hand, one can point to Hazelton and numerous other places where local receptivity has been (or become) cold, if not outright hostile. While rigorous research on this topic is emerging, it appears that the level of receptivity has profound effects on immigrants and immigrant communities. A warm and welcoming native population can ease integration into jobs and labor markets, local schools, churches, community organizations, and other social institutions However, for those places that are so inclined, national and state legislators should consider collaborating with and supporting Non-governmental organizations [NGOs] seeking to help rural immigrants and their communities cope, adjust and prosper. Funding also could be provided to offer incentives to local governments in support of programs that would bring immigrant and native populations together in joint task of community development and understanding. Finally, it should be recognized that there is significant variation within places in the level of receptivity toward new immigrants. Grey and Woodrick (2005) speak of a '20-60-20' rule, whereby 20 percent of a local population will be welcoming, 20 percent unreceptive, but the 60 percent majority ambivalent. Just what these percentages are in a given place will differ, in part according to the composition of natives. In a study of rural adolescent attitudes, Gimpel and Lay (2008:197) find that '[h]ostility to immigrants ... was concentrated among youth from well-rooted and more affluent families, not the poor.' As more comes to be known about the correlates of receptivity, policy and educational programs might be better targeted to local pressure points that can increase receptivity or reduce hostility to new immigrants to rural areas of the US.

References

Baker, P.L. and Hotek, D.R. (2003), 'Perhaps a Blessing: Skills and Contributions of Recent Mexican Immigrants in the Rural Midwest', *Hispanic Journal of Behavioral Sciences*, 25:3, 448–68.

Cantú, L. (1995), 'The Peripheralization of Rural America: A Case Study of Latino Migrants in America's Heartland', *Sociological Perspectives*, 38:3, 399–414.

Clogg, C.C. (1979), *Measuring Underemployment: Demographic Indicators for the United States* (Washington, DC: National Academic Press).

Cravey, A.J. (1997), 'The Changing South: Latino Labor and Poultry Production in Rural North Carolina', *Southeastern Geographer*, 37:2, 295–300.

Crowley, M., Lichter, D.T. and Qian, Z. (2006), 'Beyond Gateway Cities: Economic Restructuring and Poverty Among Mexican Immigrant Families and Children' *Family Relations*, 55:3, 345–60.

Davis, K. (1974), 'The Migrations of Human Populations', in Piel et al. (eds).

Easterlin, R.A. et al. (1980), *Immigration* (Cambridge, MA: Harvard University Press).

Frey, W.H. (1996), 'Immigration, Domestic Migration, and Demographic Balkanization in America: New Evidence for the 1990s', *Population and Development Review*, 22, 353–75.

Gimpel, J.G. and Lay, J.C. (2008), 'Political Socialization and Reaction to Immigration-Related Diversity in Rural America', *Rural Sociology*, 73:2, 180–204.

Gouveia, L. and Stull, D.D. (1995), 'Dances with Cows: Beefpacking's Impact on Garden City, Kansas and Lexington, Nebraska', in Stull et al. (eds).

—— (1997), *Latino Immigrants, Meatpacking, and Rural Communities: A Case Study of Lexington, Nebraska*, JSRI Research Report No, 26. (East Lansing, MI: The Julian Samora Institute, Michigan State University).

Grey, M.A. and Woodrick, A.C. (2002), 'Unofficial Sister Cities: Meatpacking Labor Migration Between Villachuato, Mexico, and Marshalltown, Iowa', *Human Organization*, 61:4, 364–76.

—— (2005), '"Latinos Have Revitalized Our Community": Mexican Migration and Anglo Responses in Marshalltown, Iowa', in Zúñiga and Hernández-León (eds).

Gunderson, T.B. (ed.) (2002), *Immigration Policy in Turmoil* (New York: Nova Science Publishers).

Handlin, O. (1951), *The Uprooted: The Epic Story of the Great Migrations that Made the American People* (Cambridge, MA: Harvard University Press).

Hauser, P. (1074), 'The Measurement of Labor Utilization', *The Malayan Economic Review*, 19: 1–17.

Jensen, L. (1988), 'Patterns of Immigration and Public Assistance Utilization, 1970–1980', *International Migration Review*, 22:1, 51–83.

—— (1989), *The New Immigration: Implications for Poverty and Public Assistance Utilization* (New York: Greenwood Press).

—— (2006), 'New Immigrant Settlements in Rural America: Problems, Prospects, and Policies', *Reports on Rural America*, 1:3, 1–32 (Durham, NH: Carsey Institute, The University of New Hampshire).

Jensen, L. and Slack, T. (2003), 'Underemployment in America: Measurement and Evidence', *American Journal of Community Psychology*, 32:1/2, 21–31.

Johnson, K.M. and Lichter, D.T. (2008), ' Natural Increase: A New Source of Population Growth in Emerging Hispanic Destinations in the US', *Population and Development Review*, 34:2, 1–20.

Jones, M.A. (1960), *American Immigration* (Chicago: University of Chicago Press).

Kandel, W. and Cromartie, J. (2004), *New Patterns of Hispanic Settlement in Rural America*, Rural Development Research Report Number 99. (Washington, DC: United State Department of Agriculture).

LeMay, M.C. (2004), *US Immigration: A Reference Book* (Santa Barbara, CA: ABC-CLIO).

Lichter, D.T. and Johnson, K.M. (2006), 'Emerging Rural Settlement Patterns and the Geographic Resdistribution of America's New Immigrants', *Rural Sociology*, 71:1, 109–31.

Lieberson, S. (1980), *A Piece of the Pie: Blacks and White Immigrants Since 1880* (Berkeley, CA: University of California Press).

Logan, J.R. (2003), *America's Newcomers*. Albany, NY: Lewis Mumford Center for Comparative and Urban Regional Research [website]. <http://mumford1.

dyndns.org/cen2000/NewComersReport/NewComer01.htm>, accessed 29 July 2008.

Martin, P. and Martin, D. (1994), *The Endless Quest: Helping America's Farmworkers* (Boulder, CO: Westview Press).

Martin, P. and Midgley, E. (2003), 'Immigration: Shaping and Reshaping America', *Population Bulletin*, 58:2, 1–50.

Martin, P., Fix, M. and Taylor, J.E. (2006), *The New Rural Poverty* (Washington, DC: The Urban Institute Press).

Mayo-Smith, R. (1980), *Emigration and Immigration: A Study in Social Science* (New York: Charles Scribner's Sons).

Piel, G. et al. (eds) (1974), *The Human Population, A Scientific American Book* (San Francisco: W.H. Freeman)

Portes, A. and Bach, R.L. (1985), *Latin Journey: Cuban and Mexican Immigrants in the United States* (Berkeley, CA: The University of California Press).

Samora, J., Bustamente, J.A. and Cardenas, G. (1971), *Los Mojados: The Wetback Story* (South Bend, IN: Notre Dame University Press).

Simon, R. (1985), *Public Opinion and the Immigrant: Print Media Coverage, 1880–1980* (Lexington, MA: Lexington Books).

Singer, A. (2004), *The Rise of New Immigrant Gateway*, The Living Cities Census Series (Washington, DC: The Brookings Institution).

Stephenson, G.M. (1926), *A History of American Immigration: 1820–1924* (Boston: Ginn and Co.).

Stull, D.D., Broadway, M.J. and Griffith, D. (eds) (1995), *Any Way You Cut It: Meat Processing and Small-Town America* (Lawrence, KS: University Press of Kansas).

Taylor, J.E., Martin, P. and Fix, M. (1997), *Poverty Amid Prosperity: Immigration and the Changing Face of Rural California* (Washington, DC: The Urban Institute Press).

Van Hook, J., Glick, J.E. and Bean, F.D. (1999), 'Immigrant and Native Public Assistance Receipt: How the Unit of Analysis Affects Research Findings', *Demography*, 36:1, 111–20.

Vialet, J.C. (2002), 'A Brief History of US Immigration Policy' in Gunderson (ed.).

Zúñiga, V. and Hernández-León, R. (2005), *New Destinations: Mexican Immigration in the US* (New York: Russell Sage Foundation).

Chapter 3

Retention and Departure Factors Influencing Highly Skilled Immigrants in Rural Areas: Medical Professionals in Quebec, Canada

Myriam Simard

Introduction

This chapter addresses a subject area which has often been neglected in the context of rural immigration, namely the situation of highly skilled immigrants. Will they settle with their families in communities which are far from large towns or cities? What do their integration processes in rural communities look like? Would they like extended work contracts in this kind of space, and if so, under what conditions? These are some of the questions to which there are few answers at present. Hence, the aim of this chapter is to shed some light on these concerns, drawing on a case study of a particular group of qualified immigrants in Quebec's rural areas, immigrant physicians. A key interest here is to identify some of the basic conditions required to maximize the retention of this group.

The chapter provides first of all the general background to the issues described above, consisting of a brief overview of the Canada-wide immigration context. This is followed by a description of the specific situation in rural Quebec, with particular reference being made to the shortage of general practitioners. Policy approaches to the recruitment of immigrant physicians are referred to. The chapter moves then on to explain the empirical study carried out to explore rural immigrant physicians' situations and views on their professional and private lives. The main part of the chapter examines the various retention and leaving factors identified (professional, socio-cultural and community, family, personal, financial, and environmental), based on the physicians' experiences. In this context, some of the solutions proposed by the physicians themselves to improve retention of professionals in rural areas are considered. Before concluding, some important points are raised which seem worthwhile taking into account if the aim is to improve the recruitment and retention of medical staff in rural areas.

General Background

Brief Overview of the Immigration Context in Canada and Quebec

It is well recognized that Canada is an immigration country, and that immigrants are an important factor in Canada's population growth. In fact, the last population census in 2006 counted a total of 6,186,950 million immigrants,[1] who resided in the ten Canadian provinces and the three Northern territories (Yukon, North-West, Nunavut). This number constituted almost a fifth (19.8 per cent) of the total Canadian population of 31.2 million. Nearly all of these foreign born individuals lived in towns and cities (94.9 per cent), with a small minority (5.1 per cent) having settled in rural areas. The urban orientation of immigrants is easily noticeable, with nearly two thirds of all immigrants (62.9 per cent) being concentrated in the three principal Canadian census metropolitan areas.[2] These are, in order of importance, Toronto (Ontario) with an immigrant population of 45.7 per cent, Vancouver (British-Colombia) with a 39.6 per cent and Montreal (Quebec) with a 20.6 per cent immigrant population (Chui et al. 2007). Other immigrants have moved to middle sized cities, such as Calgary, Ottawa-Gatineau, Winnipeg, Victoria, and Saskatoon (Frideres 2006; Statistique Canada 2007). While in the more distant past, Europe was the main region from which immigrants originated, over the last thirty years or so, the countries of origin have diversified. Asia, Europe, Central and South America, the Antilles and Africa are all represented. Members of visible minority groups represented 16.2 per cent of the Canadian population in 2006, and almost all of these (95.9 per cent) lived in a metropolitan region (Statistique Canada 2008).

It is clear that only few immigrants have settled in rural localities. For this reason, the Canadian government, together with the provinces, have developed since the 1990s a number of policies, programmes and measures to change this trend by promoting the regionalization of immigration[3] (Carter et al. 2008; CIC 2003, 2001). Given the wide expanse and diversity of Canada, from the Atlantic Ocean in the East to the Pacific Ocean in the West, each province has distinctive characteristics. As a consequence, the regional distribution of immigrants is unequal, with the more prosperous provinces being in a more favourable position,

---

1   For Statistics Canada, immigrants are people born outside of Canada, who are permanent residents, that is residents who have been granted the right to live in Canada permanently by the immigration authorities (Statistics Canada 2006 Census of Population). Hence, this definition excludes temporary migrant workers.

2   By way of comparison, in 2006, only 77.5 per cent of the population born in Canada resided in towns and cities, and 22.5 per cent in rural areas. Just over a quarter (27.1 per cent) of the population born in Canada resided in the three metropolitan regions preferred by immigrants (Chui et al. 2007).

3   See Reimer (2007) for analyses of some policies and programmes in several provinces.

such as British Columbia, Ontario and Alberta (JIMI 2008; Reimer 2007; CES 2005). At the time of the last census in 2006, Beshiri and He (2009) calculated the number of immigrants in predominantly rural regions[4] in Canada to be 628,295, compared with 580,545 ten years before in 1996 (Beshiri and He 2009; Beshiri 2004; Beshiri and Alfred 2002). These immigrants are mostly of a group that arrived over 20 years ago (that is before 1986), with the more recent arrivals having tended to settle in towns and cities. The rural immigrants came first and foremost from Europe, but also from the United States, Asia, and Central and South America. Some of the sectors of employment in which these rural immigrants have worked due to labour shortages include meatpacking plants, local agriculture, oil, tourism and services (Beshiri and He 2009; Bollman et al. 2007). Their jobs tend to be unskilled and low paying, with difficult working conditions[5] (Fairey et al. 2008; Broadway 2007; Simard 1997).

These immigrants are regarded as an important factor of demographic, economic, social and cultural revitalization in the current context in which many rural communities have experienced a decline in their ageing populations, with decreasing birthrates and an exodus of young people. They are also suffering from fragile local economies and a shortage of labour. At the same time, a growing trend in Canada comprises the recruitment of temporary foreign labour (including workers from Mexico, the Caribbean, China, the Philippines and Guatemala) in order to address labour shortages, especially in agriculture, construction and the service sector.[6] These low skilled workers must return to their countries of origin once their contracts end. Practitioners and academics have found that this group tends to suffer from inadequate housing and working conditions (such as low wages, long hours, overcrowded dwellings, health risks, unsafe transportation, exclusion from services and protections associated with citizenship) and numerous forms of exploitation and rights violations. These extremely difficult conditions, have to be accepted obediently by fear of being repatriated (CDPDJ 2008; ABE 2007; TUAC Canada 2007; Preibisch 2004). This poses fundamental questions about the rights and protection of these flexible foreign workers, who are isolated and vulnerable, without permanent resident status. They are increasingly used by

---

4   Predominantly rural regions are census divisions (CDs) where more than 50 percent of the population lives in a rural community. A rural community has a density less than 150 persons per square kilometre (Statistics Canada 2006). Here, Statistics Canada uses the regional typology of the Organization of Economic Co-operation and Development (OECD) geographic definition.

5   By the time this book was being finalized, certain detailed facts of 2006 for immigrants in rural Canada and Quebec were not yet available, especially information on their types of employment. We would like to thank here Roland Beshiri from Statistics Canada for having provided us with some supplementary information.

6   In agriculture, the number of foreign temporary workers is estimated to amount to around 20,000 per year, of whom 85 per cent can be found in Ontario. These are principally Mexican and Caribbean people. Quebec holds the second place with nearly 4,000 such workers.

certain small and middle-sized Canadian enterprises with the aim of remaining competitive in the context of globalization.

We have to remind ourselves that historically, Canada has already experienced successive waves of immigration to rural areas, the most important one being linked to the campaign of Western Canada's colonization at the beginning of the 20th century. Free land was offered to pioneers, namely, mostly American and European immigrants who settled the vast Prairie lands. Ukranian farmers belong to the most important groups to have established themselves in the West during this period. Another wave occurred following World War II, with the arrival of Dutch and Swiss farmers who were looking for good land not just in the West, but also in Ontario and Quebec.[7] Other immigrants worked in rural areas, notably in construction of the transcontinental railways, in mines, sawmills and as lumberjacks. However, the transformation in Canada from a rural economy based on agriculture and the exploitation of natural resources at the beginning of the 20th century to a more urban economy centred on manufacturing and services also resulted in changes in the countryside. Beginning with the decade around 1970 to 1980, a greater diversification of immigrants' countries of origin and skills could be observed, parallel with the fact that they felt undoubtedly attracted to the metropolitan centres (Boyd 2000; Knowles 2000).

Concerning the province of Quebec with its population of 7.4 million, census data recorded a total of 851,560 immigrants in 2006 (Statistiques Canada 2007). According to the Canadian constitution, this province shares the responsibility for immigration with the federal government, and in 1968, Quebec began to exercise this joint jurisdiction and took leadership with the creation of a Ministry of Immigration of Quebec. Following successive agreements with the federal government since 1971, Quebec acquired the entire autonomy regarding the selection of those permanent immigrants who had established themselves in the province, as well as the reception and integration of new arrivals into Quebecoise society.[8] It is worthwhile considering the specific characteristics of this province, especially the challenges it faces in promoting the sustainability of the French language and culture in North America, as well as the integration of immigrants into francophone communities. Quebec undertook special efforts to augment the proportion of francophone immigrants, but without excluding allophones (that is immigrants whose native tongue is neither French nor English) or anglophones, with a perspective of comprehensive and sustainable development (MCCI

---

7 For historical studies on Canadian rural immigration, see for example: Burnet and Palmer (1988); Ganzevoort (1988); Petryshyn (1985); Akenson (1984).

8 The agreement Canada-Quebec of 1990 confirms Quebec's support for the two principles of family reunification and international solidarity, such as the reception of refugees. Moreover, the agreement authorizes the province to determine the volume and composition of a great share of immigration to its territory, to establish its selection criteria, to promote the province and select its immigrants, as well as to decide on certain rules with regard to sponsorship (MRCI 2004).

1991). As in other parts of Canada, the province is affected by an ageing and declining population. It must urgently address its demographic developments with immigration as well as with family policies.

It is also important to note that in 1992, Quebec adopted a policy of promoting immigration to non-metropolitan areas. This policy sought to bring about the more balanced spatial distribution and long-term settlement of immigrants in Quebec's rural areas.[9] The goals of attraction and retention were central to this policy (Simard 1996). However, it has yet to yield truly significant results. In fact, the 2006 Canadian census still revealed modest changes with a high concentration of immigrants in the Montreal metropolitan area and the neighbouring cities (740,355), that is to say 87 per cent of all the immigrants in the province. This means that, nearly fifteen years after the policy was introduced, only 13 per cent of immigrants were located in non-metropolitan areas, that is, in small or medium-sized cities or towns and rural areas such as Québec (3.08 per cent of immigrants), Sherbrooke (1.22 per cent), Trois-Rivières (0.36 per cent) (Statistiques Canada 2007).

Consequently, only a small number of immigrants can be found in Quebec's rural areas. The analyst, Beshri, calculated the number to be at 33,290 in predominantly rural regions in 2006. They originate mostly from Europe, and then from Asia, Central and South America, as well as Africa.[10] Immigrants in Quebec therefore show the same urban concentration as is the case in the rest of Canada. This accentuates even more the distinction between rural and urban areas, with the latter receiving the majority of immigrants. In addition to employment in agriculture, it appears that recent rural immigrants have found jobs in the manufacturing or service sectors, where they fill labour shortages. The presence of these immigrants provides evidence of the key characteristics of contemporary rurality, such as the diversification of rural populations. This has brought about challenges related to the integration of people with different backgrounds and values in rural areas, the various types of occupations of land, and the sustainable development (SRQ 2008, 2000; Simard 2007c).

Immigration to the rural areas of Quebec is not a recent phenomenon here either, as Quebec was already familiar with different previous waves of rural

---

9   For a history and critical analysis of Quebec's policy on promoting immigration to non-metropolitan areas, see Simard (1996). See also Allen et al. (2007) for more recent developments of the policy.

10   Statistics Canada, supplementary information. Amongst these immigrants, there is a noticeable presence of refugees. They are the only group of immigrants to whom the government can assign a regional and rural destination. At the beginning of the 1980s, Quebec received refugees from the South China Sea, half of whom were allocated first of all to regional small towns, and second to rural areas. This constituted one of the first contemporary initiatives in Quebec which aimed to regionalize immigration. Their retention in those areas remained minimal, as after two years, the majority had either moved to Montreal, or had left the province (Simard 1996). The challenge of integrating and maintaining these immigrants in rural and regional areas is therefore acutely relevant.

immigration, comprising in particular immigrant farmers of European origin (for example, Germans, Belgians, Swiss and French) who arrived after World War II (SOHCCQ 1985). This kind of agricultural immigration has decreased since the 1990s as the context of the global economy has complicated the immigration of foreign farmers (Simard 2008). Farmer immigrants are considered to have integrated with particular success, not only economically, but also socially, culturally and politically. A study of these immigrant entrepreneurs has shown well their ability to profit from their extended networks, especially international ones, to introduce innovations which allow them to position themselves well in the context of opening markets. In addition, the entire family is involved in diverse local associations – the farmers, as well as their partners and children. Their impact therefore reaches well beyond the economic sphere (Simard 1995a, 1995b, 1994). The situation is completely different for the seasonal agricultural immigrant workers in Quebec (Africans, Haitians, Latin Americans, East Europeans and Vietnamese). They are well familiar with difficult working conditions and legal and social exclusion (Simard 1997; Mimeault and Simard 1999, 2001). Their situation is similar to that of other immigrant workers in agriculture in Canada, who live in precarious conditions, experiencing poverty and discrimination.[11] The Quebecoise countryside is consequently marked by a certain polarization between skilled and unskilled employment for rural immigrants.

Having provided an overview of historical and contemporary trends of rural immigration at the Canadian national and provincial level, this chapter will now turn to explore in depth the situation of rural immigrant physicians in Quebec in recent years. As will have become clear from the discussion above, immigrants in professional jobs do not constitute the majority of immigrant workers in rural areas. However, as will be demonstrated below, their role in rural development can be extremely important as they can fill important skill gaps, and are also involved in social and community life. Hence, studying issues related to the attraction and retention of immigrants with skills which are of short supply in rural areas can provide an evidence base on which policy development can be based.

Shortage of General Practitioners in Quebec Rural Areas and the
Recommendation of Recruiting Immigrant Physicians

For a number of years now, the problem of the uneven distribution of physicians in the different regions of Quebec has been widely described, highly publicized and the subject of recommendations in all reports on recruitment problems. In 2000, the Clair Commission Report raised the question of the geographic maldistribution of medical staff and the shortage of general practitioners, especially in 'peripheral and remote' areas. It recommended, in the short term, a number of targeted, exceptional measures that would allow both for an increase in medical staff where there was a real shortage and greater accessibility to healthcare for the Quebec

---

11   See among others: Cecil and Ebanks 1991; Satzewich 1988; Wong 1988.

population as a whole. In the context of meeting the needs for medical manpower, some of these recommendations made direct reference to immigrants as a possible solution and source of recruitment.[12] It is noteworthy that the shortage of medical professionals in rural areas affects other Canadian provinces to a similar extent, so that they are well familiar with this problem, as articles in medical and scientific Canadian journals confirm (Mullally et al. 2007; Grant 2006; Audas et al. 2005).

However, the lack of in-depth knowledge of the issue of immigrant physicians in Quebec's rural areas[13] afforded little solid support for the recommended measures. Despite the existence, since the early 1980s, of a program (*Diplômés hors Canada et États-Unis*, or DHCEU) that addressed physicians with credentials from outside Canada and the United States, nothing was known about the dynamics of their professional, social and family integration, nor about the factors that retained them in rural areas.[14] In 2001, in an effort to more thoroughly document the reality of immigrant physicians practicing in rural areas, *Quebec's Ministère de la Santé et des Services sociaux (the MSSS*, or health and social services ministry) therefore funded a research project on this subject, which had been designed by the author of this chapter. While this study of physicians concentrated on the territorial distribution of medical staff and their retention in the context of increasingly alarming shortages in rural areas, it also looked at the broader context of rural immigration and at policies designed to promote immigration to non-metropolitan areas. The rationale behind this approach was that in order to form an overview of the current situation regarding immigrant physicians in remote areas, the study was to analyze the issue from both angles (shortage of medical manpower and rural immigration).

Various studies on non-metropolitan immigration conducted by the author of this chapter have revealed the complexity of the factors likely to enter into immigrants' decisions to remain in these areas or return to urban centres (Simard

---

12   Clair Commission (2000), *Emerging Solutions*, Report and Recommendations, *Ministère de la Santé et des Services sociaux (MSSS)*, Quebec. See also INSPQ (2004) and the MSSS website under 'Médecin en région,' at www.msss.gouv.qc.ca/enregion, Gouvernement of Quebec.

13   For the purpose of this study, 'rural' in the context of Quebec includes both 'rural' and 'remote.' It refers to rural areas and small towns, which include urban areas of less than 10,000 inhabitants and rural areas outside the commuting zones of large urban centers (10,000 inhabitants or more) (du Plessis et al. 2002: 8).

14   It must be remembered that this program was implemented in 1983–84 for medical graduates from outside Canada and the United States. Through the *Recrutement Santé Québec* [RSQ], a department of the MSSS, physicians with foreign qualifications are offered first a residency in family medicine that will involve a contractual commitment to practice in rural areas later on. Hence, after the end of their residency, and provided the immigrant physicians are considered successful in their practice, they fulfil their contract for four years in a region that has priority needs and is a so-called MSSS-designated region. Only after completing this residency are these internationally trained physicians eligible to sit the examinations leading to a permit to practice medicine in Quebec.

2007a). Thus, not only do economic and professional factors come into play (Simard 1995a, 1995b, 1994), but also factors pertaining to the social and cultural vitality of the host community, services available and overall quality of life (Simard 2007b; Simard et al. 2001). The case of immigrant physicians practising in rural areas provides an ideal opportunity for summarizing these numerous retention and departure factors since they each play a role to varying degrees.

The Study

This qualitative study pursued two primary objectives by examining the experiences of immigrant physicians having practised in rural areas of Quebec for at least their initial four-year contract. Data was collected from the physicians through in-depth interviews. The first objective was to describe the overall socio-professional and family integration process of immigrant physicians, or physicians trained outside Canada and the United States (DHCEU), in rural areas in Quebec. The second was to highlight the main retention factors involved in this process. Through analysis of the testimonials given by these physicians, an effort was made to provide a long-term view of immigrants' contribution to solving the problem of the shortage of general practitioners in rural areas.[15] By integration, we mean in this study a complex, dynamic and comprehensive process not limited to the economic sphere but including all the others aspects of life in rural areas, such as social, cultural, community, and political. The structural factors (for example, the health system, skilled labour shortage, process of recognition of qualifications, dynamism of the region) as well as circumstantial factors (for example, family situations, children's education) that affected this integration process were all analysed to give a more nuanced and overall perspective. The multiple and diverse integration strategies of the immigrant physicians, their social networks as well as their participation activities (professional, social, cultural, and community) in rural society were scrutinized.

In this study, the term *immigrant physician* means a general practitioner having obtained his or her immigrant status and signed a contract obliging him or her to practice in an establishment located in a rural area designated by the MSSS. This DHCEU program in fact enables foreign-trained physicians to practice in Quebec on condition that their diploma is recognized, that they take postdoctoral training in a residency program offered at a Quebec university (usually two years) and that they pass the required examinations. Their participation in the program is

---

15   For a detailed overview of the results of this study, see the final report by Simard, M. and Van Schendel, N. (2004), *Les médecins immigrants et non immigrants en régions éloignées au Québec: processus d'insertion globale et facteurs de rétention,* Cahier de recherche de l'INRS-UCS, Montreal. This report may be downloaded in PDF format from the following address: http://www.ucs.inrs.ca/. See the heading *Publications and documents,* and click on *Research reports and notes.*

contingent upon their signing a contract in which they commit to practising for a four-year period in a designated area (rural and short of medical staff). This means that this medical practice in rural areas is performed on a contractual rather than voluntary basis.

It was further deemed worthwhile to compare these immigrant physicians to a control group of Quebec-trained physicians who were also required by contractual agreement to practice medicine in rural areas for a period equal to that required of their immigrant counterparts. This group comprised general practitioners having benefited from annual subsidies awarded under Quebec's *Bourses d'études en médecine (*medical studies subsidy program)*. The recipients may benefit from up to four years of financial aid in exchange for practicing medicine for an equal number of years outside the large urban centres. This comparison made it possible to explore both the similarities and differences between the two groups, thus casting clearer light on the distinct aspects of their respective experiences.

To thoroughly understand the range of possible experiences, we interviewed immigrant physicians and medical subsidy recipients who either *stayed* in rural areas after their initial contracts or *left* for the large urban centres. On the basis of two lists provided by the Quebec Ministry of Health and the social services, complying with the Law on Information Access,[16] a total of 45 semi-structured interviews were carried out in 2003, including 24 with immigrant physicians (DHCEU) and 21 with medical subsidy recipients. Of this number, 15 immigrant physicians and 11 subsidy recipients had left the rural areas at the time of the interviews, versus nine immigrant physicians and ten subsidy recipients who had remained. In other words, in total, 58 per cent of the physicians had left compared to 42 per cent who had stayed to continue practicing rural medicine. The interviews lasted an average of approximately one and a quarter hours.

What were the main characteristics of these general practitioners? The respondents, both immigrant physicians and subsidy recipients, were primarily men, as only 10 of the physicians were female and they were mainly immigrants. Most of the respondents were married and arrived in the rural areas with their spouses (78 per cent).[17] Nearly half of the immigrant physicians came from Europe, with a similar proportion coming from South America, the West Indies and Asia. Only a negligible number came from the Middle East. With regard to

---

16   We have also benefited from the collaboration with the *Fédération des médecins omnipraticiens du Québec* (FMOQ) which sent a letter to physicians to inform them about the research project and invited them to participate. This has facilitated our recruitment of study participants (see Chapter 2, Méthodologie, in Simard and Van Schendel 2004).

17   One unusual fact was that a minority of the married immigrant physicians (five cases) arrived in the rural area alone, without their spouses, who had stayed in the city with the children, notably to continue their jobs. Only one physician joined his family in the city upon completion of his initial contract, while the others remained in the rural area beyond their initial commitment and found various forms of accommodation arrangements including, for one particular physician, moving his family to join him in the rural area.

the rural or urban origin of the immigrant physicians, the majority came from an urban environment, that is they were born in cities and had mostly lived there until settling in the rural area after their medical residency in Quebec. The subsidy recipients stood apart here, as nearly half of them had rural origins. Their choice to go to a rural area was therefore partly influenced by their familiarity with such an environment, a familiarity acquired during childhood and that was not shared by most of the immigrant physicians.

An age gap of nearly 10 years differentiated the immigrant physicians from the subsidy recipients, who were significantly younger. The average age of the respondents at the time of the interviews was in fact 51 for the immigrant physicians and 41.5 for the subsidy recipients. This gap is attributable to the long processes that the immigrant physicians had to go through to obtain their permit to practice medicine in Quebec (eight years of waiting on average). In fact, their trajectory between their arrival in Quebec and the start of their medical practice in a rural area involved a long and difficult waiting period, notably marked by their having to work at underqualified jobs (in factories, restaurants, hotels, hospital maintenance, etc.) in order to survive and meet their family obligations.

Their experience was compounded by a real concern about remaining outside medicine for too long and losing their skills and knowledge through lack of practice. The loss of professional identity and fear of moving too far away from medicine were the overriding concerns expressed in the interviews. Given the problems in having their diplomas and medical expertise recognized, a large number of the immigrant physicians envisaged going to practice in the United States and had even passed their American equivalence examinations. The difficulty of obtaining the recognition of foreign credentials, the risk of de-skilling and the various barriers the highly skilled immigrants encountered when attempting to enter in the professional labour market have become increasingly documented and criticized in Quebec and the rest of Canada, in particular with regards to the specific professions of engineers, physicians, nurses, dentists, pharmacists and agronomists (Hawthorne 2007; Wong et al. 2007; Ngo et al. 2006; Krahn et al. 2000; Basran and Zong 1998) .

The prospect of practicing medicine in rural areas did not therefore have exactly the same significance for immigrant physicians and subsidy recipients. In fact, virtually all the immigrant physicians viewed the prospect positively as it gave them 'the chance' to be able to practice their profession in the host country. The concept of an 'exchange of services' came up in several interviews, with the physicians drawing on either their past experiences of public service abroad,[18] or on their feelings of loyalty and recognition toward the host country, to confirm

---

18   Unexpectedly, slightly more than half (58 per cent) of the immigrant physicians had experienced rural medicine in their country of origin, for periods ranging from one to ten years. Some had acquired this experience in the context of their public service years in their country of origin. They met this public service obligation in exchange for having had their medical training paid by the state and by way of 'recognition' for the latter. Hence the

that the contractual obligation to practice for four years in a rural area struck them as 'normal' and 'fair'. They saw it as a 'fair deal', particularly given the context of a shortage of physicians in such areas. At a more subtle level, however, some complaints regarding the contractual obligation were discernable, largely regarding its negative impact on marital and family life, the inequity with other non-immigrant physicians, or simply the rural lifestyle running contrary to their personal tastes.

By contrast, the majority of the subsidy recipients cited the challenge of running a comprehensive and multi-faceted practice as the main incentive for going to rural areas, coupled with, secondarily, a taste for discovery and adventure. Clearly, for them, practicing rural medicine seemed to provide a means of gaining greater autonomy in their profession, closer and continuous contact with their patients, as well as an opportunity to 'experience something different'. In fact, this attitude of the subsidy recipients toward the prospect of practising rural medicine was influenced by their 'youth'. As they were young when they first arrived in rural areas, they were in the phase of their lives where the idea of taking on challenge and adventure was particularly appealing. Also at play was the concept of 'overall quality of life', which is vital to today's younger generation, as I have observed in other studies (Simard 2003a). The young subsidy recipients were not indifferent to this factor, and in fact were also seeking a quality of life that met their aspirations in terms of work, less stress and an environment conducive to raising a family, outdoor access, peace and quiet.

To Stay or to Leave? Retention and Departure Factors Pertaining to Rural Areas

What emerges from analysis of the integration process of the physicians, both immigrant and subsidy recipients, is the dynamic interaction between several factors that are likely to influence their decision to stay or leave at the end of their initial contract. The importance of these factors can fluctuate over time and according to the period that the physician may be going through in life (marriage, children's teenage years, divorce, sick parents in the city, etc.). Rather than going into the details of the various trajectories followed by these physicians,[19] this chapter will concentrate only on the major trends in order to highlight the main factors at work. These factors, which are six in number, will each be analyzed in turn: professional factors, socio-cultural and community factors, family factors (spouse and children), personal factors, financial factors, and factors related to the

idea of working in a rural area after their postdoctoral training was not totally new to them since they had already served their country by practising in remote rural areas.

19   For interested readers, Chapter 4.3 of the report entitled *Les seuils de la rétention ou les conditions de la durée* presents an in-depth analysis of these trajectories and the various time intervals spent in rural areas (Simard and Van Schendel 2004).

natural environment. When pertinent, they will be discussed in conjunction with the solutions suggested by the physicians themselves to improve retention rates.

Professional Factors

Professional factors usually appear at the top of the physicians' lists of reasons for staying or leaving. They are also the factors that have attracted the greatest attention from researchers, judging from a review of the literature on this subject (L'Acteur rural 2003; Humphreys et al. 2002; Kamien 1998; Mongeau et al. 1994).[20] They concern as much the type of medical practice in the rural area, as the working conditions (workload, medical staff, successors, the welcome and support offered by colleagues…) and the possibilities of transfers.

A first observation is in order here: the physicians, both immigrants and subsidy recipients, appreciated practising rural medicine in terms of the autonomy it gave them, the broad range of care they had to administer, and the close and continuous rapport they had with their patients. The fact that they had limited access to specialists obliged them to broaden their skills (cardiology, obstetrics, orthopaedics, surgery and so on) and to become more versatile. The prior rural experience of the immigrant physicians stood out as a clear asset when the time came for them to go to a rural area in Quebec, since their foreign medical experience had helped them develop qualities, such as autonomy and versatility, that were particularly pertinent in such areas. In addition, they had had to manage in difficult contexts where there was a dire shortage of resources such as a war situation.

The required versatility and autonomy corresponded to the physicians' own concept of what a general practitioner should be: a 'true family doctor/generalist' with a more active, overall and satisfying role than in the urban context. They therefore found fulfilment as rural physicians despite the demanding nature of the practice, provided there was a good balance maintained in the working conditions. This concept of balance is fundamental to their retention. As long as these conditions were acceptable, generally speaking, they did not consider leaving. The conditions conducive to contract renewal mainly involved a reasonable workload and good team spirit among the physicians. Work relations, including mutual aid and support among colleagues, were rarely criticized by the physicians, two-thirds of whom gave this aspect a highly positive rating. This collaboration within the team would appear to have been one of the strengths in the professional working conditions for these rural physicians, and often led to friendships that extended beyond the work context.

However, when the working conditions deteriorated as the result of a chronic shortage of physicians, they then became a key factor in the physicians' departure

---

20   For a survey of the literature on the retention of general practitioners in rural areas, see Chapter 1 of the report (Simard and Van Schendel 2004). Also refer to the critical review by Humphreys et al. 2001.

from the rural areas owing to the work overload and resulting decline in their overall quality of life, from personal, family, socio-cultural, community, and professional standpoints. For not only did persistent shortages have negative impacts, such as real burnout within the local medical team, but they also hampered recruitment of potential medical successors, who avoided committing to an area facing such flagrant shortages of medical staff. The balance and stability among the base team were thus undermined and the working conditions became patently unsatisfactory.

It was this work overload, combined with the heavy responsibilities when there was a critical shortage of staff that was most often cited by several physicians (both immigrants and subsidy recipients) who had left to return to cities, as the deciding factor in their departure. This situation was exacerbated by the already precarious balance between their professional and personal lives. Among the possible solutions envisaged, the physicians asserted that an increase in medical staff in rural areas was absolutely essential to solving the problems of the work overload faced by physicians and of physician retention. Solving this problem would stabilize the local, base medical team and lead to an improvement in working conditions (fewer hours, less stress, more free time for the community and family leisure activities and so on).

Another factor concerns the freedom to make professional choices and to benefit from possible mobility and transfers in a fluctuating life trajectory. In general, physicians do not want to lock themselves in by making irreversible decisions regarding their careers. No one can predict the future, and physicians – immigrants or not – wish to keep the doors open for the different opportunities that may arise over the years, not only professionally speaking, but also on the personal and family levels. Any obstacles to these opportunities in the medium and long term risk being viewed negatively and thus represent a dissuasive factor in terms of the decision to stay in the rural area and even in the choice to go there voluntarily. The different phases of life come into play here. As the physicians get older, their career progresses and their children grow, their interests and needs also change. Nothing is set in time and everything is subject to change. Some physicians, both immigrants and subsidy recipients, therefore left the rural area at the end of their contracts, fearing that they would never have the possibility of being transferred to the city in view of the rumours circulating about the possible imposition of restrictive regulations by the government.[21]

Finally, one last and more indirect factor, but one that may facilitate integration and retention, concerns the physician's first professional contact with the target rural area during his or her reconnaissance trip and visit to the regional hospital. Several immigrant physicians attested that a positive experience during their medical residency in the rural area, a warm welcome from colleagues and the

---

21   These rumours related to possible administrative measures to be implemented by the Ministry, which were to render a return to urban centres more difficult for those physicians practicing in rural regions.

local population, and the presence of other immigrant physicians who invited them to come and settle in the area, were all crucial factors. Furthermore, the physicians suggested that structured reconnaissance trips be organized in order to give future physicians looking for a rural area to practice in, a specific, clear and comprehensive view of the area, beyond simply the visit to the regional hospital. These tours through the areas, which the spouses could join, would provide one means of obviating nasty surprises and of facilitating the long-term settlement of family physicians. This proposal is particularly pertinent for immigrant physicians, who initially know nothing of the rural areas.[22]

Socio-cultural and Community Factors

Socio-cultural and community factors often rank second among the physicians' reasons for staying or leaving, particularly when combined with the first-ranking professional factors. These factors are associated with the physician's social, cultural and community experiences in his or her living environment. Depending on the quality of his or her integration into this environment, the physician may be won over by the characteristics of the rural area and want to settle there long-term, or contrarily, may feel isolated and estranged, finding virtually no attraction or source of contentment, and may want to leave to go somewhere else. These factors frequently interact with others (mainly professional and personal) in the decision to stay or leave, as has been demonstrated in other international studies (Wulff et al. 2008; Pope et al. 1998; Cutchin et al. 1994).

A first aspect leaps out when analyzing the testimonials from most of the physicians, both immigrants and subsidy recipients, who remained beyond their first contract. The social and community life available to them in the rural area offered them several advantages: a warm welcome, solidarity and mutual aid in the neighbourhood, easy and satisfying social relations with the local population, the possibility for some of becoming involved in the community, respect and social recognition by the community for the contribution they made as both physicians and citizens, and so forth. They thus managed to form true feelings of belonging to the community in which they were living. In this regard, their status as 'village notables' conferred by the community generated original opportunities for social and community involvement for nearly one-third of the physicians.

---

22   It should be noted that 'reconnaissance trips' are a systematic practice among immigrant agricultural entrepreneurs wishing to settle in rural Quebec. Generally speaking, these immigrants pay two or three visits to the target areas, including one with their spouse. The latter's agreement is crucial to the success of their long-term settlement. Sometimes a fellow countryman (serving as an informal sponsor) or a friend who has already settled in Quebec accompanies the would-be immigrant as a goodwill gesture. Each reconnaissance trip lasts a couple of weeks. This formula usually yields positive results in that it prevents certain problems from arising when the family makes the definitive move (see Simard 1995a; 1994:47–50).

The simpler and slower pace of rural life compared to that in large urban centres is often mentioned, along with less stress, less traffic, less criminal activity and more time for in-depth social relationships. In other words, according to some physicians, it constituted an ideal context for raising children safely, apart from the lack of cultural activities such as movies and theatre. However, the narrower range of activities than in the city was often offset by other local activities, notably outdoors for example, hunting, fishing, hiking, canoeing/camping, and varied family leisure activities). A number of physicians confirmed that the rural context enabled them to achieve a good balance between their professional and private lives, thus improving their overall quality of life, except of course, during critical periods when there was a shortage of physicians.

In contrast, for the physicians who had left, certain aspects of the social and community life had not pleased them and were seen as challenges to the point of preventing them from truly appreciating and integrating into their new living environment. These aspects included fields of interest and systems of values that differed from their own, a certain closed mentality in the community, the social and cultural distance kept by the local population, and the lack of privacy in the sparsely populated area. The result was virtually no involvement in the community on the part of these physicians, both immigrants and subsidy recipients, and little feeling of belonging and rootedness. This relative detachment from the social and community life promoted their departure for large urban centres.

The following problems appear to have been more common among those immigrant physicians who left: less frequent social relations outside work, some mistrust on the part of the local population, fewer invitations from the local population for them to become involved in community life, and discrimination and racism. Their double status as 'strangers', first, as urbanites not coming from the community (a status shared by the subsidy recipients) and second, as immigrants coming from foreign countries, was sometimes prejudicial to them. A certain split between these physicians and the local population was then observed.

It is important to remember that most of the immigrant physicians come from urban environments. It is therefore not surprising that several of them returned to the city, in this case, Montreal, as soon as they could, given their greater affinity with the urban lifestyle (see section D, Personal Factors). Some did so as soon as their contracts ended, citing the importance of reconnecting with family, community of origin and the cultural, artistic and cosmopolitan environment of a big city. The isolation and solitude experienced in rural areas, the distance from familiar urban reference points, certain attitudes on the part of the local population that were sometimes offensive and unjustified only served to reinforce their decision to leave. This preference among the immigrant physicians for an urban environment has already been noted in other American and Australian studies (Simmons et al. 2002; Pathman and Konrad 1996). However, generalizations must not be made too hastily because slightly more than one-third of the immigrant physicians discussed here (37 per cent) did in fact stay beyond their first contract for several reasons, including stability for children, familiarity with rural life due to public service rendered in rural areas in their country of origin, and satisfaction with their role as a family doctor.

Family Factors

Most of the physicians interviewed, both immigrants and subsidy recipients, were married and had arrived in the rural area with their spouses (78 per cent). Of these spouses, 40 per cent were unable to find work in the area. The other spouses held jobs mainly in the health sector, primarily as nurses. Nearly half of the physicians already had children when they arrived, particularly the families of the immigrant physicians, given that they were older than the subsidy recipients. Several physicians, notably the subsidy recipients, had children during their first contract. The testimonials from all these physicians were particularly revealing in terms of the relative importance of family factors, pertaining to either spouses or children, in their decision to stay or leave. This importance has been repeatedly evidenced in the literature (Humphrey et al. 2001).

Spouse's professional fulfillment The question of the employment of the physicians' spouses, both immigrant and subsidy recipient, was not unimportant in their experiences. A reflection of the current labour context, both spouses wanted to fulfill themselves, notably through gratifying work, such that professional inactivity was generally unwelcome.[23] Over time, it became a source of tension, and in some cases, even the cause of a break-up. Neither taking care of children nor doing volunteer work in the various local associations filled the void left by a professional career that was on hold. In the long term, the impossibility of the spouse finding suitable employment became a decisive factor in the decision to leave, a point emphasized by the physicians in their interviews. The expressions they used to describe this situation suggest the severity of the loss experienced by the spouse: 'doing nothing and going around in circles', 'boredom', 'depression', 'terrible experience', 'feeling defeated', 'sacrificing his/her career', 'work opportunities wiped out'.[24]

Underlying this factor of spousal inactivity is the entire question of the decline in and destructuring of some rural areas in Quebec, where jobs are rarer than in cities, largely due to an anomic economy and a high unemployment rate.[25] This is

---

23   One exception must be noted, however. A few of the spouses of the immigrant physicians seemed perfectly satisfied to stay and home and take care of the children rather than getting a job outside the home, owing to their different cultural values.

24   Interviews with immigrant physicians and medical subsidy recipients, 2003, translation from French.

25   It is important to note that there are major regional differences in Quebec, with some rural areas enjoying good demographic and economic conditions and others – mostly remote – suffering from the decline in their economy, unemployment, poverty, the decrease

particularly applicable to high-qualification jobs, such that several well-educated spouses in the study had to abandon their promising careers in the city to accompany their partners to the rural areas. These spouses thus applied pressure to leave the area upon completion of the contract, given that they had been unable to find a job corresponding to their skill set. What emerges here is the importance of having a satisfying and gratifying job for both. As one of the physicians so aptly put it, 'if you want to retain physicians, both [physician and spouse] must be happy'.[26] In this regard, several physicians suggested strengthening support initiatives from the community to assist the spouse in her/his job search. According to these physicians, this is one of the keys to long-term settlement.

Educational opportunities for the physicians' children   The physicians faced a particular dilemma once their children were ready to begin their post-secondary education. In fact, the limitations of the rural school system in Quebec oblige children to leave home to continue their higher-level studies. Hence, this constituted one of the critical stages in which the physician's family had to decide whether to stay in the rural area without their children who had gone to study elsewhere, or to leave with them. A secondary factor was that the quality of education offered in some secondary schools did not always meet the criteria of certain parents. This may have further promoted the decision to leave the area in quest of the best possible quality of education, one that was well suited to the young person's interests and talents.

The issue of the limitations of the rural education system was more acute in certain immigrant physician families. The absence of private schools in rural areas that could offer a greater level of supervision for children, the perceived lesser value placed on education in the countryside, the problems of violence and drugs, the limited diversity of the pedagogical systems were all repeatedly mentioned as a cause of their departure from the rural area. Some of the subsidy recipients shared this viewpoint, and if they had not already left the area, they planned to do so when their children reached secondary school or the post-secondary education stage.

Despite their critical comments about the rural school system, most of these immigrant parents said how much they appreciated the quality of their children's socio-cultural integration in the rural areas prior to adolescence, which notably helped the children cultivate numerous friendships. This observation corroborates the results of another study in which young people of immigrant origin, primarily non-European, confirmed that they returned to the rural area after completing their higher education in the city precisely to regain their social connectedness and the friendlier, warmer atmosphere they had experienced during childhood. At the same

in services, aging of the population, and their exodus of young people. See among others in this regard: Conseil des affaires sociales 1989; Côté et al. 1995; Julien 1995; Leclerc and Béland 2003; MAMR 2006; Proulx 2002; Vachon et al. 1991.

26   Interview with a medical subsidy recipient, 2003, translation from French.

time, these young people said they felt greater stigmatization of immigrants and their offspring during their stay in cosmopolitan cities such as Montreal (Simard 2003b).

A personalized welcome and support for the social and community integration of the spouse and children Generally speaking, the physicians who stayed in the rural areas after their first contract, whether immigrants or subsidy recipients, stressed that they had successfully integrated in that their families felt a sense of attachment to the area. This positive assessment remained contingent upon the host community's ability to offer a personalized welcome and support to all family members, mainly by helping them overcome the difficulties faced during the first few months of their adaptation (looking for a house, registering their children at school, providing information on local resources, addressing loneliness and isolation, etc.), and by compensating for their distance from an extended-family support network. The immigrant physicians also cited the importance of there being an open-minded attitude toward foreigners. This concept of a warm welcome is crucial to promoting the families' well-being and retention right from the outset. France provides a telling example in this regard, since a number of rural areas are working to improve their hosting potential and their ability to attract and integrate new populations, against the backdrop of a *Charte nationale de l'installation en milieu rural* (national charter to promote settlement in rural areas) (CVC 2003; 2004; Exiga and Mamdy 2004; Moquay and Roussel 2002).[27]

In addition to this initial welcome, the physicians recommended another possible solution for improving retention, that is that support be offered for the social and community integration of their spouses and children, all with a view to ensuring them an overall quality of life in the rural area. This concept of 'overall quality of life' is in fact key to the issue of retention, and includes providing a rural living environment that is adequate and interesting for everyone from the social, cultural, community, educational and professional standpoints. In this respect, the physicians considered the role of community leaders and local associations crucial to facilitating the integration of their families.

A variety of community and socio-cultural activities that can make the living environment interesting, such as activities and recreational options for young people, were highly recommended to improve retention and families' long-term settlement. Here, the respondents were referring more to the cultural dimension, which they found to be a weak and neglected aspect of rural life. What is required here is an improvement in regional cultural infrastructures, failing which the gap between the vast array of activities available in Montreal and Quebec City versus the lack of cultural services in the rural areas will only induce the physicians' families to leave these areas. In fact, the issue of regional development in Quebec is implicit here. An overall living environment that is

---

27   The website of the *Collectif Ville Campagne* is extremely interesting in this regard and warrants a visit: http://www.projetsencampagne.com/.

interesting and dynamic will be better able to retain both the local population and its physicians. This is particularly so if they do not have to look elsewhere for the basic services they need.

Personal Factors

Two key personal factors pertaining to the physicians themselves would appear to have significant impact on their retention in rural areas, specifically, their rural origin or, at least some degree of familiarity or affinity with the rural environment, as well as a desire for challenges and greater autonomy. With regard to rural origin, or at least, satisfaction with the rural lifestyle, this aspect has been documented in the international literature (Kamien 1998) and in the Quebec literature (Gouin and Roy 1996). The latter authors conclude that 'a rule clearly seems to exist to the effect that we tend to return to settle in the same type of area as the one we come from' (p. 20, translation from French).

Nearly two-thirds (60 per cent) of the physicians of rural origin who were interviewed stayed in the rural area upon completion of their first contract, confirming the above conclusion. Conversely, a similar proportion (66 per cent) of the physicians of urban origin left for the big cities. However, one must be wary of overgeneralizing because some of the physicians interviewed, notably immigrants, who were of urban origin also remained in the rural areas beyond their first contract (six immigrant physicians and four subsidy recipients). A whole set of other factors may come into play here.

The rural origin of the spouses may also have an impact, since such spouses are generally likely to be less surprised and bored by the particularities of the rural environment than are urbanites, and consequently, less likely to want to leave the area. An affinity with the rural lifestyle is more likely to be present when spouses are of rural origin. Moreover, in cases where the spouses come from the same area as where the physicians practice medicine, their network of family and relatives helps facilitate the overall integration of both the physicians and their children.

This is all the truer when both spouses aspire to raising their family in the countryside and share a similar interest in nature, the landscapes, outdoor sports activities, personalized connections, the pace of rural life, in short, if they share the same enthusiasm for the quality of life available in the rural area. Clearly, this shared intention to settle on a long-term basis is a guarantee of greater retention. Interestingly, especially the oldest immigrant physicians expressed their intention to settle long-term in the rural area. They wished to put an end to their migrations and settle down definitively in their new country. As one of them put it, 'If we feel good here, we will stay because we're tired of moving around' (translation from French).

As for the physicians' desire to seek out challenges and opportunities offering greater autonomy and responsibilities, it would appear to be an asset for practicing rural medicine. In fact, a number of physicians, both immigrants and subsidy recipients, specifically mentioned the need to target physicians who are looking for a rural lifestyle, or who are predisposed to such a lifestyle by virtue of their desire for versatility and autonomy and their interest in nature and the great outdoors. According to their testimonials, this concordance and compatibility is likely to lead to longer retention.

Financial Factors

Regarding the various financial and compensatory measures intended to induce physicians to work in rural areas (higher pay, settlement and other bonuses, professional development and training days and so on), most of the physicians interviewed in the study confirmed that these incentives were important and that they had had a positive impact in the short term. However, they frequently nuanced their enthusiasm by citing the limitations and temporary or stop-gap nature of the strictly financial measures in terms mainly of long-term retention. One physician summed up this reservation, which was shared by several other colleagues, as follows: 'You won't keep people for ten years in rural areas just for the money.' However, a retention bonus for those who practice rural medicine for more than seven years would have a beneficial effect by introducing a certain form of symbolic recognition of their contribution to alleviating the shortage of medical staffpower. Moreover, it would represent a supplementary compensation for taking on a heavier, more stressful load than that in an urban environment.

The professional development and training incentives offered outside the rural area were much appreciated by the physicians, and constituted a factor that helped strengthen their sense of personal confidence in a medical practice requiring great practitioner autonomy and versatility. Moreover, given the high cost of air transport in rural areas and the need to maintain a quality of life that is acceptable to the entire family, it was suggested that such enrichment opportunities be expanded to include spouses and children. Additional enrichment excursions, other than professional in nature, were thus proposed both for the physicians themselves and for the members of their families, and in the name of 'family well-being.'

According to the physicians interviewed, beyond these financial and compensatory incentives, offering them a guarantee that they would be free to return to the city after doing a stint in a rural area and to join a medical practice of their own choosing would also provide an effective means of attracting more candidates to rural areas. Many of them in fact refuse to work in such areas because they are afraid of being trapped or locked in by irreversible choices. This again relates back to the concept of having freedom of choice in a life's trajectory that is unpredictable and subject to change, as previously mentioned in the section entitled Professional Factors. Furthermore, the physicians' views on the limitations of the financial incentives suggested the need for providing additional incentives aimed at enhancing the quality of all aspects of rural life, to truly improve retention.

Factors Related to the Natural Environment

Other, more secondary factors concerning physical characteristics of the rural area and its natural setting also influenced the physicians, both immigrants and subsidy recipients, in their decision to stay or leave. Either these factors combined with the previously mentioned positive factors had reinforced their decision to settle long-term in the area, or conversely, they had added weight to the decision to leave imminently.

The physicians who stayed found many attractions related to the natural environment in rural areas. These included the beauty of the landscapes, peace and quiet, clean air, wide-open spaces, proximity and easy access to nature, numerous opportunities to do a variety of outdoor sports in the different seasons, a source of replenishment and meditation, and various opportunities for outdoor family activities. These attractions added to the physicians' overall quality of life once their professional life had fallen into place.

On the other hand, for the physicians who left, often this pastoral context degenerated into one representing anxiety or nightmares owing, for example, to the amount of travelling required, long distances involved, harsh climate, long winters and dangerous road conditions during storms. Their anxiety in this regard was very apparent in the interviews. Moreover, the peace and quiet was not always appreciated, as several of these urbanites missed the vibrancy and energetic pace of big city life. Under these circumstances, the beauty of the landscapes and the peace and quiet did nothing to mitigate the harshness of the climate and greater dangers involved in travelling, or the lack of dynamism and entertainment.

Important Points to Consider for Recruitment and Retention

Before closing, the following points are worthwhile considering as possible means of improving recruitment and retention of the medical staff needed in rural areas. This improvement in turn will facilitate accessibility to healthcare in these regions where there is a severe shortage of general practitioners.

First, the results of the research project bring to light a host of retention and departure factors, which may be attributable, at least in part, to the different phases in the professional and personal life of physicians, be they immigrants or subsidy recipients. Whether the physicians are embarking on their careers or seeking new professional challenges, starting a family or parenting adolescents ready to begin their post-secondary education away from home, or divorced and sharing child custody with someone in another region, their trajectories are punctuated and marked by many such events, all of which weigh in their decision to stay or leave. It is therefore important to constantly bear in mind that their trajectory is in no way rectilinear, and instead, that the different phases in the life cycle also affect the lives of physicians in rural areas.

Rather than having a static vision, a flexible, more long-term perspective is needed, one that takes into account these different stages in the medical career path of general practitioners and in their married or family life. For example, it is important to ensure that they be given a constant guarantee regarding the possibility of returning to the city so that they can face the unknown challenges posed by life and benefit from some flexibility, both in terms of the length of their stay in the rural area and of their future.

Second, in any future recruitment process, it is important to take into account that the new generation of general practitioners has aspirations concerning overall quality of life. Having a balanced life that reconciles careers, family, leisure activities, family relationships and friendships is one of their chief concerns. Gone are the days of the old country doctors who were totally devoted to their patients both day and night, and even during family celebrations. Immigrant physicians are also affected by the quest for quality of life. They too mention this aspiration for a decent quality of life, in terms of workload and quality time with family and friends. We cannot impose exhausting working conditions upon them or they will not stay, as the evidence presented here showed. Care must therefore be taken to provide working conditions and work organization arrangements that prevent overload, professional burnout and the families' subsequent disillusionment.

Third, regional development policies need to be more closely tied to policies promoting non-metropolitan immigration if we wish to retain general practitioners, immigrant or not, in rural areas. These two types of policies clearly play a role in the issue, and both joint action and closer cooperation are essential. In addition, beyond purely economic measures, social and cultural measures are also required in order to meet aspirations concerning all aspects of quality of life. Hence the crucial importance of an overall regional development policy for the entire population, immigrant or not. It is only through closer ties between these policies, themselves clearly defined with an overall perspective, that ongoing efforts to retain people, medical or otherwise, in rural areas will be viable and sustainable. It is important to remember that immigrants to non-metropolitan areas do not wish to live in a cultural and social wasteland, as was revealed in earlier work on non-metropolitan immigration (Simard 2007a).

Fourth, we must focus our attention on a potential pool of immigrant medical manpower wishing, at the present time, to help remedy the shortage of medical staff in rural Quebec.[28] These physicians, who are currently waiting for their diplomas to be recognized and to receive their medical permits, display a genuine

---

28   Since 1998, a formal association has existed in Quebec that groups together foreign physicians awaiting their permit to practice medicine. Initially called the '*Association multiethnique des médecins diplômés hors Canada et États-Unis*', it was later renamed the '*Association québécoise des médecins diplômés hors Canada et Etats-Unis*'. It had 107 duly registered members at the beginning of 2004. Moreover, additional foreign-trained physicians attend the meetings without registering as members. They come from different continents: Europe, Asia, Africa, as well as Latin America and the West Indies.

openness to going anywhere in Quebec, even remote areas, to practice medicine. It is therefore an opportune time to further explore, in an innovative way, the possibilities of utilizing immigrant physicians to remedy the uneven distribution of medical staff throughout Quebec, Canada and other countries. Here, we can benefit from the various experiences gained by the physicians discussed here and from the lessons to be drawn regarding the variety of factors that must be taken into account.

Accordingly, it is important that collaboration be stepped up among the various ministries and other agencies concerned by this issue, whether at the level of health, immigration, regional development, education, the Collège des Médecins du Québec or other medical federations.[29] A comprehensive, shared vision is required among the various stakeholders and decision-makers, starting with the question of obtaining equivalences for medical studies and going as far as the measures to be taken to promote overall and sustainable integration in rural areas.

Long delays in accessing the practice of medicine prevent, to some degree, fast integration in rural areas as well as the possibility of more long-lasting rootedness. In fact, immigrant families that are waiting generally put down roots elsewhere in other contexts, usually metropolitan. It then becomes difficult for them to pick up once again and remove themselves from the community and pace of life to which they have grown accustomed. The question of the recognition of diplomas is thus at the crux of this issue as often emphasized in the literature (Hawthorne 2007; JIMI 2007; Bauder 2003; Couton 2002; CSÉ 2000). Identified as one of the principal structural barriers to immigrants' access to employment corresponding with their actual skills, this question must be examined here as diligently and efficiently as possible in order to reduce these waiting times and accelerate the process of integrating these highly skilled resources into medical practice and rural areas.

Conclusion

The study discussed here provided an in-depth look at the reality facing general practitioners, both immigrants and subsidy recipients, in rural Quebec, and at the complexity and dynamic interaction between the various retention and departure

---

29   In Quebec, since 2003, it appears that a change in attitude regarding immigrant physicians has been taking place among the main authorities concerned, notably, the Collège des médecins du Québec, medical federations and the provincial government (mainly the health and immigration departments). Some openness can be discerned, and various tools are being put in place to better inform applicants and facilitate the process of recognizing equivalences in diplomas and access to the practice of medicine. (Among other documents, see: MICC 2004, 2005; CRI 2004; *Groupe de travail sur l'accès aux professions et métiers réglementés* 2005; Gouvernement du Québec 2003). A number of information documents are also available on the following website: www.immigration-quebec.gouv.qc.ca, see the heading *Emploi and Profession de médicin.*

factors likely to come into play. It also showed the positive impact that these physicians can have in attenuating the shortage of medical staff in rural areas. In addition, it led to a more nuanced understanding of the integration process, going beyond the initial results to bring to light certain variables and factors that were not anticipated at the outset. It thus helped to dissipate two myths, the first being that immigrant physicians are not interested in practising in rural areas or in settling there after completing their initial contract, and the second, that physicians – whether immigrants or not – from urban backgrounds are intent on returning to cities as soon as possible since their customary way of life does not motivate them to stay long in rural areas. Some of the findings of this research project would appear to contradict these premature assertions.

Obligation or Incentive?

The question of solutions for the problematic shortage of general practitioners in rural areas is a complex and difficult one, particularly when linked to the issue of freedom of choice. Nearly half of the physicians interviewed, including equal numbers of immigrants and subsidy recipients, were open to the prospect of making it compulsory for all graduates, whether immigrants or not, to do a stint in rural areas. However, they emphasized the condition that this stay in the rural area must be of reasonable duration[30] and that guarantees must be given that a return to the city is possible upon completion of the contract, if the physician so wishes. Also, they stated that the choice of rural area should be made in light of the physicians' interests and affinities to ensure the greatest possible compatibility between their aspirations and the characteristics of the rural area. Lastly, the importance of the spouse in the decision to settle or not in the area must not be overlooked. Thus, new formulas must be sought that will successfully reconcile the couple's interests when fulfilling contractual obligations in rural areas.

This obligation to practice medicine in rural areas is justified on several grounds. The subsidy recipients cite the concepts of *duty, gift, fair return* or *fair exchange* in a context of critical shortage. For their part, the immigrant physicians based their opinions on their past *public service* experience and affirmed that it was a service they owed the people in exchange for their training. These concepts of *exchange* or *public service* put forward by the physicians require a closer look. I shall leave the last word in this regard to two immigrant physicians:

> If you take the example of Europe, [there are countries where] you are obliged
> to do mandatory social service of two years. No one objects because it's part of
> their training [...]. This is for the benefit of the rural areas, so that everyone has

---

30   A period of between two and four years is suggested in order to give the physician enough time to become familiar with and adapt to the new environment (one year is considered insufficient in this regard), and to take personal constraints into account (four years would appear to be too long in some cases).

access […]. It's more of a moral obligation (Immigrant physician who stayed in the rural area, translation from French).

Quebec and Canadian students must be sent [to rural areas]… go into exile, so that they understand the beauty, need and even privilege of working in rural areas […]. In my country, new graduates are required to work in rural areas [for two, three or even four years]. They aren't allowed to settle [first] in the capital city. And there's no increase [in salary] […]. It's just a matter of repaying your debt in rural areas (Immigrant physician who left the rural area, translation from French).

References

Akenson, D. (1984), *The Irish in Ontario: A Study in Rural History* (Kingston and Montréal: McGill-Queen's University Press).

Allen, B. and Troestler, H. (2007), 'L'application sur le terrain de la stratégie du gouvernement du Québec en régionalisation de l'immigration', *Nos Diverse Cités*, 3, été, 69–75.

Au bas de l'échelle [ABE] (2007), *Mémoire présenté à la Commission sur l'avenir de l'agriculture et de l'agroalimentaire québécois* (Montréal).

Audas, R., Ross, A. and Vardy, D. (2005), 'The use of provisionally licensed international medical graduates in Canada', *Canadian Medical Association Journal*, 10:11, 1315–1316.

Basran, G.S. and Zong L. (1998), 'Devaluation of Foreign Credentials as Perceived by Visible Minority Professional Immigrants', *Canadian Ethnic Studies/Etudes Ethniques au Canada*, 30: 3, 6–23.

Bauder, H. (2003) '"Brain abuse", or the devaluation of immigrant labour in Canada', *Antipode*, 35:4, 699–717.

Beshiri, R. and He, J. (2009), 'Immigrants in Rural Canada: 2006', *Rural and Small Town Canada Analysis Bulletin*, 8:2 (Ottawa: Statistics Canada, Catalogue no.21-006-XIE).

Beshiri, R. (2004), 'Immigrants in rural Canada: 2001 update', *Rural and Small Town Canada Analysis Bulletin*, 5:4, 1–27. <http://www.statcan.ca/english/freepub/21-006-XIE/21-006-XIE2004004.pdf>.

Beshiri, R. and Alfred, E. (2002), 'Immigrants in rural Canada', *Rural and Small Town Canada Analysis Bulletin*, 4:2, 1–20.

Bollman, Ray, D., Beshiri, R. and Clemenson, H. (2007), 'Immigrants to rural Canada', in Reimer B. (ed.) special issue on Rural Communities, *Our Diverse Cities*, Summer, 3, 9–15.

Boyd, M. and Vickers, M. (2000), 'Cent ans d'immigration au Canada', *Tendances Sociales Canadiennes*, Ottawa 58, fall, 2–13.

Broadway, M. (2007), 'Meatpacking and the Transformation of Rural Communities: A Comparison of Brooks, Alberta and Garden City, Kansas', *Rural Sociology*, 72:4, 560–82.

Burnet J.R. and Palmer, H. (1988), *'Coming Canadians', An Introduction to a History of Canada's Peoples*, McClelland and Steward and Department of the Secretary of State of Canada (Coll. 'Generations: A history of Canada's peoples')

Canadian Ethnic Studies (CES) (2005), *Thinking about Immigration Outside Canada's Metropolitan Centres*, special issue, 37:3.

Carter, T., Morrish, M. and Amoyaw, B. (2008), 'Attracting immigrants to smaller urban and rural communities: Lessons learned from the Manitoba provincial nominee program', *Journal of International Migration and Integration*, 9:2, 161–83.

Cecil, R.G. and Ebanks, G.E. (1991), 'The Human Condition of West Indian Migrant Farm Labour in South Western Ontario', *International Migration/ Migrations internationales*, 27:3, September, 38–405.

Chui, T., Tran, K. and Maheux, H. (2007), Immigration au Canada: un portrait de la population née à l'étranger, Recensement de 2006. *Statistique Canada*, no 97-557-XIF au catalogue (Ontario: Ottawa).

Citoyenneté et Immigration Canada [CIC] (2003), *Metropolis-Série de conversation 9: Régionalisation de l'immigration*, Ottawa, 25 p. <http://www.canada.metropolis.net>.

Citoyenneté et Immigration Canada [CIC] (2001), *Vers une répartition géographique mieux équilibrée des immigrants*, Recherche et examen stratégique, Ministère des Travaux publics et Services gouvernementaux du Canada, Canada.

Collectif Ville Campagne [CVP] (2004), *Campagnes en mouvement*. Synthèse de la rencontre des acteurs de l'installation en milieu rural du 15 et 16 décembre à Saint-Brieuc/Côtes d'Armor (Aixe-sur-Vienne, France).

Collectif Ville Campagne [CVC] (2003), *Bilan des actions en faveur de l'accueil de nouveaux actifs en milieu rural, synthèse de l'étude réalisée pour la DATAR* (Aixe-sur-Vienne, France).

Commission des droits de la personne et des droits de la jeunesse [CDPDJ] (2008), *Notes de présentation aux audiences pan canadiennes du Comité permanent des communes sur la citoyenneté et l'immigration: les travailleurs étrangers temporaires*, Québec, 9 p.

Conseil des affaires sociales [CAS] (1989), *Deux Québec dans un. Rapport sur le développement social et démographique* (Montreal, Gaëtan Morin éditeur).

Conseil des relations interculturelles[CRI] (2004), *Commentaires sur le document de consultation concernant les personnes immigrantes formées à l'étranger et l'accès aux professions et métiers réglementés*, October.

Conseil supérieur de l'éducation [CSÉ] (2000), *La reconnaissance des acquis, une responsabilité politique et sociale*, Avis du CSÉ au ministre de l'Éducation, June.

Côté, S., Klein, J-L. and Proulx, M-U. (1995), *Et les régions qui perdent... ? Tendance et débats en développement régional* (Rimouski: GRIDEQ, Université du Québec à Rimouski).

Couton, P. (2002), 'Highly skilled immigrants. Recent trends and issues', *ISUMA: Canadian Journal of Policy Research/Revue canadienne de recherche sur les politiques*, 3:2, fall, 114–23 (Québec: Presses de l'Université de Montréal).

Cutchin, M.P., Norton, J.C., Quan, M.M., Bolt, D., Hughes, S. and Linderman, B. (1994), 'To stay or not to stay: issues in rural primary care physician retention in eastern Kentucky', *Journal of Rural Health*, 10: 4, 273–78.

du Plessis, V., Beshiri, R., Bollman, R.D. and Clemenson, H. (2002), *Definitions of 'rural'. Agriculture and rural working paper series*, working paper no. 61. (Ottawa: Statistics Canada: Agriculture Division).

Exiga, I. and Mamdy, J.F. (Coord.) (2004), 'Dossier Cap sur la campagne', *Revue Pour*, 182, 51–243.

Fairey, D., Hanson, C. et al. (2008), 'Cultivating Farmworker Rights: Ending the exploitation of immigrant and migrant farmworkers', BC, *Canadian Centre for Policy Alternatives*, Canada. <http://www.policyalternatives.ca>.

Frideres, J.S. (2006), 'L'intégration des immigrants dans les villes: l'avenir des centres de deuxième et de troisième rangs', *Nos Diverse Cités*, 2: été, Métropolis, Canada, 3–9.

Ganzevoort, H. (1988), *A Bittersweet Land: The Dutch Experience in Canada, 1890–1980* (Toronto: McClelland and Stewart).

Gouin, U-M. and Roy, F. (1996), *Recherche sur la région d'origine des étudiantes et étudiants québécois en médecine et sur la relation avec le lieu de pratique*, Université Laval.

Gouvernement du Québec (2003), *Recours aux infirmières et aux médecins formés à l'étranger. Les ministres Michelle Courchesne et Philippe Couillard présentent leurs mesures*, Communiqué, November. Quebec, 3 p.

Grant, H. (2006), 'From the transvaal to the Prairies: The migration of South African physicians to Canada', *Journal of Ethnic and Migration Studies*, 32:4, 681–95.

Groupe de travail sur l'accès aux professions et métiers réglementés (2005), *Les personnes immigrantes formées à l'étranger et l'accès aux professions et métiers réglementés*, Rapport, February. Quebec.

Hawthorne, L., guest editor (2007, Spring), *Foreign Credential Recognition, Canadian Issues*, Association for Canadian Studies.

Humphreys, J., Jones, J., Jones, M., Graeme, H., Bamford, E., and Taylor, D. (2001), 'A critical review of rural medical workforce retention in Australia', *Australian Health Review*, 24:4, 91–102.

Humphreys, J., Jones, J., Jones, M. and Mara, P. (2002), 'Workforce retention in rural and remote Australia: determining the factors that influence length of practice', *Rural Health*, 176, 472–76.

Institut national de santé publique du Québec (INSPQ) (2004), *Vivre dans une collectivité rurale plutôt qu'en ville fait-il vraiment une différence en matière de santé et de bien-être?*, Quebec.

Journal of International Migration and Integration (JIMI) (2008), *Attracting new arrivals to smaller cities and rural communities: findings from Australia, Canada and New Zealand*, special issue, 9:2, June, Springer Netherlands.

Journal of International Migration and Integration (JIMI) (2007), *Accessing the higher echelons of a host country's labour market: policy directions from the personal experiences of skilled immigrants*, special issue, 8:2, June, Springer Netherlands.

Julien, P-A. (1995), 'Régions et sous-développement économique: voies de solution', in Dumont, F., langlois, S. and Martin, Y. (dir.) *Le traité des problèmes sociaux* (Sainte-Foy: Institut québécois de recherche sur la culture), 127–43.

Kamien, M. (1998), 'Staying in or leaving rural practice: 1996 outcomes of rural doctors' 1986 intentions', *Medical Journal of Australia*, 169, 318–21.

Knowles, V. (2000), *Les artisans de notre partrimoine: La citoyenneté et l'immigration au Canada de 1900 à 1977* (Ottawa:Citoyenneté et Immigration Canada).

Krahn, H., Derwing, T., Mulder M. and Wilkinson L. (2000), 'Educated and Underemployed: Refugee Integration into the Canadian Labour Market', *Journal of International Migration and Integration* 1:1, 59–84.

L'Acteur rural (2003), 'Attirer des professionnels de la santé sur son territoire', La lettre de l'Acteur rural, *L'accompagnateur de projet* 2: 181, October, France.

Leclerc, Y. and Béland, C. (dir.) (2003). *La voie citoyenne. Pour renouveler le modèle québécois*, coll. Économie et humanisme (Montreal: Éditions Plurimédia).

Mimeault, I. and Simard, M. (2001), 'Travail agricole saisonnier occasionnel au Québec: espace d'inclusion ou d'exclusion?', *Études ethniques au Canada/ Canadian Ethnic Studies*, 33:1, 25–45.

Mimeault, I. and Simard, M. (1999), 'Exclusions légales et sociales des travailleurs agricoles saisonniers véhiculés quotidiennement au Québec', *Relations Industrielles/ Industrial Relations*, 54:2, 388–410.

Ministère des Affaires Municipales et des Régions (MAMR) (2006), *Politique nationale de la ruralité 2007–2014. Une force pour tout le Québec* (Québec: Ministère des Régions).

Ministère des Communautés culturelles et de l'Immigration du Québec [MCCI] (1991). *Au Québec pour bâtir ensemble. Énoncé de politique en matière d'immigration et d'intégration*, Québec.

Ministère de l'Immigration et des Communautés culturelles [MICC] (2005), *Projets visant à faciliter l'accès aux professions et métiers réglementés mis en œuvre par le ministère de l'Immigration et des Communautés culturelles [MICC] et ses partenaires*, June.

Ministère de l'Immigration et des Communautés culturelles [MICC] (2004). *Les personnes immigrantes formées à l'étranger et l'accès aux professions et métiers réglementés, Document de consultation préparé par le Groupe de travail sur l'accès aux professions et métiers réglementés.*

Ministère des Relations avec les Citoyens et de l'Immigration [MRCI] (2004*). Des valeurs partagées, des intérêts communs. Pour assurer la pleine participation des Québécois des communautés culturelles au développement du Québec, Plan d'action*, 2004–2007.

Mongeau, P., Lapointe, S. and Claveau, L. (1994), *Facteurs de stabilité et profil des omnipraticiens en régions éloignées (le cas du Bas-Saint-Laurent)*, Quebec.

Moquay, P. and Roussel, V. (eds) (2002), *Les politiques d'accueil dans les territoires ruraux* (France, Clermont-Ferrand: Éditions ENITA, Collection Actes numéro 10, Engref et Cemagref).

Mullally, S. and Wright D. (2007), 'La Grande séduction? The immigration of foreign-trained physicians to Canada, c. 1954–76', *Journal of Canadian Studies/Revue des Études Canadiennes*, 41: 3, Fall, 67–89.

Ngo, H.V. and Este, D. (2006), 'Professional Re-entry for Foreign-Trained Immigrants', *Journal of International Migration and Integration*, 7:1, winter, 27–50.

Pathman, D.E. and Konrad, T.R. (1996), 'Minority physicians serving in rural National Health Service Corps sites', *Medical Care*, 34: 5, 439–54.

Petryshyn, J. (1985), *Peasants in the Promised Land: Canada and the Ukrainians 1891–1914* (Toronto: James Lorimer & Co).

Pope, Alison S.A., Garry, D.G., Whiteside, C.B.C. and Kazanjian, A. (1998), 'Retention of rural physicians: tipping the decision-making scales', *Canadian Journal of Rural Medicine*, 3: 4, 209–16.

Preibisch, K. (2004), 'Migrant agricultural workers and processes of social inclusion in rural Canada: encuentros and desencuentros', *Canadian Journal of Latin American and Caibbean Studies*, 29:57–8, 203–39.

Proulx, M-U. (2002), *L'économie des territoires au Québec, coll. Science régionale* (Sainte-Foy, Quebec: Presses de l'Université du Québec).

Reimer, B. (ed.) (2007), 'Rural communities'*, Our Diverse Cities* Summer, 3, Métropolis. Canada.

Satzewich, V. (1988), 'The Canadian State and the Racialization of Caribbean Migrant Farm Labour 1947–1966', *Ethnic and Racial Studies*, 11:3, July, 282–304.

Simard, M. (2008), 'Les nouveaux habitants dans la campagne québécoise: le cas des entrepreneurs agricoles d'origine européenne', *Les Étrangers dans les campagnes*, Centre d'études et de recherches appliquées au Massif Central (CERAMAC), (Clermont-Ferrand, France: Presses Universitaires Blaise Pascal), 443–56.

Simard, M. (2007a), 'Immigrant Integration Outside Montréal', *Our Diverse Cities*, in Reiner, B. (ed.), Special issue on rural communities, 3 (Summer) (Concordia University), 109–14.

Simard, M. (2007b), 'Pratiques novatrices des jeunes d'origine immigrée dans les régions au Québec', in Potvin, M., Eid, P. and Venel, N. (ed.), *La deuxième génération issue de l'immigration. Une comparaison France-Québec*, Preface by Dubet, F. (Quebec: Athéna éditions), 103–17.

Simard M. (2007c), 'Nouvelles populations rurales et conflits au Québec: regards croisés avec la France et le Royaume-Uni', *Géographie, Économie, Société*, numéro spécial sur Conflits d'usages et dynamiques spatiales: les antagonismes dans l'occupation des espaces périurbains et ruraux (dir. T. Kirat et A.Torre, CNRS et INRA), 9: 2 (April–June), Lavoisier, France, 187–213.

Simard, M. (2003a), 'Regional youth of immigrant origin in Quebec: innovative relationship to work', in Roulleau-Berger, L. (dir.), *Youth and Work in the Post-Industrial City of North America and Europe* (USA: Brill Leiden-Boston), 217–31.

Simard, M. (2003b), 'Le rapport à l'espace des jeunes issus de parents immigrés en région au Québec: un bricolage inédit ?' *Recherches sociographiques, special issue on youth migration*, XLIV: 1, 57–91, (January–April), Université Laval.

Simard, M., Mimeault, I. and Lévesque, M. (2001), 'Insertion en emploi et pratiques migratoires des jeunes d'origine immigrée en région au Québec', in Roulleau-Berger, L. and Gauthier, M. (dir.), *Les jeunes et l'emploi dans les villes d'Europe et d'Amérique du Nord* (France, Lyon: Éditions de l'Aube), 229–42.

Simard, M. (with the collaboration of Isabelle Mimeault) (1997), *La main-d'oeuvre agricole saisonnière transportée quotidiennement de la région de Montréal: profil socio-économique et insertion professionnelle*, Cahier de recherche de l'INRS-Culture et Société.

Simard, M. (1996), 'La politique québécoise de régionalisation de l'immigration: enjeux et paradoxes', *Recherches sociographiques*, XXXVII: 3, 439–69.

Simard, M. (1995a), 'La régionalisation de l'immigration: les entrepreneurs agricoles immigrants dans la société rurale québécoise', *Recherches sociographiques*, XXXVI: 2, 215–42.

Simard, M. (1995b), 'Immigration agricole au Québec: impact sur le milieu rural et le développement régional', *Revue canadienne des sciences régionales/ Canadian Journal of Regional Science*, XVIII: 3, 307–32, (fall) (University of New Brunswick).

Simard, M. (1994), *Les entrepreneurs agricoles immigrants européens: insertion dans la société rurale québécoise* (Montreal, Ministère des Affaires internationales, de l'Immigration et des Communautés culturelles [MAIICC]), (Études et recherches, no. 11).

Simmons, D., Bolitho, Les E., Phelps, G.J., Ziffer, R. and Disher, G.J. (2002), 'Dispelling the myths about rural consultant physician practice: the Victorian physicians survey', *Rural Health*, 176, 477–81.

Solidarité rurale du Québec [SRQ] (2008), *Études de cas sur la néoruralité et les transformations des collectivités rurales,* Rapport de recherche, Québec.

Solidarité rurale du Québec [SRQ] (2000), *L'immigration en milieu rural*, Document de réflexion, Québec.

Société d'histoire des communautés culturelles du Québec (SHCCQ) (1985), *Originaires de l'Europe centrale et de l'Europe du Sud, Fides*, vol 1.

Statistique Canada (2007), *Population selon le statut d'immigrant et la période d'immigration, chiffres de 2006, pour le Canada, les provinces et les territoires, et les régions métropolitaines de recensement et les agglomérations de recensement, Canada.*

Statistique Canada (2008), *La mosaïque ethnoculturelle du Canada, Recensement de 2006*, produit no 97-562-XWF2006001 au catalogue de Statistique Canada, Ottawa, Ontario, 9 avril, Série 'Analyses', Recensement de 2006, http://www12.statcan.ca/francais/census06/analysis/ethnicorigin/index.cfm, accessed 28 January 2009.

TUAC Canada (Syndicat des travailleurs et travailleuses unis de l'alimentation et du commerce, (2007), *Situation des travailleurs agricoles migrants au Canada 2006–2007*, Rapport.

Vachon, B. (dir.) (1991), *Le Québec rural dans tous ses états* (Quebec: Éditions du Boréal).

Wong, A. and Lohfeld I. (2008), 'Recertifying as a doctor in Canada: international medical graduates and the journey from entry to adaptation', *Medical Education* 42:1, January, 53–60.

Wong, L. (1988), *Migrant Seasonal Agricultural Labour: Race and Ethnic Relations in the Okanagan Valley, thèse de doctorat en sociologie, Faculté des études graduées* (Ontario: Université York).

Wulff, M. and Dharmalingam, A. (2008), 'Retaining skilled migrants in regional Australia: the role of social connectedness', *Journal of International Migration and Integration*, 9:2, June, 147–60.

Chapter 4

From Enthusiasm to Perplexity and Scepticism: International Migrants in the Rural Regions of Greece and Southern Europe

Charalambos Kasimis

Introduction

International migration flows to the Southern European countries of Greece, Italy, Portugal and Spain (henceforth referred to as Southern Europe) have increased considerably since the late 1980s. As a result, all Southern European countries have evolved from senders of migrants to migrant receivers and permanent migrant destinations. A crucial dimension of this international process is the engagement of migrants in agricultural employment often connected with their settlement in rural regions where they seem to undertake a 'multifunctional' role surpassing agriculture itself.

Migrant employment in agriculture specifically, and the rural economy in general, is no longer a secondary phenomenon. Rural areas themselves have become 'multifunctional'. Non-agricultural activities like tourism and housing construction have developed, urban dwellers have returned to their land of origin, and new consumption patterns connected to leisure and recreation have grown. In Greece migrants have become almost the exclusive contributors of wage labour in agriculture. Their role, however, is not restricted to agriculture only. In the mountainous regions, in particular, they provide also an overall support to old-age households.

This paper draws, almost exclusively, on the findings of two research projects carried out by the author in the same three paradigmatic rural regions of the country in two distinct periods: the first in 2000–2002, before the implementation of a 'regularization programme', and the second after the implementation of this programme in 2004–06. The study showed that more than half of the total number of rural households and two-thirds of the farm households employed migrant labour.

Migrant workers have addressed structural developments in rural Greece, including longstanding labour shortages due to emigration and changes in the rural economy, the younger generation's increasing rejection of rural life and jobs, and the native rural population's growing tendency to obtain non-agricultural employment.

The chapter starts with the presentation of the Southern European context of migration towards rural regions. It then moves to a discussion of the phenomenon in Greece in the context of the Common Agricultural Policy (CAP) reform of 2003. Following this, the empirical findings of the afore-mentioned two research projects are being considered. A number of regional differentiations are revealed concerning the socio-economic implications of migrant employment and of migrants' settlement in the regions studied over the two time periods. These implications are examined at the level of both, the farm unit and the farm household. Furthermore, they are discussed in the light of the implementation of a 'regularization programme'. The chapter ends with a discussion of Greek people's perceptions and attitudes towards the migrant population.

Southern European Context

The integration of South European countries into the European Union (EU) (in 1981 for Greece, 1986 for Spain and Portugal and 1958 for Italy as a founding member) and the rapid transformation of their economies have narrowed the economic and social distance between Southern and Northern Europe. A number of factors have generated a demand for flexible labour power, independent of trade union practices and legislation. These factors include the expansion of the tertiary sector (an economic development specific to Southern European countries), namely of seasonal industries like tourism, agriculture and construction, as well as the large size of an informal and family-based economy (i.e. an economy which relies widely upon family controlled capital, labour and management). Furthermore, the fluid nature of southern economies based on tourism, commerce and shipping, has often allowed the legal entry of migrants as tourists and visitors, who went on to stay illegally upon their visas' expiration. Extended coastlines and easily crossed borders facilitated migrants' entry as did the healthy demographic character of the migrants' countries of origin *vis-á-vis* the negative demographic developments of Southern European countries. Finally, an unsatisfactorily run and poorly financed administrative bureaucracy for the management of migration has contributed to the difficulties of controlling irregular flows and stocks (Arango and Jachimowicz 2005).

For King (2000) Southern Europe constitutes a 'special case' of European capitalism characterized by late industrialization, large agricultural and tourist sectors, speculative urban development and an extensive family-based informal economy. All these characteristics make up the framework for the construction of the so-called 'Southern European model of migration' (King 2000). Key characteristics of this model include its wide 'illegality' due to migration controls and restrictive policies imposed by EU countries; the multiplicity and heterogeneity of nationalities migrating towards Southern Europe; the asymmetry of their gender composition (being overwhelmingly male); the differentiation of the geographic, social and cultural origin of migrants; and finally the coexistence of migration with high unemployment and underemployment (i.e. involuntary part-time employment) in the receiver countries. Despite having had the highest unemployment rates in Europe (close to 10 per cent), Spain, Italy and Greece have continued to attract great numbers of migrants.

Unemployment in Southern Europe affects less the middle-aged, low-skilled heads of households than is the case in Northern Europe. This is due to the fact that certain groups of unemployed people are not in direct competition with migrants in the labour market. Opportunities of accessing the labour market are often not taken advantage of, unless they correspond with education levels and family status. Additionally, the restructuring of the economy and the increasing integration of women into the labour market have led to the creation of jobs of a kind often rejected by local populations (King 2000). Consequently, the aspiration for 'secure and decent' jobs by the national population has led to an unwillingness to accept less well-paid and demanding jobs, opening up spaces for incoming migrants (King 2000; Labrianidis and Lyberaki 2001; Baldwin-Edwards 2004).

In such an environment, migrants come and fill the gaps left in the labour market by the national population. For Hoggart and Mendoza (1999) these gaps are socially defined and regulated rather than economically prescribed. Accounting for this situation, they refer to the 'segmentation theory', which suggests that the labour market is segregated into sectors, with access to specific employment positions being defined by social positions of power. Hence, employees end up in different segments on the basis of their ethnicity, gender and class (Bradley 1984; Peck 1996). For migrants, these sectors consist mainly of agriculture, construction, family handicraft, tourism, and domestic services in which they provide their labour for the marginal, least secure, highly exploitative, under-paid and non-insured jobs.

However, once we examine the phenomenon of immigration cross-nationally, it becomes clear that the countries under consideration do not constitute a homogeneous frame of reference. Thus, the theoretical construct of a 'Southern European model of migration' can be challenged. First, Southern European countries are not a 'unified' geographical entity and within each of them – especially Italy and Spain – regional differences are substantial (Mendoza 2001). Second, more emphasis should be placed upon the differences observed between the Southern European countries, mostly in relation to the composition of the migrant population and the relations between the recipient country and the countries of origin.

The changes observed in the past few years – mostly in the demographic composition of migrant population – could lead to a revision of a number of characteristics of the Southern European model of migration. For example, in relation to gender issues of migration and the observed asymmetry of proportions of men and women migrants, recent evidence shows that the proportions are becoming increasingly equal (Bell 2002; Baldwin-Edwards 2004; Fuentes 2005; ISMU 2005).

Hence, the theoretical model discussed above cannot be treated as a static model given the development of the phenomenon and the changes which processes of family unification can bring to most countries. A question to be answered in the future is whether the particularity of the Southern European model of migration will persist. Alternatively, the changes in the socio-economic and the demographic situations of migration, as well as the discussion on integration and diversity in the European South, could lead to a convergence of the characteristics of the Southern and the Northern models of migration.

Despite the changes observed above, a number of interdependent factors like globalization, EU enlargement and the particular socio-economic developments in Southern European countries (improvement of living standards and education, women's integration into the labour market, expansion of the tertiary sector and finally the extended informal economy) have transformed Southern European countries from senders to receivers of migration flows.

Migrants in Rural Southern Europe

One of the particularities of Southern European migration flows is their extensive direction towards rural regions, i.e. regions comprising a relatively high percentage of local communities with a low population density.[1] Evidence shows a rapid increase in migrant employment in both. agricultural and non-agricultural activities over the past two decades (Reyneri 2001; King 2002; de Zulueta 2003; Kasimis 2006).

Migrants arriving from the Balkans, Africa and even Asia have boosted these often labour-intensive regional economies by working in increasingly specializing seasonal agriculture and economically restructured rural areas. In fact, in the year 2000, more than two-thirds of the farm holdings and of the agriculturally employed population of the EU-15 were concentrated in the European South (European Commission 2004). This situation can partly be explained with this sector's special weight in Southern European economies and societies. In the economically restructured rural areas, migrants are also engaged in non-agricultural economic activities, such as in hospitality, construction and food processing (Kasimis 2008; Daly 2003; Kasimis, Nitsiakos, Zacopoulou and Papadopoulos 2002).

In Italy, migrants are over-represented in agricultural employment when compared with the economically active population of the country (13.1 per cent

---

1   The OECD distinguishes between 2 levels of geographic detail: the *local community* level and the *regional* level. Local communities are classified as rural or urban according to their population density (< > 150 inhabitants per sq km). Regions are classified according to the proportion of the population living in rural or urban communes: regions are defined as predominately urbanized (PU) when they have <15 per cent population in rural communes, as significantly rural (SR) with 15–49 per cent population in rural communes and as predominately rural (PR) with >50 per cent population (SERA 2006).

versus 5.3 per cent). They make up 60 per cent of the total seasonal labour force in agriculture – the majority of them being undocumented. Two-thirds of this workforce originates from Poland, Slovakia, the Czech Republic and Romania (King 2002; de Zulueta 2003).

The role of migrant workers in the Italian labour market varies by sector and region. In Northern Italy, regularized foreign labour is in demand. Moroccan migrants are mostly employed in pig and cattle farms. Migrants from Central and Eastern European countries are mostly employed in vineyards and the fruit and vegetable sectors. In the South, because of the massive, continuous arrival of migrants and the seasonal characteristics of the regional economy, the demand is for illegal, highly exploitable labour (de Zulueta 2003; King 2002; Pugliese 1993).

Spain's 2001 Census showed that nearly one fifth of all migrants are settled in rural areas concentrated in regions like Alicante, Malaga, Las Palmas, Tenerife, the Balearic Islands, Murcia, and Almeria. They are mostly employed in agriculture (OECD 2004a). Recent evidence also shows that Romanians and Bulgarians have nowadays supplanted the once-dominant African migrants in the Spanish labour market. Such trends are also evident in Greece and Italy (Hoggart, Mendoza 1999; Mendoza 2001; Cánovas Pedreño 2003).

Only in Portugal has migrant employment played a marginal role, in this case due to very strong cooperative networks among locals. A recent exception seems to be Portugal's large-scale agriculture, which now reportedly relies heavily on inexpensive migrant labour. A qualitative change in migration inflows to Portugal has also been observed in recent years. All previous inflows were part of an international migratory system united by the Portuguese language. However, migration flows from Eastern European countries like Ukraine, Moldova, Romania and Russia, and to a lesser extent from Southeast Asia, have been on the rise. Non-EU Eastern European migrants are concentrated in the Lisbon metropolitan area and the region of the Algarve, but they are also spread out to rural regions. In rural areas, they are employed in construction and the agricultural sector (especially in the Alentejo, Ribatejo, and Oeste regions). Brazilians and 'traditional' migrants from PALOP (Portuguese-speaking African) countries generally are employed in construction and the service sector (Fonseca, Alegria and Nunes 2004; Baganha and Fonseca 2004; Malheiros 2002; Peixoto 2002).

In Greece, migrants provide nearly one-fifth of the total labour supply in the sector. They have become almost the exclusive contributors of wage labour in Greek agriculture. In intensive cultivations, such as sultana grapes, asparagus, tobacco, greenhouse and flower production, and the fruit industry in general, migrants' labour contribution is approaching one-third of the total labour expended. Their role, however, is extended to other non-agricultural activities too (Kasimis 2005; National Statistical Service of Greece 2001).

Research in rural Southern Europe has brought to light a number of issues. For example, evidence has shown that large numbers of migrants perform less specialized jobs in conditions of ethnic segregation and under a gender division of labour differentiated regionally (Reyneri 2001; King 2002; Parini 2002; Toronjo 2004; Cánovas 2005). Despite the fact that a large proportion of them do not have a rural background, they show quick adjustment to farm work. By contrast, the continuous arrival of illegal migrants contributes to the maintenance of a model of agricultural production which inhibits the smooth process of labour and social integration of older migrants in these rural regions through their displacement and the downward pressure on wages. The replacement of 'old regularized migrants' with irregular 'newcomers' has often been linked with state/institutional and employers' attempts to restrict collective action and bargaining for higher wages and better working conditions sought by 'regularized migrants'. Migrant workers in rural regions seem to constitute a 'new rural class' the presence of which has caused social tensions connected directly with their way of life and their claims for regularization, better working conditions and higher payments. One common feature for all Southern European countries comprises the common strategies of migrants to move to other economic sectors after their regularization (Pedone 2005; Mendoza 2001).

Despite a widespread acknowledgement of migrants' positive contribution by the rural populations of the receiving countries, insecurity is still expressed, and negative stereotypes have been maintained. In addition, some locally established people find it difficult to accept the cultural differences which migrants' presence implies (Kasimis and Papadopoulos 2005).

A number of these observations apply also to Greece. The Greek experience is a valuable frame of reference for policymakers of most Southern European countries – and indeed, some in Northern Europe – as they grapple with the challenges and opportunities of migration. Policymakers need to cope with Southern Europe's persistent demographic and structural problems, the informality of rural labour markets, and the exodus of native-born workers from rural areas as a result of increased social and economic expectations. If not tackled, these issues are expected to negatively affect the future of rural areas at a time of severe global pressure on farmers, resulting from World Trade Organisation (WTO) negotiations, CAP reforms and EU enlargement, as discussed in detail below.

Migrants in Rural Greece and the CAP Reform

The population of Greece increased from 10,259,900 in 1991 to 10,964,020 in 2001. This increase can almost exclusively be attributed to immigration in the past decade. The census shows that the foreign population of Greece in 2001 was 762,191, making up approximately seven per cent of the total population (National Statistical Service of Greece 2003).

It is estimated that the real number of migrants is higher. Many analysts believe that migrants make up as much as 10 per cent of the population because unauthorized migrants were not included in the census (Kasimis and Kassimi 2004; Kasimis 2005). Almost two-thirds of the foreign population are from Albania, Bulgaria and Romania. Of these, Albania accounts for 57.5 per cent of the total, with second-placed Bulgaria at 4.6 per cent. Common borders with both of these countries have facilitated migration. Most of the jobs migrants undertake comprise basic skilled, manual work well below their education and qualifications. Although they are mainly employed in construction (24.5 per cent), about 17.5 per cent work in agriculture. The agricultural workers, who are mostly from Albania, entered the country illegally in the 1990s following the collapse of the communist regime. Most of them were regularized in the past four years under the provisions of *Act 2910/2001*, otherwise referred to as Greece's second regularization programme (Kasimis and Kassimi 2004). Regional and global developments have important implications for Greece's family-centric farming, which still holds an important position in both the economy and society of rural regions (European Commission 2007; Demoussis 2003).

As the agricultural sector changed in response to national and international developments, migration patterns could also be expected to evolve. More specifically, the most relevant recent development was the 2003 introduction of reforms to the CAP – a system of EU agricultural programmes and subsidies. The need for the CAP reform was pushed to the forefront with the EU's enlargement in May 2004. Ten new states joined the union, but the total EU financial support for agriculture was not to be increased before 2013. WTO negotiations for a new agreement on agriculture, which have meant adjustments to the level of agricultural subsidies, have also played a role. Additional factors created pressure for the CAP reform, including European citizens' increasing demands for the production of safe food and the protection of the environment.

In terms of the contents of the CAP reform, perhaps most importantly, there have been changes in the great majority of subsidies. Emphasis was placed on producers' orientation towards the market and the development of non-agricultural activities for the supplementation of household incomes. In contrast to arrangements before the reform, subsidies are now being paid independently from the volume of production. These new single farm payments are linked to the respect of standards relating to the environment, food safety and animal welfare. However, member states are given the option to maintain some limited link between subsidy and production (Kasimis 2005).

The implications of the CAP reform for the future of European agriculture are difficult to foresee and quantify. Some early studies carried out for the EU predict extensive restructuring of cultivation, reduction of agricultural production in some sectors, extension of both crop and animal production. All this is expected to result in an increase in agricultural incomes of no more than 1.7 per cent by 2009 (European Commission 2003; European Commission 2002). On the other hand, it is expected that the continued restructuring and modernization of Europe's agriculture will lead to a reduction of some two million workers on a full time basis in EU-15 countries by 2014. Additionally, one to two million full-time workers are expected to leave the sector in the ten new member states, and one to two million workers in Bulgaria and Romania (SERA 2006).

For Greece in particular, contradictions seem to be on the horizon. On the one hand, no serious reduction is expected in the total financial support for agriculture until 2013. On the other hand, certain producer groups (for example, cotton cultivators) have already experienced important income cuts and others (for example, tobacco cultivators) have almost entirely moved out of tobacco cultivation, finding it extremely difficult to adjust to the new conditions (OECD 2004b).

More specifically, after a period of substantial rise in agricultural incomes due to the support of the CAP, the currently declining competitiveness of Greek agriculture can be attributed to a cutback in private investments, irrational management of EU funds (allocated mostly to consumption and/or to investments outside agriculture and rural regions), and ineffective structural policy (Demoussis 2003; Louloudis and Maraveyas 1997). The reform of the CAP and the readjustment of national agricultural policy created serious problems for agricultural incomes. The pressures for technological modernization and the restructuring of agriculture in favour of intensive crops resulted simultaneously in the growth of off-farm employment of family members and in greater seasonal demands for labour (Kasimis and Stathakis 2003; Zacopoulou 1999).

This development was reinforced by the demographic deficiency of rural labour created by a massive rural exodus in the 1950s and 1960s, and by the restructuring of rural areas. The expansion of other, non-agricultural activities like tourism, housing construction, the return of urban dwellers to their place of origin and the growth of new consumption patterns connected to leisure and recreation, have created a 'multifunctional' environment in rural Greece which has exerted pressures for types of labour not available from the local population (Kasimis and Papadopoulos 2001).

Such labour deficiencies are explained not only by demographic and structural factors but also by social factors, such as the rejection by the younger generation of low-status, unskilled and poorly-paid jobs in rural areas. The improved level of education and standard of living as well as the spreading out of urban consumption patterns has led to the creation of high expectations by the younger generation, who have looked for jobs outside the agricultural sector and outside rural areas, too. Moreover, the integration of women into the labour market, accompanying changes in family structures and the lack of adequate social infrastructures have resulted in increased demands for domestic support work (King 2000; Lazaridis and Psimmenos 2000).

What impact can these developments have on migration? In Greece, despite the increase in migration in-flows, relevant research in rural areas has been limited. Most studies have focused primarily on issues of migrants' employment and social integration in urban centres and on the resulting economic and social implications for the domestic labour market and communities. For this reason, two independent interdisciplinary studies have been conducted in the time periods of 2000–02 and 2004–06, on the socio-economic impacts of migrant employment in three paradigmatic rural regions of Greece.

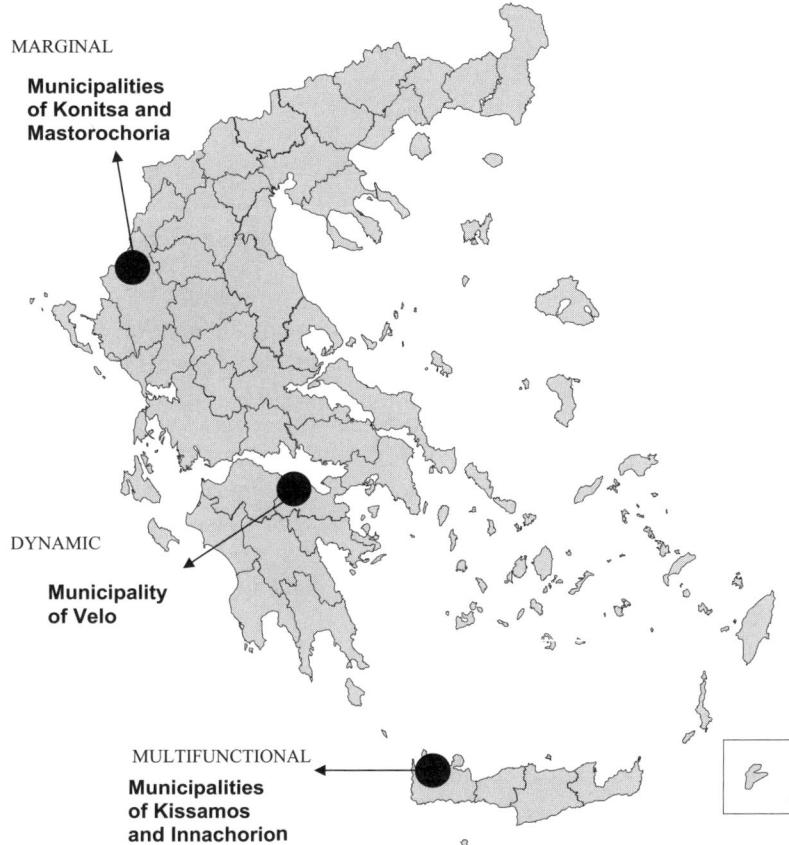

MARGINAL

**Municipalities
of Konitsa and
Mastorochoria**

DYNAMIC

**Municipality
of Velo**

MULTIFUNCTIONAL

**Municipalities
of Kissamos
and Innachorion**

Figure 4.1   The three paradigmatic rural study regions in Greece

The Case Studies: Methods and Findings

The main hypothesis of the two studies mentioned above has been that migrant
workers have addressed four structural developments in rural Greece: first, the
longstanding shortages of labour in rural Greece that have resulted from the
restructuring of its agricultural sector and rural economy; second, the demographic
crisis experienced by the rural population as a result of the rural exodus due
to emigration in the period 1950–70; third, the social rejection by the younger
generation of life and labour in rural areas; and fourth, increased opportunities of
the rural population for off-farm employment. All selected regions have similar
population sizes (approximately 4,000 households) (Figure 4.1).

These regions were:

A 'Marginal/Mountainous' Region (Municipalities of Konitsa and Mastorochoria), which runs along the Albanian border in the prefecture of Ioannina, has been the main gate for both legal and illegal migrants entering Greece. It is characterized by an elderly population left behind by the massive rural exodus of the 1950s and 1960s and by limited productive activities concentrated in agriculture and stock farming. Its marginality results not only from its geography and economy, but also from the Cold-war climate in the region developed after the defeat of the left in the 1946–49 civil war and the establishment of communist Albania. The recent development of the mountainous communities as 'return sites' for older Greeks and as 'recreation sites' for the young, the rebuilding of the region after a devastating earthquake in 1996, and the increasing support needs of the aged population have heightened the demand for labour and set the context for the reception of migrants.

A 'Dynamic' Region (Municipality of Velo), in coastal Peloponnese, in the prefecture of Corinthia, which has a long history of market integration and export-driven agricultural development. Cultivation of sultana grapes, the dominant crop, has expanded rapidly over the past few years, occupying a large part of the cultivable land. Processing and commercial companies in the region are involved in the export of this product. The seasonality of the grape harvest has spurred intensive demand for labour, particularly during the summer. The region is characterized by a balanced age structure and increased educational levels which have often led the locally established people into off-farm employment.

A 'Multifunctional/Pluriactive' Region (Municipalities of Kissamos and Innachorion) on the island of Crete in the prefecture of Chania, which combines traditional agriculture, such as olive groves, 'dynamic' agriculture, such as greenhouse cultivation, and non-agricultural businesses, particularly small-scale tourism. These activities take place at both individual and household levels. The local population is ageing without being satisfactorily replaced by a younger generation. These elements have created the need for a low-skilled, flexible labour force.

Three empirical studies were carried out in each region, involving different rural actors such as local leaders, rural household members and migrants themselves. The studies had both quantitative and qualitative elements. More specifically:

- A qualitative study consisting of semi-structured interviews covered 58 local/regional administrators and opinion leaders.
- A questionnaire was distributed to a representative sample of 293 households of the well established population, two thirds of which were farming households. The questionnaire collected information on the role of migrants and the implications of migrant employment for the operation of farms, family businesses, and the overall support of households. The same questionnaire also registered the attitudes of local people towards migrants

and opinions on the prospects for migrants' integration.
- Finally, a qualitative study was conducted with 65 migrants, employing semi-structured interviews. These interviews aimed to document the social, economic, and cultural experiences of these migrants, as well as their future plans.

In the follow-up study of 2004–06, the three regions were revisited and a qualitative study on local/regional administrators and the migrant population (35 semi-structured interviews) was carried out.

The findings presented below have resulted mainly from an analysis of the questionnaires, which were completed by heads of households in the regions under investigation. Thus, references to the local population are predominantly based on the questionnaire responses of this group. Other, qualitative, material is used only in limited cases.

Implications of International Migration for Farms and Households

In the past two decades, a series of important changes have been observed in the Greek countryside such as the rapid restructuring of farm holdings, the tendency towards the professionalization of farming activity, the substitution of family labour by non-family labour, the changing gender division of labour within farm holdings and the feminization of smaller farms. The evolution of agricultural restructuring caused by the implementation of CAP measures and by the mass inflow of migrants in rural areas has contributed to the intensification of the social and spatial differentiation in rural Greece. More specifically, there is an expanding gap between the larger and the smaller farm holdings and also between the plain, favoured rural areas and the mountainous, marginal, less favoured. Nevertheless, despite the overall declining agricultural employment and the expanding 'multifunctionality' of the Greek countryside, agriculture still remains a central feature of the social and economic life of the rural population. Characteristically, two thirds of rural households still have a farm holding in rural Greece.

On the one hand, the study revealed the structural, multivariate role of migrants in the survival of Greek agriculture and the maintenance of the social fibre of rural regions. On the other hand, a lack of any significant and tailored policy initiatives at local or national level (other than the recent regularization programme) can be observed which would facilitate the social and economic integration[2] of the migrant population in the rural environment. More specifically, the study revealed

---

2 By social integration of migrants we mean the acquisition of access to the opportunities, rights and services available to the members of the mainstream society and by economic integration the acquisition of access to the right to work with all the accompanying formal labour rights.

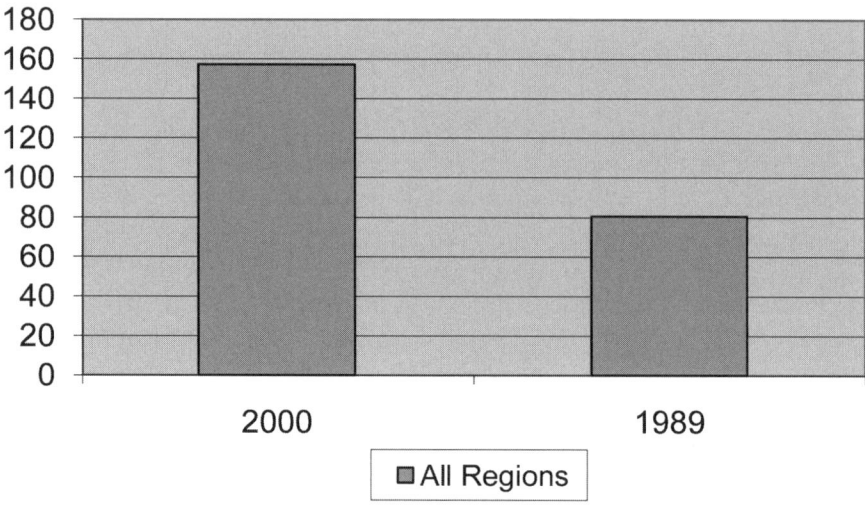

Figure 4.2   **Average number of non-family labour days in 2000 and before the arrival of migrants in 1989**

Source: Household survey, conducted in the study regions of Konitsa and Mastochoria, Velo and Kissamos and Innachorion in 2001.

that more than half of the total number of households and two thirds of the farm households employed migrant labour.

Wage labour in Greek agriculture doubled its size in the 1990s and became almost entirely migrant labour of Albanian nationality (Figure 4.2).

The weight of the geographical presence of Albanians, however, differed between regions. While Albanians offered 77 per cent of the total migrant labour in Greek agriculture, this percentage is 98 per cent in the 'marginal', 87 per cent in the 'dynamic' and only 55 per cent in the 'multifunctional' region. The latter owes the relatively low percentage to the historically long presence of other nationalities (Egyptians and Syrians) and the recent arrival of other nationalities (Georgians, Greek Pontians, Romanians and Bulgarians). Overall non-family labour constituted one-fourth of total labour expended in the farms (Figure 4.3).

The contribution and spreading of migrant labour varied in degree in accordance with the weight and role of the agricultural sector in rural regions. In the 'dynamic' agricultural region of Corinthia this contribution was 33 per cent of the total labour expended, in the 'multifunctional' 21 per cent and in the 'marginal' 8 per cent. In Corinthia international migrant labour was primarily concentrated in agricultural production and processing and secondarily in construction. In the 'multifunctional' region of Chania, combining agricultural and non-agricultural activities, migrants' contribution was diffused to all sectors. In the 'marginal' and mountain region migrants had adopted both, the role of worker and caretaker. More specifically, in the latter region, migrants worked in the revival of the traditional housing

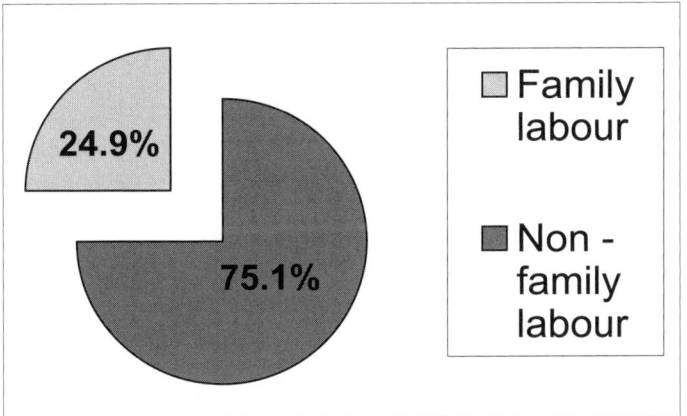

Figure 4.3   Family and non-family labour per farm

Source: Household survey, conducted in the study regions of Konitsa and Mastorochoria, Velo and Kissamos and Innachorion in 2001.

environment with the use of traditional materials, contributing to the conservation of the rural landscape. At the same time, they provided households of the elderly with the labour necessary to preserve the traditional way of living the older people would otherwise have been likely to lose. In other words, in the absence of a satisfactory public social welfare system in these areas, migrants undertook the support role hitherto played by family members.

The use of migrant labour contributed to the modernization and technological development of Greek agriculture. The expected competition between farm modernization, technological development and the employment of migrant labour failed to materialize. Significantly, in the 'dynamic' region, the expansion and technological upgrading of sultana grape cultivation owes much to the availability of migrant labour. This applies similarly to the modernization and expansion of greenhouses in the region of Chania in Crete and to the few cases of intensive livestock farming in the 'marginal' region. In other words, the mass supply of low cost labour has implied a reduced cost of investment in modernization and expansion of agricultural activities making it worthwhile undertaking.

Migrants supported both the survival and the expansion of farms. The employment of migrant labour was, in economic terms, more significant for the larger, 'entrepreneurial' farms. It is evident that while the average numbers of wage labour days per farm below the size of 5 hectares were approximately 60 per year, this number increased almost three times for farms over 10 hectares. In the 'dynamic' region in particular, the average non-family wage labour days per farm more than doubled after the arrival of migrants. Thus, despite the fact migrant employment was spread among larger strata of rural population, the process of socio-economic differentiation in the countryside seems to have become accentuated after their arrival. Migrant labour did not substitute other rural wage labour. Arriving migrants did not compete with indigenous labour for the same jobs. Instead they covered long established demands resulting from the seasonal fluctuations of the agricultural and non-agricultural sectors, the demographic deficits and the social rejection of work and life in rural regions. Migrants acted complementarily to family labour by filling seasonal deficits and meeting increasing demands in both agriculture and the rural regions in general. Simultaneously, migrant labour led to a new family division of labour on and off the farm. It facilitated the partial withdrawal of family labour and the adoption of new family employment strategies. Farm operators reduced their workload and devoted more time to farm organization and management; spouses either reduced their work or returned exclusively to housework while other members of the family sought employment outside agriculture.

Two interconnected processes illustrate the implications of migrant labour upon gender employment in family farms. At one level, migrant labour favoured the expansion of larger farm holdings, located in plain rural areas, allowing them to compete in the market, expand and modernize their cultivation and increase their production. At another, the availability of migrant labour resulted in the 'masculinization' of the larger farms. This helped female family members to withdraw from farm work, and to opt either for off-farm employment or for leaving the labour market.

However, migrant labour also contributed to the 'feminization' of small farm holdings. It provided the seasonal labour necessary to preserve the farm while allowing the males of the family to seek full time, off-farm employment. This development facilitated the transfer of farm management to women, giving them the opportunity to obtain a professional farmer identity.

On the large farms, 'trusted' migrants worked as permanent labour and in peak periods found labourers and undertook the role of supervisor responsible for the organization and supervision of farm work. Seasonal, non-family labour in Greek agriculture existed prior to the arrival of migrants. It was provided by those ethnic groups who were travelling seasonally to meet labour demands (Rom, Pomac Muslims from northern Greece) and/or by poor land workers form other rural regions. These ethnic groups and poor Greek land workers had already moved out of the sector before the arrival of new migrants. They had exploited opportunities of better employment and pay in expanding industry and tourism causing labour deficits in the agricultural sector. Similarly to the situation in Spain, migrants in Greece have replaced and expanded pre-existing models of seasonal employment which were part of cyclical movements of internal migration.

Since their arrival, migrants have not only met real labour demands. They often fulfilled symbolic roles satisfying the social prestige of the newly shaped role of the 'farmer-boss'. Our research material (both quantitative and qualitative) showed that, at least in the first few years of migrants' arrival, farmers were often in 'competition' with each other for the confirmation of their social and economic position in the local society through their withdrawal from manual work and the employment of migrant labour.

Migrants have contributed positively to the demography of rural areas. The rural population has welcomed both the infusion of eligible women and the increased availability of labour. It is indicative that in the 'multifunctional/ pluriactive' study area, out of 482 marriages which were registered in the period 1996–2004, one quarter of them was not between Greeks. Marriages of Greeks with migrants or other foreigners represented 55 per cent of that quarter. Of similar importance were mixed marriages for stock farmers in the 'marginal' region. Of even greater significance for the demography of the rural regions was the presence of migrant children in all types of primary and secondary education schools. In the 'multifunctional/pluriactive' study area, there were primary schools where the proportion of pupils of a foreign nationality was over one-third of the total number of pupils. In the 'marginal' region their number was over two-thirds. In a number of villages schools re-opened for the first time in years to receive the children of migrants.

'Times are Changing...': Perplexity and Scepticism from Farmers and Migrants

In recent years, deep scepticism has been expressed by the farming community about the direct or indirect changes resulting from the CAP reform. How would the changes in the crop structure and the reductions of EU subsidies affect farmers and migrants? Changes had taken different directions in the study regions.

For example, in the regions involving dynamic agriculture (Corinthia and Chania), it was found in the first phase of the research that the expansion of farming was directly connected to the availability of cheap migrant labour. In the second phase, it was reported by the farmers themselves that their often 'irrational' expansion was now facing heavy pressure from increasing labour costs, low market prices and the strong competition from imported agricultural products. In other words, it was claimed that the availability of cheap labour had supported an extensive expansion and modernisation of the farms beyond the size they could manage as family farmers.

Farmers have found themselves in worsening market conditions facing increasing pressures to either scale down, or to involve family members more heavily in order to reduce labour costs. Such a development implied a redefinition of the position and the role of the Greek farmer and of the migrants themselves within the farm.

A return to heavier family labour involvement was noted in both the 'dynamic' and the 'multifunctional/pluriactive' regions. It will be interesting to see in the future how the situation will develop if young Greeks are 'forced' by the developments to start working next to migrants in the same farms and regions.

Important changes were identified in the composition of the migrant population. In Crete, in particular, Georgians and Pontians (former USSR citizens of Greek origin) have now the strongest presence, while Romanians and Bulgarians are showing a continuously increasing presence in all regions. These developments have put migrants in a contradictory situation over the past few years. On the one hand, the continuous regularisation programmes have created a more secure environment, (despite all the problems of bureaucracy and slow administration procedures). On the other hand, the increasing costs of living and the pressure upon wage-levels, which resulted from the continuous arrivals of new waves of migrants, have contributed to growing insecurity.

On-going research in other parts of the country has confirmed new arrivals of undocumented migrants mostly from Bangladesh, Pakistan, India, Bulgaria and Romania. It is worthwhile pointing out that since January 2007, large numbers of Bulgarian and Romanian citizens have arrived as EU citizens. Although they cannot be legally employed, they have worked seasonally living in very poor conditions, and earning wages as low as 23 euros/day.

The continuous casual and irregular hiring of new agricultural migrant labourers from the lowest strata of the job market, who are assigned to unskilled jobs, has become an attractive option with the restructuring of Greek agriculture towards labour intensive cultivations. The new migrants provide the cheap irregular labour that keeps the cost of production low, securing a more competitive position for Greek products in the national and international markets. One of the consequences includes a growing pressure on the regular migrants and the formal labour markets, which affect wages and insurances. Despite the legal requirement on employers to provide a minimum wage and social insurance, compliance with these stipulations are poorly policed, and controls by public authorities have been limited and often ineffective.

Albanians, in particular, are under pressure from two fronts. While they feel the pressure of the increasing costs of integration for example, and family demands for a better standard of living, there is also pressure from the new pool of irregular labour that pushes wages down and encourages their movement out of the agricultural sector (Kasimis 2008).

Regarding migrants' progression opportunities, between the two study periods, there are some indicators of upward mobility of a number of 'older' migrants. They moved from jobs in agriculture to employment offering greater stability, and also found improved school education for their children. Albanians have shown higher professional and social mobility when compared to other nationalities. They have increasingly moved away from seasonal and opportunistic jobs and have sought more regular and permanent employment.

Albanians often concentrate their efforts on accessing jobs in construction or in setting up their own businesses in either trade, services (tourism) or agriculture through either land renting or sharecropping. Such behaviour tends to depend on the length of residence in the region and the requirements in the life cycle of the migrant family.

These developments have contributed to the occurrence of social differentiations and the formation of new social groups of migrants in rural Greece. An early analysis for the Greek case would allow the construction of the following four main types:

1. *Migrant families employed as permanent or semi-permanent farm labour showing a clear gender division of labour.* The husband is normally employed as a permanent wage labourer in agriculture and the wife in domestic services and/or in the agro-food processing industry.
2. *Migrants directly engaged as family farmers themselves.* The husband has settled for a long time in the rural regions and has either become an independent farmer or sharecropper while his wife is helping on the farm or is working in domestic services.
3. *Migrant families holding off-farm employment.* The husband is often employed as an unskilled/semi-skilled construction worker and his wife is employed in the tourism industry. In some regions, however, there is a seasonal sectoral alternation of migrant employment from tourism to agriculture and from agriculture to construction. This demonstrates how local economies and labour markets complement each other, with migrants executing many functions.
4. *Migrants employed as seasonal labour without families.* Undocumented male migrants often live in conditions of insecurity and social exclusion without any clear migration plans. The institutional framework of permit provisions has shaped this situation. The limited prospects for regularisation in Greece have led to a lack of direction. Some migrants want to return home and others prefer to move to another European country.

Perceptions and Attitudes of the Local Population

In all three regions, household members thought that the presence of migrants had a positive effect on the local economy, mainly because labour supply increased, labour costs fell, and consumption expanded. More specifically, almost half of the households surveyed called the impact on the local economy 'positive', 30 per cent assessed it as both 'positive and negative', and only 17 per cent characterized it solely as 'negative' (Figure 4.4).

The household respondents attributed the positive impact of migrants primarily to the acquisition of workers, and secondarily to lower labour costs. Those respondents who claimed negative implications mostly referred to a reduction of work available to locals. However, such a consequence was not identified by our research in the regions surveyed. In other words, in both our quantitative and qualitative research it became evident that migrants did not substitute local wage labour but rather covered labour deficits caused by the factors outlined before. Both groups of respondents, older people and employers of migrants, had the most positive attitude of all the respondents towards the newcomers. The perhaps surprisingly positive response from older people can be accounted for

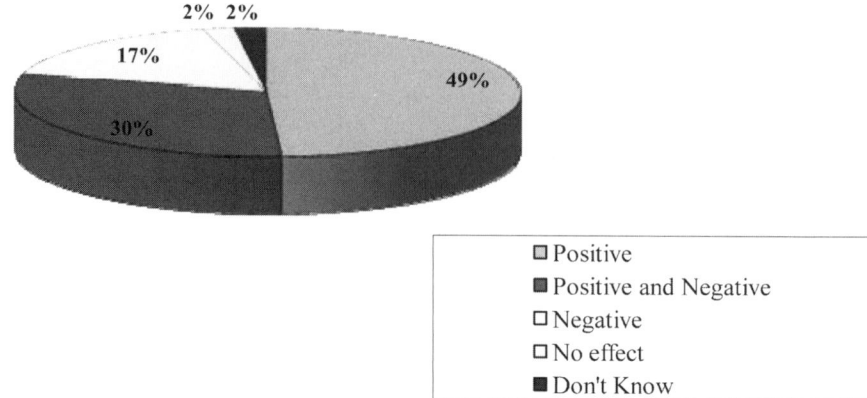

Figure 4.4   Household members' perception of the impact of migrant employment on the local economy

Source: Household survey, conducted in the study regions of Konitsa and Mastorochoria, Velo and Kissamos and Innachorion in 2001.

by explanations provided by some of them that the deprivation experienced by migrants reminded them of their own difficult lives. Another factor reinforcing more positive attitudes among the older generation appears to be the close relationships experienced because of many migrants' roles as caregivers to the elderly.

More negative attitudes were found in younger respondents and those who did not hire migrants. These respondents showed a lack of experience with migration and deprivation. Coupled with fear of a perceived economic, social, and cultural 'threat' seemed to have led to expressions of xenophobia.

Respondents expressed the belief that the local economic sectors that benefited the most from migrant labour were primarily agriculture and secondarily construction. As a consequence, farm holders had positive impressions about migrant labour on their land. The majority of respondents (60 per cent) saw only 'positive' impacts and a large number (29 per cent) 'no impact' at all. 'Negative' implications were only noted by a limited number (10 per cent) of respondents (Figure 4.5).

There were, however, negative stereotypes common to all three regions studied, mainly concerning Albanian migrants. The stereotype of the rough, non-obliging, highly demanding Albanian was the most common. These stereotypes appeared to reflect national stereotypes, all largely shaped by the mass media, rather than stereotypes developed locally as a product of the respondents' everyday social experiences. Positive local stereotypes included those of the hard working, family-caring migrant.

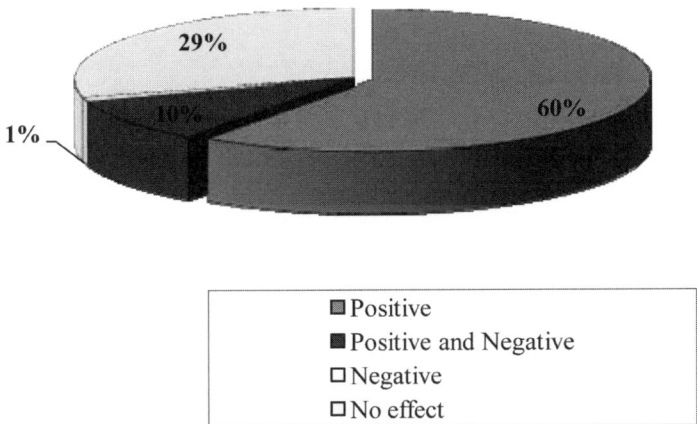

Figure 4.5   Farm holders' evaluation of impact of migrant employment on operation of farm

Source: Household survey, conducted in the study regions of Konitsa and Mastorochoria, Velo and Kissamos and Innachorion in 2001.

Findings from interviews with household heads and local agents indicated that migrant workers were relatively more positively received in the less-developed rural regions than in the developed ones. This appeared to be related to the proportion of migrants in the total population of each region (i.e. the higher the proportion of migrants, the more negative the attitudes), their family status, and their job characteristics. There seemed to be a greater acceptance of migrants who lived permanently in one region together with their families, as opposed to seasonal/ irregular labourers travelling without families.

Migrants and the local population had largely overlapping opinions about the prospects for integration. Both populations believed that the prospects for integration were much better for migrants who lived in the countryside with their families. These migrants adopted strategies that were immediately related to the future of their children. They also often allowed Greeks to become godfathers or godmothers of their children, therby developing close relations with them. Additionally, having established independent economic activities, they developed economic relations with locals which again contributed to more successful integration.

However, the prospects and expectations differed by age. The younger generation of migrants wished to stay in Greece and showed willingness to move to the cities in search of a more regular and higher employment status, often pursued through better education and training. The older generation were often happy with regular employment irrespective of other conditions and employment prospects.

Conclusion

The main aim of this chapter was to analyse the implications of the expanding employment of migrants in the rural regions of Southern Europe in general, and in Greece in particular. On the basis of empirical research material, these implications were examined at the level of the farm unit and the rural household. In addition, perceptions and attitudes of the rural population towards migrants were explored. In Greece and Southern Europe, where agriculture still holds an important position for both the economy and society, migrants play a crucial role in the development of the sector and the preservation of the material conditions for a satisfactory standard of living of the rural population. In the case of Greece, migrant labour has contributed, first, towards avoiding a perceived 'inevitable' crisis of Greek agriculture and rural regions due to demographically, structurally and socially created labour deficits. Secondly, migrants supported the maintenance of the social fabric in rural regions.

More specifically, the following contribution of migrants could be identified: first, migrants have been very important for the agricultural and wider economic development of rural areas. They have been employed for many tasks requiring varying skills and significant geographic mobility over the seasons. In short, they have provided a highly flexible labour force. They have not replaced native wage labourers; rather, they have complemented family labour, improving the organisation and management of farms, relieving family members of manual tasks, and facilitating the search for off-farm employment. Hired to do the arduous, health-threatening, and low-paid jobs that the native population has long ago declined for social and economic reasons, they have greatly served agriculture and other sectors such as construction and tourism by providing the necessary labour.

Second, in regions where agriculture holds a significant position in the local economy, the positive consequences of migrant labour have ranged from farm preservation to farm expansion and modernisation. This has applied in particular to large-scale farms and businesses, which depend heavily on the availability of migrant labour. For smaller and pluriactive farms, migrants have offered the opportunity to preserve the farm while the farm operator and/or family members hold off-farm jobs. In marginal areas, migrants have provided rural households with the labour necessary for the maintenance of their traditional and cultural life. This last contribution is key to understanding the social and demographic implications of migrants' presence in rural Greece.

Third, migrants have offered great services in other forms of rural economic activities such as construction, tourism, and personal/domestic services. The generally positive view of migrants' contributions to the local economy has been further strengthened through migrants' support for the maintenance of social and economic continuity in the Greek countryside.

However, international trade pressures, the reform of the CAP and the consequent reduction of subsidies and crop changes have led to increasing pressures to either reduce the size of migrant employment or to re-engage more family members in order to cut down labour costs. Such a development would imply a redefinition of the family division of labour on and off the family farm, and may have important consequences for the future of migrants in rural regions.

The persisting problems of Southern Europe's agricultural sector and rural regions require policies that will regulate and monitor the integration of migrants. These policies need to adhere to principles of social justice, and should resolve the problems of regularisation, of equal pay for jobs of equal value and of social rights. They should promote economic efficiency through job training and education. Such an approach must also support the restructuring of the agricultural sector and the development of the countryside. It must recognize the fact that apart from international pressures, rural areas also need to deal with the new EU policies of rural environmental protection, the production of quality agricultural goods, and the requirements for multifunctional agriculture, which in addition to producing food and fibre, will preserve the landscape and create rural employment.

Acknowledgements

This chapter draws on the findings of a completed research project entitled 'The Implications of the Settlement and Employment of Migrant Labour in Rural Greece' by Kasimis, Nitsiakos, Zacopoulou and Papadopoulos (2002) and a follow-up study 'The Multifunctional Role of Migrants in Rural Greece and Rural Southern Europe' by Kasimis and Papadopoulos (2006). The author would like to thank the John D. and Catherine T. MacArthur Foundation (USA) for supporting the latter project.

References

Arango, J. and Jachimowicz, M. (2005), 'Regularizing Immigrants in Spain: A New Approach', *Migration Information Source* (published online September 2005) <http://www.migrationinformation.org>, accessed 7 May 2008.

Baldwin-Edwards, M. (2004), 'The Changing Mosaic of Mediterranean Migrations', *Migration Information Source* (published online June 2004) <http://www.migrationinformation.org>, accessed 7 May 2008.

Baganha, M.I. and Fonseca, M.L. (eds) (2004), *New Waves: Migration from Eastern Europe to Southern Europe* (Lisbon: Luso-American Foundation).

Bell, N. (2002), 'The Exploitation of Migrants in Europe', *Conference on 'Borders and Migration'* organized by the Austrian League for Human Rights, Vienna, 29–30 October 2002.

Bradley, T. (1984), 'Segmentation in local labour markets', in Bradley, T. and Lowe, P. (eds), *Locality and Rurality: Economy and Society in Rural Regions* (Norwich: GEO Books), 65–90.

Cánovas Pedreño, A. (2005), 'Sociedades etnofragmentadas', in Cánovas Pedreño, A. and Pedreño Hernández, M. (coord.), *La condición Inmigrante. Exploraciones e investigaciones desde la Región de Murcia*, (Universidad de Murcia, Aula de Debate, Servicio de Publicaciones), 75–103.

Cánovas Pedreño, A. (2003), 'Trabajadores inmigrantes y agricultura intensiva: por qué vinieron a recolectar frutas y hortalizas a los campos del mediterráneo español y cómo fueron convertidos en fuerza de trabajo vulnerable y disponible', in Cubillo Tornos, A. (ed.), *Los inmigrantes y el mundo del trabajo* (Madrid: Universidad Pontificia de Comillas).

Daly, E. (2003), 'By enticing foreigners, villages grow young again', *The New York Times*, July 31.

de Zulueta, T. (2003), 'Migrants in Irregular Employment in the Agricultural Sector of Southern European Countries', *Report for the Debate in the Standing Committee* (Council of Europe).

Demoussis, M. (2003), 'Transformations of the CAP and the Need for Reorganizing Agricultural Policy in Greece', in Kasimis, C. and Stathakis, G. (eds), *The Reform of the CAP and Rural Development in Southern Europe* (Aldershot: Ashgate), 173–85.

European Commission (2007), *Agriculture in the European Union – Statistical and Economic Information 2007* (published online http://ec.europa.eu/agriculture/ agrista/2007/table_en/2012.pdf.

European Commission (2004), *Eurostat Yearbook 2004: The Statistical Guide to Europe*, 234–35.

European Commission (2003), *Impact assessment of the mid-term review proposals for agricultural markets and revenues in the EU-15 and in the EU-25 using the ESIM model*, Directorate General for Agriculture, Brussels.

European Commission (2002), *Impact assessment of the mid-term review proposals for agricultural markets and revenues in the EU-15 2004–2009*, Directorate General for Agriculture, Brussels.

Fonseca, M.L., Alegria, J. and Nunes, A. (2004), 'Immigration to Medium Sized and Rural Areas: The Case of Eastern Europeans in the Évora Region (Southern Portugal)', in Baganha, M.I. and Fonseca, M.L. (eds), *New Waves: Migration from Eastern Europe to Southern Europe* (Lisbon: Luso-American Foundation), 91–118.

Fuentes Moreno, F.J. (2005), 'The regularization of undocumented migrants as a mechanism for the "emerging" of the Spanish underground economy', *Working Paper 05-06*, Unidad de Políticas Comparadas (CSIC).

Hoggart, K. and Mendoza, C. (1999), 'African immigrant workers in Spanish agriculture', *Sociologia Ruralis*, 37:4, 538–62.

ISMU (2005), *X Rapporto sulle Migrazioni*.

Kasimis, C. (2008), 'Diagnostic and qualitative study for the immigration movements in Greece', paper presented in the *INTERREG III, ARCHIMED HuReDePIS Project's Final Progress and Management Meeting*, Patras, Greece (25 February 2008).

Kasimis, C. and Papadopoulos, A.G. (2006), *The Multifunctional Role of Migrants in Rural Greece and Rural Southern Europe*, John D. and Catherine T. MacArthur Foundation, project report (USA).

Kasimis, C. (2006), 'The New Role of Migrants in the Rural Economies of Southern Europe', in Papademetriou, D. (ed.), *Europe and its Immigrants in 21st Century: A New Deal or a Continuing Dialogue of the Deaf?*, Migration Policy Institute-Luso-American Foundation (USA).

Kasimis, C. (2005), 'Migrants in the Rural Economies of Greece and Southern Europe', *Migration Information Source* (published online October 2005) <http://www.migrationinformation.org>, accessed 7 May 2008.

Kasimis, C. and Kassimi, C. (2004), 'Greece: A History of Migration', *Migration Information Source* (published online June 2004) <http://www.migrationinformation.org/Profiles>, accessed 7 May 2008.

Kasimis, C. and Stathakis, G. (eds), (2003), *The Reform of the CAP and Rural Development in Southern Europe* (Aldershot: Ashgate).

Kasimis, C., Nitsiakos, V., Zacopoulou, E. and Papadopoulos, AG. (2002), *The Implications of the Settlement and Employment of Migrants in Rural Greece* (Patras: Universities of Patras and Ioannina) [in Greek].

Kasimis, C. and Papadopoulos, A.G. (2001) 'The de-agriculturalisation of the Greek countryside: the changing characteristics of an ongoing socio-economic transformation', in Granberg, L., Kovacs, I. and Tovey, H. (eds), *Europe's 'Green Ring'* (Aldershot: Ashgate), 197–218.

King, R. (2002), 'Tracking immigration into Italy: Ten years of the *Immigrazione Dossier Statistico*', *Journal of Ethnic and Migration Studies*, 28:1, 173–80.

King, R. (2000), 'Southern Europe in the changing global map of migration', in King, R., Lazaridis, G. and Tsardanidis, C. (eds), *Eldorado or Fortress? Migration in Southern Europe* (Basingstoke: Macmillan), 1–26.

Labrianidis, L. and Lyberaki, A. (2001), *Albanian Migrants in Thessaloniki* (Thessaloniki: Papazisis) [in Greek].

Lazaridis, G. and Psimmenos, I. (2000), 'Migrant flows from Albania to Greece: economic, social and spatial exclusion', in King, R., Lazaridis, G., Tsardanidis, C. (eds), *Eldorado or Fortress? Migration in Southern Europe* (Basingstoke: Macmillan), 170–85.

Lianos, T., Sarris, A. and Katseli, L. (1996), 'Illegal migration and local labour markets: the case of Northern Greece', *International Migration*, 34:3, 449–84.

Louloudis, L. and Maraveyas, N. (1997), 'Farmers and agricultural policy in Greece since the accession to the European Union', *Sociologia Ruralis*, 37:3, 270–86.

Malheiros, J. (2002), 'Portugal seeks balance of emigration, immigration', *Migration Information Source* (published online 12 February 2002) <http://www.migrationinformation.org>, accessed 7 May 2008.

Mendoza, C. (2001), 'Cultural dimensions of African immigrants in Iberian labour markets: a comparative approach', in King, R. (ed.), *The Mediterranean*

Passage. Migration and New Cultural Encounters in Southern Europe (Liverpool: Liverpool University Press), 41–65.

National Statistical Service of Greece (2003), *Population Census 2001* [website], (updated May 2008) <http://www.statistics.gr>, accessed 7 May 2008.

National Statistical Service of Greece (2001), *Preliminary Results of the Census of Agriculture and Livestock 1999/2000 and General Conclusions*, Athens [in Greek].

OECD (2004a), *Trends in International Migration: Annual Report*, SOPEMI (2003 Edition).

OECD (2004b), '*Analysis of the 2003 CAP Reform*', Paris.

Parini, E.G. (2002), *I Posti delle Fragole: Innovazioni e Lavoro nella Fragolicoltura della California e della Calabria* (Rubbettino: Soveria Manelli).

Peck, J. (1996), *Work-Place: The Social Regulation of Labour Markets* (New York: Guilford Press).

Pedone, C. (2005), Diversificación de las cadenzas migratorias ecuatorianas hacia el mercado de trabajo agrícola de Murcia, España, in Cánovas Pedreño, A. and Pedreño Hernández, M. (coord.), *La condición Inmigrante. Exploraciones e investigaciones desde la Región de Murcia*, Universidad de Murcia, Aula de Debate, Servicio de Publicaciones, 255–71.

Peixoto, J. (2002), 'Strong market, weak state: the case of recent foreign immigration in Portugal', *Journal of Ethnic and Migration Studies*, 28:3, 483–97.

Pugliese, E. (1993), 'Restructuring of the labour market and the role of the Third World migrations in Europe', *Environment & Planning D: Society and Space* 11:5, 513–22.

Reyneri, E. (2001), *Migrants' Involvement in Irregular Employment in the Mediterranean Countries of the European Union*, Working Paper, IMP, (Geneva: International Labour Organization).

SERA (Study on Employment in Rural Areas) (2006), SAC, European Commission, Directorate General for Agriculture.

Toronjo Redondo, D. (2004), 'Nouvelle réalité d'un vieux problème social? L'immigration dans les marchés de travail locaux. Le cas de Huelva (Espagne)', *Colloque International: Les Migrations de l'Est vers l'Ouest. Entre mobilité et installation* (Université Libre de Bruxelles).

Zacopoulou, E. (1999), 'Pluriactive population and agriculture: first unravellings of a complex phenomenon', in Kasimis, C. and Louloudis, L. (eds), *Countryside in Greece: Late 20th Century Greek Rural Society* (Athens: EKKE/Plethron), 115–47 [in Greek].

Chapter 5

Migration to Rural Ireland: A North Cork Case Study

Liam Coakley and Piaras Mac Éinrí

Introduction

Immigration to Ireland increased substantially in the years between 1997 and 2007. In part, this was a Europe-wide phenomenon, but Ireland was exceptional in terms of the rapid, recent and significant nature of the change. Today, non-Irish nationals account for almost 16 per cent (355,000 people) of the Irish labour force (Central Statistics Office[1] 2007a) and Ireland has one of the highest percentages of immigrants in the European Union (Watt and McGaughey 2006, 15). Estimates from the Quarterly National Household Survey confirmed these ongoing high rates of immigration. Gross immigration into Ireland for 2006/2007, at 109,500, was the highest on record (CSO 2007b).

Up until very recently, the rhythms of life in Ireland were influenced more by the prospect of emigration than by any equivalent pattern of immigration. The arrival, in the late 1990s, of relatively large numbers of labour migrants and asylum seekers first brought this changing pattern to the attention of the public at large.[2] However, these immigrants have been eclipsed since May 2004 by the arrival of significant numbers of labour migrants from the original EU15,[3] and from the new

---

1 Ireland's specialist national statistics agency, designated as CSO from here on, charged with the collection, compilation, extraction and dissemination for statistical purposes of information relating to economic, social and general activities and conditions in the State.

2 Before this, the largest groups of refugees who came to Ireland were what are nowadays called programme refugees, for example persons admitted under Ireland's participation in refugee resettlement programme (for example, Hungary in 1956; Chile in 1973; Vietnam in 1979; Iranian Bahá'í in the mid-1980s; Bosnia-Herzgovina and Kosovo in the 1990s).

3 EU15 refers to the member countries in the European Union prior 1 May 2004, comprising the following 15 countries: Austria, Belgium, Denmark, Finland, France, Germany, Greece, Ireland, Italy, Luxembourg, Netherlands, Portugal, Spain, Sweden, United Kingdom.

EU accession states of Hungary, the Czech Republic, Lithuania, Latvia, Estonia, Poland, Malta and Cyprus.[4]

Immigrants from Eastern European 'accession states' are by far the most significant population here. Curiously, although Romanian and Bulgarian nationals do not have automatic admission to the Irish labour market, 17,371 Romanians had been issued with Personal Public Service Numbers – national insurance – by end April 2008, the vast majority since Romanian accession in 2007 (Department of Social and Family Affairs 2008[5]).

Because of the organised and pre-approved nature of refugee arrivals in earlier times and the relatively limited numbers involved, it was possible for Irish planners to implement a managerial approach based on advance planning. These earlier groups had a relatively minimal impact on the host society and on service providers. However, Irish planners were unprepared for the larger numbers arriving in the last ten years and Ireland's immigration policies and practices have been overburdened. While individual targeted initiatives have been common, and indeed highly successful on occasion, there has been a lack of strategic planning, a shortfall in funding and a lack of reliable research upon which to base future approaches.

This chapter will first of all provide an overview of the legislative and policy background relating to immigration to Ireland. This constitutes the context of the second part of the chapter, an account of an empirical study, which was carried out in North Cork – a strongly agricultural and rural part of Ireland. The study's central aims were to assess immigrant needs, expose the barriers to integration and highlight any facilitating factors. The purpose of the research was to provide evidence to inform effective inter-agency engagement with the dynamics of new communities in North Cork and beyond. The Conclusion evaluates Irish achievements with regard to immigrant integration, also in the light of research findings at local level.

Immigration to Ireland – Legislative and Policy Background

Immigration policy in Ireland needs to be understood in terms of the country's early to mid-20th century history of relative underdevelopment and impoverishment, the

---

4   In May 2004, European Union membership was extended to include the ten countries of Cyprus, Czech Republic, Estonia, Hungary, Latvia, Lithuania, Malta, Poland, Slovakia and Slovenia. While nationals from Cyprus and Malta have had full free movement rights and have been able to work throughout the EU, transitional measures were put in place to restrict movements by nationals from the other eight (Accession 8 or A8) countries. For the first two years, only Ireland, Sweden and the UK granted full access to their labour markets to these new EU citizens.

5   The Irish Government's Department of Social and Family Affairs (hereinafter D/ SFA). This department formulates appropriate social protection policies and administers and manages the delivery of a range of social insurance and social assistance schemes including provision for unemployment, illness, maternity, caring, widowhood, retirement and old age. Over 1.5 million people directly benefit from such payments.

presence of an inward-looking and isolationist culture and an economy which up to the very recent past could not provide sufficient employment for Irish people, not to mention immigrants. With the obvious exception of British people, the number of people immigrating to Ireland in the period before the 1960s was therefore very modest and Irish immigration policy was consequently conducted more by *ad hoc* ministerial orders, statutory instructions and confidential rules and procedures than by enlightened legislation. This had the unfortunate result that parliamentary scrutiny only took place on rare occasions and civil society had little opportunity to develop an informed view of Irish immigration policy. The core legislation for non-European Economic Area (EEA) workers and residents in Ireland is still the *Aliens Act* of 1935 and the *Aliens Order* of 1946. While the *Aliens Order* was somewhat modified following a court challenge in 2004, these acts are draconian in some of their provisions, reflecting their origins in First World War British legislation, adopted at a time when all foreigners were regarded with suspicion. Extraordinary, far-ranging and discretionary powers concerning immigration are conferred upon the Minister of the day, who may take his or her decisions without explanation and without appeal.

It is not intended to suggest that the original harsh measures provided for in the legislation have not been blunted over the years by some degree of emerging custom and practice and a gradual opening of decision-making more generally to a greater degree of transparency and external scrutiny. In the recent past, a range of rights-based legislation and policy greatly improved conditions for all in terms of employment rights, the right to equality of treatment in service provision and enhanced protection and redress against racism and discrimination. Nevertheless, it remains the case that the majority of non-EEA migrants, other than those married to Irish or EU citizens, are present in Ireland on terms and conditions which are usually temporary, conditional and discretionary.

While immigration policy has gradually been adjusted in a relatively flexible manner and has usually kept pace with the changing needs of the labour market, it could not be said that Ireland has a clear and well-resourced integration policy as yet. Although substantial immigration has been occurring now for more than a decade, the only official definition of integration used by the Irish State was drawn from a 1999 report concerned solely with refugees,[6] to be discussed further in the following section.

Nevertheless, after this slow start, Irish policy makers have gradually begun to engage with the need to legislate for the reality of various forms of immigration as well as the presence of an emerging multi-cultural society in Ireland. The *Refugee Act* was passed in 1996, establishing the mechanisms for the granting of refugee status. Another four Acts, mostly dealing with immigration control, were passed between 1999 and 2004. Unfortunately, these legislative developments are

---

6 'Integration means the ability to participate to the extent that a person needs and wishes in all of the major components of society, without having to relinquish his or her own cultural identity' (Department of Justice, Equality and Law Reform 1999).

generally considered to be piecemeal and *ad hoc* in nature (Ryan 2005, 2). Ireland's Department of Justice, Equality and Law Reform[7] therefore proposed a radical overhaul of the system in April 2005 when it published its *Outline Proposals for an Immigration and Residency Bill*. This discussion document led ultimately to a consolidated legislative bill, the *Immigration, Residence and Protection Bill* in 2007 While that Bill lapsed because of the 2007 General Election, a revised version of it has since been tabled by the current Government but has yet to be enacted in law.

The promotion of equality and inclusion is now central to many efforts in the public domain. Three initiatives are of particular importance. These are i) the document already mentioned *Integration: a two-way process* (D/JELR 1999), ii) *National Action Plan Against Racism* or NPAR (D/JELR 2005) and iii) The appointment of a Minister for Integration.

Integration: A Two-Way Process

The first significant report to be produced in this area in Ireland was *Integration: a Two-Way Process* (D/JELR 1999). This report was produced at a time when Ireland's experience of immigration was new and relatively limited. It did not recommend 'hard targets' in achieving the aims set out and no public review and evaluation mechanism was put in place to monitor implementation of the report. However, the it did make a series of modest recommendations and some progress was made.

Significantly, this report recognised the need to make mainstream services accessible to immigrants. Language assessments and skills training assessments were put forward as key objectives. A recognition of the need to provide immigrants with information on accessing mainstream services was made. The provision of interpretation services, training programmes for service providers and information in various languages were also seen to be key.

While these recommendations applied directly only to refugees and persons with leave to remain in Ireland, working definitions of integration associated with these recommendations came to have a wider relevance. However, *Integration: A Two Way Process* lacked an appreciation of the fact that there would need to be a more fundamental shift in attitudes, structures and services if its goals were to be achieved. It was not appreciated that it was not simply a question of making public services more user friendly for migrants. The nature of the relationship between the migrant and Irish society needed to be assessed in a more fundamental manner

---

7 The Irish Government's Department of Justice, Equality and Law Reform (D/JELR). Agencies controlled by D/JELR impact on every aspect of life in Ireland, from child protection and involvement in inquiries and tribunals to all elements involved in crime and punishment and the courts system, from the buying and selling of property to a range of immigration services and the areas of disability and diversity.

if social cohesion was to be preserved and migrants successfully integrated into a society which had hitherto seen itself as largely monocultural in composition.

National Action Plan Against Racism (NPAR)

In many respects, *The National Action Plan against Racism in Ireland* (D/JELR 2005) developed the themes first set out in *Integration: A Two Way Process*. Every area of statutory activity was addressed (Mac Éinrí and Coakley 2006, 8). The framework underpinning the NPAR was based on the following elements: i) effective protection and redress against racism, ii) economic inclusion and equality of opportunity, iii) the accommodation of diversity in service provision, iv) the recognition and awareness of diversity and v) full participation in Irish society.

The methods to be used to achieve the aims of the Framework included: i) mainstreaming of an intercultural approach to policy-making, ii) targeting strategies to overcome inequalities, iii) benchmarking progress made and significantly iv) an engagement with key stake-holders and drivers to support the implementation of the NPAR. 'Intercultural' was understood to mean the promotion of an active engagement between different cultural communities, recognising and seeking to validate difference within an agreed framework. In that sense it was seen as representing a qualitatively different approach than that implied by the word 'multicultural', which in admittedly reductionist terms could be seen as merely the factual recognition that people lived in an ethnically mixed society. It must be said that this relatively subtle distinction was not always understood in public and political discourses.

There were other problems. For example, even this latter document lacked a solid statutory basis for action, and the National Consultative Committee on Racism in Ireland (NCCRI)[8] does not have the same status, budget or powers as, for example, its UK counterpart – the Equality and Human Rights Commission (which subsumes the former Commission for Racial Equality (CRE)). Equally, although there was a growing recognition of the crucial role of the voluntary sector, the precise manner in which they would be involved was not spelled out.

Appointment of Minister with Special Responsibility for Integration

In June 2007, the incoming Government appointed Mr Conor Lenihan as Minister for State with Special Responsibility for Integration. It could not be said, however, that Ireland has a full-fledged integration policy as yet. In his first major policy statement *Migration Nation* (Diversity Ireland 2008), the Minister announced

---

8   Ireland's National Consultative Committee on Racism and Interculturalism (NCCRI) was established in 1998 as an independent expert body focusing on racism and interculturalism. It is a partnership body which brings together government and non-government organisations to combat racism and foster an intercultural society.

the creation of a Commission on Integration, drawn from appropriate academic and professional sectors, to engage in a series of public consultations as well as advising the Minister. A Ministerial Council on Integration, drawn from ethnic communities, was also announced. Unfortunately, to date, neither the Commission nor the Council has been created.

Critiquing the Multicultural Model

European and other approaches to the integration of migrants have tended to be defined as a spectrum of responses from the 'assimilationist' model espoused traditionally by countries such as France (Bertossi 2007) and the 'multicultural' one first developed in Canada (Taylor 1994; Kymclicka 1995) and later adopted in some form or another in countries as diverse as Australia (Hage 1998), the Netherlands, Britain (Hewitt 2005; Modood 2007) and Sweden. Recent events, such as the riots in Britain in 2002, the London suicide bombings of 7 July 2005 and the murders of Pym Fortuyn in 2002 and Theo Van Gogh in 2004 in the Netherlands, as well as the backwash from 9/11 in the USA, have suggested to some critics that all is not well with the multicultural model (Goodhart 2004). Some oppose it on the grounds that certain minorities – many would instance fundamentalist Muslims – allegedly cannot be accommodated within the western liberal democratic model.

Others argue against multiculturalism for an entirely different reason, holding that it encloses individuals within communities and ghettoises them, making integration more difficult by emphasising communal rights over individual ones (Wieviorka 2002). In this perspective, the 1998 Belfast Agreement (Northern Office 1998) between the UK and Ireland, exemplifies an approach where an emphasis on 'parity of esteem' not only failed to attend to underlying issues of power and inequality, but arguably made the gulf between communities deeper than before by refusing to recognise the more complex and hybrid nature of many people's sense of identity, not easily pigeonholed into preconceived categories (McVeigh 2002).

The following research project carried out in the rural area of North Cork will provide some insights into immigrants' needs, the extent to which they were met, and the reasons for immigrants' integration, or the lack of the same.

Project Overview: Immigrant Communities in North Cork

More specifically, the research focused on assessing the extent to which immigrants feel 'at home' in this area and how Irish organisations can help smooth their transition from a life of uncertainty as an immigrant. An analysis of the barriers to the integration of new communities into wider Irish society was central to the project, as was a consideration of the effectiveness of service provision in the area.

We 'cast our net wide'. Drawing on a definition of integration that pivots on 'the ability to participate to the extent that a person needs and wishes in all of the major components of society, without having to relinquish his or her own cultural identity' (D/JELR 1999) we sought to study the experiences of new communities in North Cork in as comprehensive a manner as possible. The project thus sought to address the socio-cultural and economic experiences of immigrant communities in the Avondhu area of North Cork and to contexualise this information at local level.

Our key objectives were to:

• Provide a description of the immigrant communities in North Cork with a view to informing the development of an evidence-based approach to the needs of these communities.

• Provide a description of patterns of economic, political and social integration prevalent among these communities and outline the challenges and obstacles to integration that remain.

• Inform evidence-based policy and encourage an effective inter-agency engagement with the dynamics of new communities in this country.

Methods

The following methods were used in the field: semi-structured interviews and focus group discussions with immigrant community members, and interviews with front-line staff employed by statutory and non-statutory agencies.

Semi-structured interviews   The experiences of the communities under study were examined using semi-structured interviews. 155 interviews were conducted on a one-to-one basis by a team of four research assistants who, in turn, were drawn from the predominant immigrant communities resident in North Cork – those from West Africa and Eastern/Central Europe. Interviewers were trained for this purpose. Interviews were conducted in English. All participants were asked the same questions, ensuring that broadly replicable types of data were produced. However, individuals were allowed to speak in their own words and add information deemed relevant by them, allowing for each individual experience to be recorded as comprehensively as possible. The act of verbalising responses to asked questions was also important as such verbalisation can prompt research participants to make associations across time, and maybe even to evaluate and represent life-events in a manner that is unexpected to them personally.[9]

The need to engage with a diverse population was of primary importance here. Historically, probability-style sampling methods have been used to obtain as representative a picture of such diverse populations as possible, subject to quantifiable and acceptable margins of error. Such sampling methods were not

---

9   See for example, Coakley and Healy (2009).

feasible in this instance as the research team's ability to engage in an adequately rigorous pattern of random selection was hampered by the lack of a clear sample frame. Two vital conditions did not apply: precise data about the population under study was lacking, and a reliable random sampling approach could not be employed. First, accurate data on immigrants is not available at sub-regional level, at least in intercensal periods, and second, no reliable sampling frame could have been constructed due to data protection restrictions.

Previous research attempted to address this data issue by operating in conjunction with organisations active in the area. Ward (2002) for example, drew her sample from the records of relevant statutory organisations, while Phelan and Kuon (2005) constructed their sample frame from records kept by the non-statutory organisation, Doras Luimní.[10]

The feasibility of harnessing a similar approach was examined in North Cork but the research proceeded from the premise that such an approach is necessarily a distorted one, as there is no way of knowing how representative of their respective communities the persons interfacing with specific services providers might be. It may be, for instance, that they are among the more active and aware among their coevals of the range and depth of such services. But it may also be the case that their self-selecting use of such services is actually reflective of quite a different tendency, namely a level of dissatisfaction or of specific needs not, in general, shared by those who do not seek out such services and such organisations.

A multi-stage, proportional style of quota sampling was therefore used. A broad profile of the target population was developed during initial contacts made with relevant agencies. A degree of stratified sampling was then applied. This was achieved using a variety of access points into the target population. The most significant of these were: i) specialist non-governmental organizations (NGOs), ii) faith-based communities active in the area and iii) charities that engage in outreach-style work. We then drew on best practice when seeking to engage with 'inaccessible' populations by snowball sampling from these starting points in order to achieve a wider spread.

This chosen method was more laborious than operating within the contact networks of specific NGOs, as it involved an attempt to map the whole target community, through its own internal structures as well as through NGOs and other service providers, but an engagement with absolute representation was not of central concern. Rather, this approach was followed as it was deemed to offer the most intellectually honest method of engaging with issues of respondent selection, given our initially imperfect understanding of the nature of our target

---

10 Doras Luimní is a non-governmental organisation that works among the immigrant community in Limerick, Ireland. Their stated aims include the desire to open doors for those seeking asylum and refuge, to inform and involve the local community in dealing with issues of asylum-seekers, multiculturalism and racism, and to work with the statutory and voluntary bodies in planning and implementing programmes to support asylum seekers and refugees.

population. The sampling method used is thus best described as a pattern of sound theoretical respondent selection rather than an engagement with notions of absolute representation. We are, however, satisfied that the approach was justified and has yielded results which fairly reflect how the target community see themselves and their place in Irish society.

Focus groups   Three focus group discussions were held with members of the immigrant community. The intention was that these groups would provide a more informal setting for data production than the one-to-one interview. This proved to be the case. On occasion, significant insights arose when the region-wide patterns gleaned from the interview surveys were subjected to the more nuanced conversational exploration inherent in such group interactions. This method had the added benefit of allowing research participants to reclaim some ownership of their data. Broad patterns in the data were discussed, initial analysis was considered, and a right of reply was fostered among survey participants. This also allowed the research team to revisit and challenge their own assumptions.

Informal interviews with service providers   A series of informal and often quite lengthy, qualitative interviews were conducted with front-line staff employed by statutory and non-statutory agencies active in the region and comment was invited on the patterns of need uncovered. Staff consulted here included people employed in education, health and welfare, employment, policing, social care, public administration and social activism.

Profile of the Study Area

North Cork is a predominantly rural and agricultural area, with two substantial local towns. These are Mallow (population including environs 10,056, Census 2006) and Fermoy (population including environs, 5,722, Census 2006). The economy of Cork county has undergone substantial changes in recent decades. Older industries in the Cork City and Cork harbour area – shipbuilding, car assembly, steel and manufacturing – have all been phased out. In turn, strong new sectors have emerged, notably in the areas of pharmachem, manufacturing and information technology. By contrast, the present study is located in rural North Cork. Mixed farming, construction and services have been the main types of economic activity in recent years, in contrast, for instance, to rural West Cork, which has been able to develop a much stronger tourist industry.

The increase in the number of migrant workers in the study area has been dramatic. Taking the two main towns as examples, the number of persons of foreign nationality has grown from 488 in Mallow in 2002 (5.6 per cent of the town population) to 1,212 (12.3 per cent of the population) in 2006. In Fermoy the migrant population grew from 237 in 2002 (5.1 per cent of the population) to 996 (17.9 per cent of the population) in 2006.

These increases illustrate a key pattern in recent immigration into Ireland – that although there are high concentrations of migrants in inner city and urban areas generally, there is also a notable pattern of rural dispersal, so that many smaller rural towns and surrounding hinterlands have experienced relatively high rates of in-migration even though the absolute numbers in parts of Ireland with relatively low rates of population density are not that high. The figures cited in the preceding paragraph may be compared with the percentage of migrants in Ireland as a whole, at just over 10 per cent in 2006. As a result, what can be stated with some degree of certainty, is that the immigrant population resident in North Cork is diverse and significant (people from 29 different countries were interviewed during the course of this project). In many respects, this population falls strongly in line with national patterns. The vast majority of migrants in Ireland are from other European Union (EU) countries and the largest single national group are United Kingdom (UK) citizens. Apart from UK nationals, the other most significant foreign population in the study area consists of Polish nationals (5 per cent of population of Fermoy and 3 per cent of Mallow, 2006). Established West African communities also reside here, most of whom have come to Ireland via the asylum/refugee process, and significant populations of immigrants from the accession states of the EU10 and new European citizens from Eastern Europe and the Baltic are also visible.

This population is not homogenous in nature. Significant linguistic, ethnic and cultural diversity is present and immigrant groups are internally differentiated along many lines (some of which may not be easily accessible to an Irish-born observer). This must be borne in mind when seeking to engage with the idea of new communities in Ireland. Nevertheless, many statutory and non-statutory organizations maintain a presence in North Cork and an often wide-ranging engagement with immigrant need is in evidence.

Research Findings: Integration in North Cork

What were the findings of the research with regard to all the key axes of immigrant integration which were examined, in particular immigrant experiences of: i) education, ii) employment, iii) housing, iv) health and welfare as well as v) non-statutory service providers in North Cork?

Ireland's Department of Social and Family Affairs (D/SFA) is often the first port of call for people immigrating to North Cork. Apart from its role in the provision of social security (PPS) numbers to new workers, this organisation hosts an information section on social welfare benefits available to immigrants. A range of other service providers also maintain a presence in rural North Cork and immigrant groups interact with such service providers at many levels as they seek to settle in Ireland. Foras Áiseanna Saothair (FAS), Ireland's national employment authority,[11] the Health Service Executive – Southern area[12] and An Garda Síochána (the national police force) all commonly interact with immigrant groups. For example, Community Gárdaí, police officers tasked with working closely with the public, have been proactively 'humanising' their interactions with immigrants and individual Community Gárdai and immigration Gárdai have made efforts to 'be a friendly force' by maintaining a visible and approachable presence in the area and working closely with immigrant organisations active in the area (Community Garda, Mallow).

Unfortunately, such services and service providers can be inaccessible to immigrants. The Department of Social and Family Affairs (D/SFA) for example, provide some translated leaflets for use but this department's work is conducted in English and language difficulties arise.

> It's difficult for ourselves to follow it, let alone someone who can't speak English. Social welfare itself is not straight forward, it's very complex (Staff member, D/SFA, Mallow).

Immigrant attempts to integrate in Ireland can be profoundly affected by such difficulties, as the subsequent sections demonstrate.

Education

The design and delivery of educational services in Ireland has always reflected a recognition of the need to accommodate people with different ethnic/cultural backgrounds (see for example, Murray 2006; Tormey 2005). However, with the exception of work on 'Irish Travellers'[13] very little research has been carried out on the needs of minority groups in general and almost nothing is known about the specificities of educational service provision for migrants in rural areas.

---

11   Ireland's national employment authority seeks to enhance the skills and competencies of individuals and enterprises in order for Ireland to further develop as a competitive, inclusive, knowledge-based economy. The provision of tailored training and employment programmes is central to its mission.

12   The Health Service Executive (HSE) is the single body responsible for providing Health and Personal Social Services for everyone living in the Republic of Ireland. As such, the HSE provides thousands of different services in hospitals and communities across the country. These services range from public health nurses treating older people in the community to caring for children with challenging behaviour; from educating people how to live healthier lives to performing highly-complex brain surgery; from planning for major emergencies to controlling the spread of infectious diseases.

13   Irish Travellers are a highly excluded ethnic minority group who have been part of Irish society for many centuries. Irish Travellers are recognised in UK law as an ethnic group and protected under the Race Relations Act.

Education for children   The provision of educational services of immigrant children is set out in law. *Ireland's Education (Welfare) Act 2000* requires that an education is made available to all children resident in Ireland between the ages of six and 16 years (Coakley and Mac Éinrí 2007, 2). In this regard, the Department of Education and Science (DES)[14] does not differentiate between those children born in Ireland and those born elsewhere. This is strongly in keeping with international law. The *EU Convention of Human Rights* (Protocol 1, Article 2) states that children are subject to compulsory education, irrespective of legal status (Lodge and Lynch 2004) and the state is required to extend the right to education to all persons resident in the country, not just to citizens of Ireland (Pobal 2006). As a result, often large numbers of foreign-born children are being educated in Irish schools. These pupils tend to be integrated into the student body in general and are invariably placed in the 'correct' age group, irrespective of language ability (Christian Brothers et al. 2002, 18).

Insofar as the State has sought to meet the specific needs of migrant children in a targeted way, most emphasis is focused on the provision of language support. Ireland's Department of Education and Science (DES) has made resources available for schools catering for non-English speaking pupils. Both primary and post-primary schools are eligible to receive this support and any school that has 14 or more immigrant pupils with 'significant English language deficits'[15] is entitled to funding equivalent to an additional temporary teacher for a period of up to two years. Schools with 28 or more such pupils will be entitled to the equivalent of two temporary teachers (see Coakley and Mac Éinrí 2007).

This system seems to work well in North Cork. We found very little evidence of difficulty among immigrant children resident here. Twenty seven research participants have children of school-going age. Only a very small number (three people) refer to difficulties faced. Two of these people feel that language is a problem while one person refers to problems associated with money. Interestingly, contrary to patterns uncovered in nearby Cork city, no person referred to cultural difficulties or racist incidents here.

A different picture emerges when patterns of adult and continuing education are examined. Contrary to expectations, the people interviewed during this project do not make use of the educational opportunities available to them in North Cork.

---

14   The Irish government's Department of Education and Science. Key priorities are the promotion of equity and inclusion, quality outcomes and lifelong learning; planning for education that is relevant to personal, social, cultural and economic needs; and enhancement of the capacity of the Department for service delivery, policy formulation, research and evaluation.

15   Students are deemed to have 'significant English language deficits if the are adjudged to have 'very poor comprehension of English' and 'very little spoken English' or if they only 'understand some English and can speak enough English for basic communication.' (http://www.citizensinformation.ie/categories/education/primary-and-post-primary-education/educational-supports/non_nationals_and_non_english_speakers)

Adult and continuing education The need to address the English language training needs of immigrants is well recognised. As early as July 2000 the Irish government published a white paper on adult education entitled 'learning for life' (DES 2000). This document proposes that asylum seekers should have 'free access to adult literacy, English language and mother culture supports' (Section 8.13). In research springing from this paper, Ward (2002) stresses that language and literacy are linked to the experience of equality and interculturalism and recommends the delivery of such programmes through mainstream state adult education providers and the provision of supports to community based programmes. Ireland's national social partnership agreement further reflects this prioritisation.

It is unsurprising therefore, that a range of services are provided for immigrants resident in North Cork. Beginners are catered for through Cork County Vocational Educational Committees' (VEC) literacy scheme.[16] Twenty hours basic English for Speakers of Other Languages (ESOL) tuition is provided, free of charge, in each of five centres in the North Cork area. All comers are given tuition, irrespective of status, or previous educational attainment. This provision is 'subject to budgets being available' and inconsistencies arise (in nearby Cork city for example, the VEC does not accept 'highly educated' people on their basic ESOL schemes as they believe that these do not fall within the remit of the literacy budget (Adult Lteracy Officer, Cork County VEC)). Intermediate students can access ESOL through the VEC's Back To Education Initiative (BTEI) schemes. However, the requirement to pay a once-off payment of €30 may be prohibitive in this instance. Various faith-based organisations and NGOs also provide specific targeted interventions in the region and language training is available via specialist service providers in Cork city.

Many wider further education opportunities are available in North Cork. Both colleges, *Colaiste an Craoibhin* in Fermoy and Davis College in Mallow provide Post Leaving certificate (PLC) level courses to adult learners (the Leaving Certificate is the certificate examination taken by all students in Ireland at the end of the second level educational cycle). There is a strong expectation that these courses will lead to a qualification useful in the world of work. Courses are varied and are certified.

Reasonably low levels of uptake are seen among the migrant population. Only a small number of people have availed of English language training (20) and only just over one third of research participants (58 people) have availed of educational opportunities and gained educational/professional qualifications since coming to

---

16   There are 33 VECs in Ireland. These organisations were established in accordance with the provisions of the Vocational Education Act 1930 to provide education, training and support services in local communities. These education and training programmes include second level, adult, community and second chance education, post-leaving certificate programmes, prison education, traveller education and a variety of EU funded and co-operative training programmes.

live in Ireland. The majority of these qualifications were achieved at certificate or diploma level (81 per cent).

Some groups are certainly less motivated to avail of educational opportunities than others.

> Most Polish people don't speak English, I'd say 70 per cent of community in Mallow, they don't (Male, EU10, Focus group 1).

> They simply don't want to learn English (in response, Female, EU10, Focus group 1).

This lack of engagement is difficult to explain. Similar research carried out in nearby Cork city (Mac Éinrí and Coakley 2006) shows that educational interventions are valued by immigrant communities in general. Pressure of work, among a population that is singularly motivated to engage in waged work, may be significant. Eight research participants were clear in their view that they would not be availing of educational opportunities as a result of their desire to engage in waged work. However, structural deficiencies may also be influential.

Many educational schemes are over-subscribed and service providers operational in North Cork are under-funded. Cork County VEC's literacy service for example, is funded to cater for 250 students on a part-time basis, in this area. Staggeringly, this organisation catered for over 900 learners in 2006, half of whom were ESOL students. This scheme was in receipt of:

> No extra funding for ESOL ... not one penny. ESOL dropped in the lap of literacy without any funding being earmarked (Adult Literacy Organiser (ALO), Cork County VEC).

Pressures on staff are significant.

> The service is being bombarded by something that they never expected to take the weight of, the pressure is unbelievable. There isn't any money there (ALO, Cork County VEC).

Furthermore, staff often feel that they are operating in a policy vacuum and there is a sense that local staff are left to interpret vague regulations without backup. This has inevitably led to inconsistencies across the region.

> There is no guidance on admission. Nobody is saying anything. Someone in the west, the east and Bandon will have different ideas on what a beginner is (ALO, Cork County VEC),

This factor is further reflected by at least one service provider active in this field who states that the '*bureaucracy we have here is a minefield*'. The prevalence of an unwieldy bureaucracy is seen as a problem by 13 people (over one third of all answers given) and people feel that barriers can be placed in their way on foot of an unwieldy and often uncaring system.

> In Ireland, people say the system is not good, it is not good (Female, Africa, Focus group 1),

Frustrations result. As this immigrant woman suggests:.

> The courses they offer us are English and basic computer courses, a lot of people know how to use a computer, I think it is an insult. They are teaching us the level of my daughter. You do the basic computers and then that's where it stops. We are here doing nothing, they don't want us to work I think they should offer courses that will help us in the future and not just basic courses (Female, Africa, Focus group 2),

Challenges with application forms and a misunderstanding of eligibility criteria are particularly prevalent, leading inevitably to confrontation and resistance on both sides of the service provider – user relationship. Other obstacles include: i) language (eight people), ii) money (four people), iii) the prohibitive influence of distance (one person), iv) lack of time (five people), and v) problems with the recognition of qualifications (four people).

Difficulties with the recognition of prior learning (RPL) as with the recognition of qualifications and experience in the realm of waged labour, can constitute a significant impediment to an individual's participation in further/higher education in Ireland. This is especially so in instances when an individual may lack the necessary documentary proof of learning. The salience of such difficulties has long been accepted (see, Integrating Ireland 2005, for example) and guidelines are in place in Ireland since 2005 (Further Education and Training Awards Council (FETAC) 2005).[17]

In this light, it is unsurprising that only a very small minority of research participants have attained university-level educational opportunities whilst resident in Ireland. One person has gained a post-graduate diploma from University College Cork (UCC) and two have attained qualifications from Cork Institute of Technology (CIT). This seeming lack of engagement with third level education is understandable. Issues of eligibility dominate but personal difficulties are also significant. For example, the existing three-year residency rule, which stipulates that those with refugee status are required to pay non-EU student fees until they

---

17 Ireland's Further Education, Training and Awards Council (FETAC) was established as a statutory body in 2001 to make quality assured education and training awards in accordance with national standards, creating opportunities for all learners in further education and training to have their achievements recognised and providing access to systematic progression pathways.

have been resident in this country for a period of 36 months, constitutes a significant obstacle for this sub-group of the immigrant population. Structural impediments are also likely to be influential. The National Office for Equity of Access to Higher Education (2006) for example, states that 'equity of access remains for the most part on the margins in higher education, it is not yet part of the day to day practical agenda of institutions'. Pobal (2006, 31) offer evidence to support this point when they state that all five major Higher Education Authority (HEA) reports on access to 3rd level education commissioned between 1980 and 2003 do not examine the position of ethnic minorities. In this light, in spite of stipulation contained in the *Universities Act* (1997) to promote equality of opportunity, difficulties to entry remain for many.

A fractured landscape exists in North Cork and many potential learners must either feel precluded from engaging with educational service providers or are not being accessed by providers themselves. Both service providers and policy makers must seek to integrate their efforts and endeavour to encourage the development of an integrated educational landscape in this regard. If education remains one of the crucial avenues to integration, the desire to access it must be facilitated and clear local initiatives be put in place to allow individuals to engage successfully with Irish society, at this level.

Employment

Most immigrants resident in North Cork who participated in this research work in the waged labour force (94 people, 61 per cent of the sample). This engagement is heavily dependent on a person's status.[18] The vast majority of economic migrants (from the EU10 as well as from further afield) are employed (88 per cent and 77 per cent respectively). Only 33 per cent of those with refugee status and 50 per cent of those whose residency is dependent on their status as parents of a child born in Ireland work in the waged labour force.

A difficult labour market exists in North Cork. Despite the fact that 48 people state that they worked in either professional or skilled work in their country of origin (31 per cent of the sample) many people are working in 'lower status'/ lower paying sectors of the economy in Ireland than they were used to in their home country and the vast majority of people work in unskilled sectors in North Cork (68 per cent, 64 people). Indeed, 25 per cent of people who state that they worked in professional/higher professional careers in their countries of origin are unemployed in Ireland (six people).

> I know personally people who have their status (refugee status) four or five years and have never worked a day (Female, Africa, Focus group 3).

---

18   For example, people who have asylum seeker status are precluded from working in the waged labour force

Common labour categories of the study participants include: i) general operatives (26 people, seven of whom worked in either skilled or professional sectors in their country of origin), ii) shop assistants (21 people, three of whom worked in professional areas in their country of origin), iii) cleaners (five people), iv) garage workers (three people), v) one car wash attendant, vi) one security man, vii) nurse's aids (three people), viii) kitchen porters (two people), ix) one 'store-man', and x) one administrator.

Research participants are conscious of migrants' underemployment. Frustrations arise.

> You know what is actually funny [is that employers say] oh you people are very hard working people, but you will never find a Polish person in an office, it is very rare. The thing is that most of them work in factory or in a shop or [a supermarket] (Female, EU10, Focus group 3).

> In [a supermarket], you can see many Nigerians there, at the counter or merchandising (Male, economic migrant Focus group 2).

It is unsurprising therefore that a large number of interviewees (133 people, 86 per cent) feel that immigrants face difficulties when accessing the waged labour market in North Cork.

Difficulties Experienced in the Waged Labour Force

Many report on difficulties arising from their lack of proficiency in English (45 per cent of those who are engaged in paid employment – 43 people – feel this way). Certainly, it is well recognised that lack of information on employment rights as a result of inadequate language skills can leave workers vulnerable to exploitation (see for example, Mac Éinrí 2006, 125).

> Polish workers are discriminated against, being paid a lower rate. Within the construction industry there are a lot of individuals who are being exploited. That is a reality' (Assistant Manager, FÁS Employment Services, Mallow).

> They are saying that in this country we work until 12.00 at night, and everybody does it (Manager, FÁS Business Services, Cork).

After language, the recognition of qualifications and experience is of pivotal importance in determining the level of success that a person is likely to enjoy when seeking to engage with the waged labour force. Many of the people who participated in this survey are highly qualified and experienced but many (especially those who have come to this country through the refugee process) may have departed from their country of origin without adequate preparation or forward planning. This can constitute a significant impediment to an individual's potential in Ireland. This is especially so in instances when an individual may lack the necessary documentary proof of learning.

> They don't allow you to get a good job, the job maybe you like to do. Back home, maybe you have a degree. Here you go school, they don't accept it, and I don't know, I don't know this system (Female, Africa, Focus group 3).

Inadequate access to childcare is also referenced here. However, this factor is identified far more prominently by those who are not engaged in waged labour (25 per cent of this group) than by those who work (only 7 per cent of this sample).

'Resistance' is also noted at a more general level and some people relate their experiences of difficulty whilst trying to source waged work.

> My sister didn't have a job and I went to a café with some information for a job they were looking for. I asked the lady for the job, and I said what kind of vacancy do you have, and she said this job is for someone who speaks English and I can't understand you. I said everything I wanted to say, and she said she couldn't understand. She was definitely looking for some Irish person, it was just some excuse for her (Male, EU10, Focus group 1).

While overt racism may be experienced, discrimination manifests itself in many different ways. Sometimes, a person's experience of waged work can be coloured by negative interactions with their work colleagues.

Employment advice services   The fact that migrants tend to work in a narrowly defined number of areas and at a regularly low level demonstrates that the pool of potential ability present in North Cork is not being used to best effect. However, Irish legislators have long been mindful of the fact that people's successful participation in the waged labour force will determine their ability to live and integrate in Irish society more strongly than their participation in any other area of endeavour. Hence, a wide range of policies and strategies that aim to facilitate migrant groups' access to the waged labour force (WLF) are in evidence, and statutory service providers are active on the ground in North Cork.

FÁS Employment Services maintain offices in Mallow and are '*the first port of call*' for many immigrants living in North Cork (Assistant Manager, FÁS Employment Services, Mallow). This organisation also holds a fortnightly clinic in nearby Fermoy. Migrants who are working in Ireland as a result of their Stamp 1 work permit status are not entitled to access such services but people with full Stamp 4 status and people from locations in the EU10 are entitled to full access to services and the numbers using these services are deemed to be high.[19]

---

19   Non-EU nationals wishing to stay in Ireland are required to register with Ireland's Police Service. On registration each person will receive a 'stamp' on their passport, indicating the rights and entitlements available to them. There are seven different stamps

> In the last year and a half, frontline staff say that 50 per cent of our clients coming into our offices in Cork city and Mallow were immigrants (Assistant Manager, FÁS Employment Services, Mallow).

Training opportunities, broadly based, are offered to migrants here. FETAC[20] approved English language courses and introductory courses that cover the culture of work in Ireland are available. Such training interventions are not commonly accessed.[21] Aid with job search is by far the most commonly accessed service in North Cork.

> Of that 50 per cent, 99 per cent were looking for a job. (Assistant Manager, FÁS Employment Services, Mallow)

Migrants use FÁS job search facilities in an entirely predictable manner. A free-to-access, automated information service is provided in FÁS's Mallow office via 'touch screen kiosks'. Information on job vacancies is provided here and service users are allowed to access this information at their own discretion. A hard-copy index is present in every FÁS office and a list of key terms has been translated into Polish (in response to the volume of Polish people using the service). Clients are allowed access to telephones and they 'can sit in the office all day and submit a CV'. In this way, FÁS acts as intermediary between prospective employers and job seekers. No advice is given. In FÁS's opinion, this represents the provision of as complete a service to immigrant job seekers as is possible within the remit set out for the organisation (Assistant Manager, FÁS Employment Services, Mallow).

In this way, FÁS offers no targeted job-search advice to immigrants. No interpretation service is provided, and automated screens contain information that is presented in English only. Service users are left to cope as best they can. Service users generally circumvent this difficulty by attending at the FÁS office in a group.

> I can remember one incident, last summer. A Polish group of seven came into our office in Mallow, one fella had English and he spoke to employers for them.

---

available – Stamp 1, Stamp 2, Stamp 2aA, Stamp 3, Stamp 4, Stamp A and Stamp 6. Each has a different set of entitlements (www.mrci.ie/know_rights).

20 Ireland's Further Education, Training and Awards Council (FETAC) was established as a statutory body in 2001 to make quality assured education and training awards in accordance with national standards, creating opportunities for all learners in further education and training to have their achievements recognised and providing access to systematic progression pathways.

21 Other interventions, such as FAS's Customised Training Fund are available to immigrants. However, as resources are limited, FÁS does not advertise this fund, and its application is left at the discretion of individual officers on the ground (Manager, FÁS Business Services, Cork).

> ... Often you would see three lads together and one guy would have English and
> he would interpret (Assistant Manager, FÁS Employment Services, Mallow).

Frontline staff recognise that individual service users may require more assistance than is on offer at present. However, staff feel constrained by the organisation's position that its remit does not extend beyond the provision of non-directive information services for clients and that any attempt to engage more fundamentally with immigrant groups would compromise their core ethos and move towards the provision of segregated service. As a FÁS Employment Service staff member in Mallow noted: 'The non-Irish worker is a client same as everybody else' and that no targeted interventions can be delivered to specific groups.

Housing

The immigrant housing market has not been subjected to academic analysis in Ireland (Humphreys 2006, 1) and almost nothing is known about the housing experiences of immigrants resident in more rural areas, but a very clear pattern can be seen in North Cork. Immigrants resident in this rural area are predominantly housed in the private rental sector (84 per cent of all participants in the current research rent their accommodation from a private landlord, 113 people). Only a small number of people either own their own homes or are housed in social housing (four and two people respectively, nearly five per cent in total). This is unsurprising. On leaving direct provision or on arrival in Ireland, most immigrants are faced with a stark choice and often limited time in which to operate. The vast majority do not have the financial means to purchase their own accommodation and the immediate nature of housing need is such that time spent on local authority accommodation waiting lists is prohibitive. Most are thus channelled towards the private rental sector and most meet their housing needs here.

The house search process can be challenging. A person's status is especially important. Immigrants who are engaged in paid employment occupy a reasonably strong position in this housing market. Those requiring assistance from statutory service providers are more likely to experience difficulty. For example, many landlords may not look favourably on prospective tenants in receipt of rent assistance. People leaving direct provision and people unable to engage in paid employment might be especially vulnerable here.

Housing assistance   Immigrants in receipt of social welfare payments interact with three different sets of people: i) the Health Service Executive (HSE) community welfare officers (CWOs),[22] ii) Cork County Council Housing Office/

---

22 Community Welfare Officers (CWOs) are employed throughout Ireland by the Health Service Executive (HSE). These workers are based in communities and are responsible for the day to day administration of Community Welfare Services such as Medical cards and supplementary welfare allowances.

housing assessment officers and iii) landlords.

HSE staff seek to smooth the path to housing as best they can but very few resources are placed at the disposal of prospective tenants. In this regard, Health Service Executive – Southern Area, community welfare officers play a key role. The means-tested Rental Allowance scheme is of pivotal importance. Qualification requirements are strict and are enforced by CWOs.

> Eligibility, that's what our job is. It is not a discretionary payment. This is written down in law, there is an actual set of rules there and you are either in or out (frontline HSE staff, North Cork).

Difficulties are common. One staff member makes reference to the Settlement Agreement that service users are obliged to sign. She states that immigrants regularly have:

> No idea of what they are signing. It is a probability they don't know what they are signing. It is a problem (Frontline staff member, Cork County Council Housing Office, Mallow).

Interpretation services are available to CWOs but due to limited funds, are only used in an emergency. Individual HSE staff deliver their services as best they can.

> With their broken English and my sign language. I have schoolgirl French, I know that they understand a lot of the time. I find we understand each other, but they still may not be happy (frontline HSE staff, North Cork).

At Cork County Council's local housing office, staff seem even less engaged. No translation/interpretation service is available. Each interaction is functional in nature and no investment is made by staff in each individual consultation. Equally, no translator service is provided during subsequent assessment visits by housing officers.[23]

Once housed however, most people state that they are happy with their housing and that they like the area in which they live (118 people, nearly 90 per cent of those interviewed). Only a minority of the sample feel that they have experienced challenges and obstacles in relation to accommodation in Ireland (52 people, 39 per cent of the sample).

> I would say that all our friends are in a brilliant place [concerning their] accommodation (Male, EU10, Focus Group 1).

---

23 Follow up visits to clients to ensure that all is in order with their accommodation.

Some evidence of over-crowding was uncovered amongst particular national groups. Nevertheless, in this regard, the residential market in rural North Cork appears to be reasonably normal in nature. This is somewhat at odds with the literature. Organisations such as Threshold (cited in Humphreys 2006, 7) refer to the prevalence of poor accommodation standards in this sector.[24]

Continuing financial difficulties may contribute to ongoing difficulties here, especially in this type of predominantly rural area where the range of accommodation available will inevitably be less significant than in large urban areas, but in the absence of a valid alternative, most people will continue to gravitate towards private rented accommodation here. This situation may very well resolve itself in the medium/long term as many people who are eligible have applied for social housing.

Health and Welfare

Immigrants to Ireland are entitled to access the same health and welfare services as Irish born people. The HSE, through its commitment to develop a National Health Strategy recognises this (Mac Éinri 2006, 116) and health professionals are keen to deliver an effective health service to a changing population. The development in 2005 of the *General Practice Care in a Multi-cultural Society Information Pack* is symptomatic of this orientation towards new communities, as are plans to pilot a useable interpretation service for General Practitioners.

In North Cork, local medical services (general practitioners) are orientating themselves towards the delivery of effective medical care for immigrant groups. Everyone is catered for. One medical practice staff member states that services are offered to all and that:

> Most people simply register on the day when they want to see the doctor. I've never witnessed anyone being refused (Frontline staff member 1, Family Practice, Mallow).

Individual medical practitioners and their staff are conscious of the changing nature of the population resident in the region and are taking steps to improve their effectiveness here.

> We have a simple patient information leaflet in Polish. We've trained ourselves on it. We have a book on it (Frontline staff member 2, general medical practice, Mallow).

---

24   Threshold is a not-for-profit organisation, founded in 1978, whose aim is to secure a right to housing, particularly for households experiencing the problems of poverty and exclusion.

The views of research participants reflect this pattern. When asked directly about their experience of medical service delivery in Ireland, only a small number of people either elaborated on the difficulties that they experienced while accessing health care in Ireland or gave reasons for not being satisfied with the care that they received (14 people, nine per cent of the sample). Most of these relate to the expense of medical care. Medical care is certainly expensive in Ireland, especially when compared with the equivalent costs in many immigrants' countries of origin. All those who have come through the asylum/refugee process are entitled to a medical card.[25] Ninety two per cent of these (59 people) are very happy with the Irish health care system. Economic migrants who are in paid employment are less likely to feel the same. Most of these people do not qualify, by right, for a medical card and are required to pay for medical services

> We'd have a lot of Polish, Ukrainian, Lithuanians in here, without insurance, it's all cash (Frontline staff member 2, medical practice, Mallow).

Dissatisfaction is greatest here. Only 50 per cent of economic migrants from outside the EU are either very satisfied or satisfied with the level of medical service provision available in Ireland. A higher percentage of those from EU contexts are satisfied however (75 percent). Legal status in Ireland and economic ability are important here and this situation is likely to be a reflection of different client groups' independent financial means. Although, when need is deemed to be great, it must be noted that:

> There are more and more non-nationals getting the card, the GP visit card, if they are not working. All qualify, it is not subject to habitual residency, it's means tested (CWO, Mallow).

Equally however, frustrations are voiced. As is common, the lack of an adequate interpretation service is a strong impediment to the delivery of effective services. One general practitioner refers to his patients' use of:

> Informal translation. Patients bring their own translators. Children mostly (General practitioner 1, Mallow).

The scope for an untrained person to make mistakes is significant. The use of paraphrasing and summary are particularly common in such instances. Furthermore, it is highly likely that a minor with even good English will not have the detailed

---

25 A medical card issued by the Health Service Executive (HSE) enables the bearer to receive certain health services free of charge for example, holders of a medical card are entitled to free GP (family doctor) services. Medical cards are tested and normally cover the bearer and his/her dependent spouse and child dependants. Everyone over 70 years and normally resident in Ireland, is entitled to a medical card, regardless of means.

medical vocabulary necessary for such interactions at his/her disposal nor is it appropriate in certain contexts for a minor to interpret, say, for a parent. Medical staff are placed in a difficult position in this regard. They are aware that such a situation is unsatisfactory but often feel that there is no alternative in place.

> Parents would bring their children in with them. If that's the only person available to translate then we rely on them to relay the information correctly (General practitioner 2, Mallow).

As in other sectors, training is required. Staff are aware that difficulties exist, both for themselves and for service users. Gender for example, is one area of concern. HSE staff active in the area state that:

> African men do not like being told what to do by females (HSE staff, Mallow).

Training courses that could equip staff to interface more effectively with clients from other cultural backgrounds are available (see Mac Éinrí 2006, 119) but no interviewees living in North Cork have attended such a course.

Medical service providers operational in North Cork are motivated to deliver services to immigrant groups but difficulties come to light. At present, frontline medical staff are '*muddling along*', providing services as best they can in the absence of properly structured support. Migrant practices are complex however. For example, significant numbers of people from the immigrant community (from EU 10 countries) continue to access medical care in their country of origin (29 people, 18 per cent of the sample).

Non-statutory Service Providers

In many ways, the non-statutory sector fills many gaps. Through its North Cork Immigrant Forum, the local development organisation in North Cork – Avondhu Development – has been working on behalf of immigrants over the past number of years. In many ways, Avondhu Development aims to act as a proactive information hub in the area, used by service providers and service users alike.

> We have very regular contact with Avondhu. If we come across an immigrant when we need advice we would go to (name), our first port of call. From day one, we would have been very aware of Avondhu (Staff member, Le Chéile Family Resource Centre, Mallow).

Citizen's information services have also reached out to immigrant populations. This organisation's efforts are not widely regarded however. The Citizen's Information service does not have the capacity to operate effectively here. No foreign language skills are present within the local organisation and –'we don't have the capacity to translate.' (Manager, Citizens Information Service, North Cork[26]) This experience may possibly be symptomatic of many wider issues. This organisation has, until very recently, been volunteer-led in nature. One full-time regional manager is based in Fermoy, but the five centres for which she has responsibility are staffed by motivated volunteers. Training has been provided. The Immigrant Council of Ireland[27] hosted a two day training event for volunteers in North Cork in 2006 but the capacity to operate effectively in a challenging environment is not, as yet, present within the organisation, at local level. Staff are aware of this difficulty and some measures have been instituted to help address this situation. One Polish worker has been employed on work experience in the Fermoy office and an information officer has been employed on a half-time basis in the Mallow office.

Conclusions

Ireland's economy contracted in late 2008, for the first time since 1983. Significantly, a relatively severe correction in the construction industry, which as recently as early 2007 employed nearly 23 per cent of the active male labour force, has been experienced as well. It is likely, in these terms, that a net outward flow of migration will occur, for the first time since the mid-1990s. Equally, it seems likely that some proportion of those migrants will consist of recently arrived New Accession state nationals, particularly in cases such as Poland. The Polish economy is beginning to show signs of accelerating growth and increasing salary levels, which have encouraged returns (Taylor 2006). As a consequence, difficulties experienced in Ireland whilst trying to legislate for the presence of immigrants may be proportionately lessened. Certainly, it is likely that there will be less pressure on services. Nevertheless, it remains that this new diversity, in ethnic and cultural terms, constitutes one of the most significant axes of socio-cultural change experienced in Ireland since the advent of mass urbanisation/ industrialisation in the middle of the 20th century. The successful integration of these groups remains of profound importance for the future.

Successive Irish governments were initially caught unawares by the scale of immigration to Ireland. Moreover, initial attention, in political, media and public discourses, was very largely focused on the numbers of asylum seekers arriving in Ireland at that time, to the extent that for several years there was little debate about other types of immigrants, such as labour migrants and their families. Nevertheless, much policy infrastructure is now in place in Ireland and those

---

26   Citizen's Information is a national network of 42 organizations that seek to provide a free and confidential information service to the public in Ireland. Information is delivered through three channels: Online, Telephone and Face-to-face.

27   The Immigrant Council of Ireland (ICI) is an independent Irish non-governmental organisation that promotes the rights of migrants through information, legal advice, advocacy, lobbying, research and training work. The ICI is also an Independent Law Centre.

active in political life frequently claim that Ireland's migration regime is one of the most open and flexible in the EU and beyond. Insofar as it is market- and employer-driven, the regime has proven relatively fast and responsive and has enabled the economy to cope with a prolonged period of rapid growth. A strong landscape of vibrant organizations has also emerged in recent years. As well as National Consultative Committee on Racism and Interculturalism (NCCRI) there is now a range of NGOs, which engage in advocacy and support as well as service provision for migrants and new communities in Ireland. Migrants themselves are now organising and a strong MELO (migrant and ethnic led organisation) sector is emerging. Integrating Ireland, an independent network of such organisations, lists over 180 groups that have the explicit aim of

> working in mutual solidarity to promote and realise the human rights, equality and full integration in Irish society of asylum seekers, refugees and immigrants (Integrating Ireland 2008).

However, there is a recognition that a more comprehensive and durable drive towards integration is needed. Indeed, some critics argue that Ireland is effectively operating a regime which, in *de facto* terms, is discriminatory in its general unwillingness to accept the 'other' in Irish society. The immigrant experience can certainly be negative at local level. Some of these difficulties are intangible. The fight against racism and discrimination for example, must be at the forefront of action nationally (indeed, progress is being made in this area) but there is a need also to address integration in terms of the emerging realities of an intercultural society, at local level. Basic requirements in the areas of housing, access to employment, education and training (including language acquisition and the acquisition of educational qualifications) are central here and there is a pressing need to address difficulties and shortcomings in service provision at this level. This is especially pertinent in rural contexts. The geographical spread of migrants in Ireland is highly dispersed and in many rural areas, the scale of social change precipitated by this is immense.

As seen in North Cork, service provision for minority immigrant populations resident in these areas is lacking. Services should be mainstreamed and providers should be mindful of the different and diverse needs of new communities and tailor their processes to ensure more inclusivity of access at local level.

References

Barrett, A, Kearney, I. and O'Brien, M. (2008), *Quarterly Economic Commentary Summer 2008* (Dublin: Economic and Social Research Institute).

Bertossi, C. (2007), *French and British Models of Integration. Public Philosophies, Policies and State Institutions.* ESRC Centre on Migration, Policy and Society, Working Paper no. 46 (Oxford: University of Oxford).

Central Statistics Office (CSO) (2007a), *Quarterly National House Survey Quarter 4 2007. ILO Labour Force* (Dublin: CSO).

Central Statistics Office (CSO) (2007b), *Population and Migration Estimates April 2007* (Dublin: CSO).

Christian Brothers, Mercy Sisters and Presentation Sisters Schools (2002/3), *Dialogue on Diversity: An intercultural initiative at primary level* (Dublin: Christian Brothers Education Office).

Coakley, L. and Mac Éinrí, P. (2007), 'Scoping Paper: Education and Integration', Unpublished position paper commissioned by Immigrant Council of Ireland, Dublin.

Central Statistics Office (2007b), *Quarterly National Household Survey Quarter 4 2007. ILO Labour Force* (Dublin: CSO).

Department of Education and Science (2000), *Learning for Life: White Paper on Adult Education*. Department of Education and Science. Athlone.

Department of Justice, Equality and Law Reform (DJELR) (1999), *Integration: A Two-way Process. Report to the Minister for Justice, Equality and Law Reform* (Dublin: Department of Justice, Equality and Law Reform).

Department of Justice, Equality and Law Reform (DJELR) (2005), *Planning for Diversity: The National Action Plan Against Racism* (Dublin: Department of Justice, Equality and Law Reform).

Department of Social and Family Affairs (DSFA) (2008), *Statistics on the number of PPSNs issued.* <http://www.welfare.ie/topics/ppsn/ppsstat. html#euten040506>, accessed 1 July 2008.

Diversity Ireland (2008), *Migration Nation: Statement on Integration Strategy and Diversity Management* (Dublin: Office of the Minister for Integration).

Further Education Training and Awards Council (FETAC) (2005), *RPL Policy and Guidelines* (Dublin: Further Education and Training Awards Council).

Goodhart, D. (2004), 'Too Diverse?' *Prospect*.

Hage, G. (1998), *White Nation* (Annadale NSW: Pluto Press).

Hewitt, R. (2005), *White Backlash and the Politics of Multiculturalism* (Cambridge: Cambridge University Press).

Humphreys, N. (2006), *Housing and Integration. Immigrant Council of Ireland Scoping Paper* (Dublin: Immigrant Council of Ireland).

Integrating Ireland (2005), *International Students and Professionals in Ireland: An Analysis of Higher Education and Recognition of Professional Qualifications* (Dublin: Integrating Ireland).

Kymlicka, W. (1995), *Multicultural Citizenship* (Oxford: Clarendon Press).

Lodge, A. and Lynch, K. (eds) (2004), *Diversity at School* (Dublin: The Equality Authority).

Mac Éinrí, P. and Coakley, L. (2006), 'Islands of Difference or Intercultural City? A Study of asylum seekers and persons with leave to remain in Cork', unpublished report submitted to the Reception and Integration Agency (Dublin: Department of Justice Equality and Law Reform).

Mac Éinrí, P. (2006), 'Ireland', in Watt, P. and McGaughey, F. (eds) (2006), *Improving Government Service Delivery to Minority Ethnic Groups: Northern Ireland, Republic of Ireland, Scotland* (Dublin: National Consultative Committee on Racism in Ireland).

McVeigh, R. (2002), 'Between reconciliation and pacification: the British state and community relations in the north of Ireland.' *Community Dev. J.*, 37(1): 47–59.

Modood, T. (2007), *Multiculturalism: A Civic Idea* (Cambridge: Polity).

Murray, C. (2006), 'Diversity and Equality in Early Childhood Care Education and Training', in *Spectrum 13* (Dublin: NCCRI).

Northern Ireland Office (1998), The Agreement <http://www.nio.gov.uk/the-agreement>, accessed 9 February 2009.

Phelan, H. and Kuon N. (2005), *A study of asylum seekers and those with leave to remain in Limerick* (Dublin: Reception and Integration Agency, Department of Justice Equality and Law Reform).

Pobal (2006), *Barriers to Access to Further Education for Non-EU Nationals Resident in Ireland* (Dublin: POBAL).

Ryan, A. (2005), 'Reform Issues in Irish Law and Practice'. Paper presented 15 October 2005 at the Conference on Migrant Workers and Human Rights Law, The Law Society of Ireland.

Taylor, J. (2006), 'The rebirth of Lodz draws Poland's young emigrants back', in *The Independent* (London), 28 October.

Taylor, C. (1994), *Multiculturalism: Examining the Politics of Recognition* (Princeton: Princeton University Press).

Tormey, R. (2005), *Intercultural Education in the Primary School* (Dublin: National Council for Curriculum and Assessment).

Ward, T. (2002), *Asylum Seekers in Education: A Study of Language and Literacy Needs* (Dublin: City of Dublin VEC and County Dublin VEC).

Watt, P. and McGaughey, F. (2006), How public authorities provide services to minority ethnic groups: Northern Ireland, Republic of Ireland, Scotland (Dublin: National Consultative Committee on Racism).

Wieviorka, M. (2002), *The Development of Racism in Europe: A Companion to Racial and Ethnic Studies* (London: Blackwell).

Chapter 6

The New Scottish Rural Labour Market: Processes of Inclusion and Exclusion

Mike Danson and Birgit Jentsch

Introduction

Scotland's immigration history stretches back thousands of years. Indeed, the term 'Scot' has its origin in people who migrated to Scotland from Northern Ireland around 500 AD. In terms of Scotland's recent history, immigration flows in the twentieth century included Poles who arrived during World War II and stayed on. German and Italian prisoners of war were employed in agriculture, and some also stayed. Moreover, a work permit scheme under the Attlee government (1945–1951) recruited Germans, Italians, Ukranians, Austrians and Poles to the UK (McConnachie 2002). Some of these migrant workers will have come to Scotland, but a lack of reliable data sources means that it is difficult to provide an estimate on numbers.

The 2001 Census provided the following information on the Scottish population by ethnic group: 88 per cent (about 4,500,000 people) of the population were recorded as White Scottish, seven per cent as White British and one per cent as White Irish. 1.5 per cent (78,000) of the population had been recorded as Any Other White Background. The minority ethnic population constituted the small percentage of two per cent (100,000), mainly comprising people from Pakistani, Chinese, Indian and mixed ethnic groups (Scottish Executive 2004).

Given its rather homogeneous population coupled with a relatively large migrant outflow, it is not surprising that Scotland was known as a country of emigration, rather than immigration. While trends in Scotland and the UK have shown similar patterns of net migration over the past 50 years, Scotland has experienced greater variations. It had higher negative rates prior to 2004, with a loss of 850,000 people through migration over the period – an experience only comparable to that of Ireland. By contrast, since May 2004, Scotland has enjoyed stronger positive migration rates than the UK as a whole (Wright 2008). Migrant workers – people from abroad exclusively coming to work – have had an increasingly large presence in Scotland. National Insurance Number (NINo) registrations of overseas workers have nearly quadrupled since 2002/03 from 14,790 to 52,460 in 2006/07,[1] while

---

1 National Insurance Number Registrations in respect of non-UK Nationals in 2006/07 by Government Office Region and country of origin. http://www.dwp.gov.uk/asd/asd1/niall/registration_tables2007.xls.

those from the A8 countries[2] recorded under the Workers Registration Scheme (WRS)[3] have risen from 25,035 in May 2004 to 44,565 in May 2007.

Such developments have been supported by, and are complementary to, Scottish Government policies, which were designed to attract migrant workers to Scotland to fill skill gaps and shortages, and to contribute to addressing demographic decline. In contrast to past patterns of immigration, when those entering the country would include asylum seekers, refugees, workers with families and those seeking work, those registering were going into employment with, or soon after, entry to the UK. They also continue to show high proportions registering in the more peripheral parts, for example the Highlands and Islands, and lower proportions[4] than expected being attracted to London and the common destinations within Scotland: namely the four cities of Edinburgh, Glasgow, Aberdeen and Dundee.

At least up to 2006, some Scottish rural NHS Boards reported that they were dealing with 800 to 1,000 new migrants each month (Watt and McGaughey 2006). Polish workers are, by far, the largest national grouping in Scotland. Approximately 70 per cent (31,305) of registered workers have come from Poland between May 2004 and March 2007. These migrant workers in particular and their immigrant groups in general have been welcomed, certainly by employers, but also often by the rural population who may see the new members as contributors to the sustainability of their community. However, as nationally (Anderson et al. 2006), there have been some negative comments, for example, around competition for jobs and housing.

---

2   The European Union has expanded progressively from its original six founders, through a series of enlargements. After a period of consolidation and institutional reform through the 1990s by its fifteen western European members, reflecting the massive changes in Central and Eastern Europe in May 2004, European Union membership was extended to include the ten countries of Cyprus, Czech Republic, Estonia, Hungary, Latvia, Lithuania, Malta, Poland, Slovakia and Slovenia. While nationals from Cyprus and Malta have had full free movement rights and have been able to work throughout the EU, transitional measures were put in place to restrict movements by nationals from the other eight (Accession 8 or A8) countries. For the first two years, only Ireland, Sweden and the UK granted full access to their labour markets to these new EU citizens. In May 2006, Finland, Greece, Portugal and Spain lifted all restrictions, followed by Italy in July 2006, and the Netherlands in May 2007.

3   The UK Government put in place transitional measures to regulate the A8 nationals' access to the labour market (via the Worker Registration Scheme or WRS) and to restrict access to benefits.

4   Since 1980, most migrants seeking work have entered the UK in London and, where they have moved onto other destinations, these have been fairly close to the capital. Changes in demand for labour have been concentrated in the Greater London economy and in the other major cities across the country. Precise information on migrants' movements is not available as they rely on data sources which are based on sampling, incomplete recordings of final destinations, etc. Estimations and commentaries on such issues are offered by, for example, Champion (2006).

To inform this debate, clear evidence to assess whether and to what extent immigrants, both short- and long-term, displace (especially vulnerable) locally established groups of the labour force has remained scarce. There is general agreement, however, that migrants have tended to fill positions which UK workers are not prepared to take up under the employment conditions offered (Anderson et al. 2006; Scottish Enterprise 2006). Within this complex environment, where there is a need for better labour market intelligence and understanding, possible subtle, indirect processes of inclusion and exclusion have rarely been examined. While a common question addressed in the literature has been whether migrants displace locally established people, this chapter will explore factors and processes which are likely to prevent groups of people from accessing the labour market altogether. Moreover, it will examine factors and structures which seem to confine the employability of locally established[5] and migrant groups to the secondary labour market.

The social groups whose employment situation will be examined comprise, firstly, immigrants themselves. To provide context and insight, evidence drawn from recent studies on changes in the job opportunities for migrants from the A8 countries in the Scottish rural labour market will be considered, as well as the reasons for those changes. In addition, immigrants' prospects of obtaining employment where they can utilise their existing qualifications, skills and experiences will be analysed. Although migrants from the A8 countries appear to have higher levels of education and training than their Scottish equivalents and so to be well qualified to work in a range of higher level occupations, they have a disproportionately high representation in semi-skilled or unskilled employment, especially in rural areas.[6,7]

Secondly, there is some evidence to suggest that a vulnerable pool of labour, including older workers, workers with a disability, those with caring commitments

---

5   While a definition of this group would in principle be desirable, any such definition would inevitably be partial in that it is trying to gauge whether individuals consider themselves to be established or still visiting. In addition, and especially relevant for rural areas, there is the difficult and sensitive issue whether community members regard individuals as established or as 'newcomers'.

6   There are crucial geographical variations to the role of migrant workers. A study in Edinburgh and Lothian established that 45 per cent of migrants were in managerial or professional occupations, and 51 per cent in elementary occupations, possibly highlighting urban-rural divisions (Scottish Enterprise 2006). See also, CoSLA Refugee and Asylum Seekers Consortium (2006) and Anderson et al. (2006).

7   Our working definition of 'rural' in this chapter is based on the Scottish Government's definition of 'rural Scotland' as settlements with a population of less than 3,000. The term 'remote rural' applies to those areas with a greater than 30-minute drive time to the nearest community with a population larger than 10,000. By contrast, accessible rural refers to those settlements that can reach a community with a population of greater than 10,000 in less than 30 minutes drive time.<http://www.scotland.gov.uk/Topics/Rural/rural-policy/16780/6661>, accessed 15 February 2009.

and members of minority ethnic groups have experienced increasing difficulties in competing in the labour market. Issues of employers' direct discrimination have been raised, as well as concerns about indirect discrimination processes. Predominant working conditions, especially in rural labour markets, are such that it is very difficult to secure jobs which allow for some work – life (family) balance, and which secure an income on which individuals, and families, can participate in societal life. Such factors need to be taken into consideration when assessing employers' claims that there is a lack of willingness and motivation on the part of the locally established workforce to take up local jobs.

Such processes of inclusion and exclusion highlight some significant challenges rural labour markets face. Formerly, debates on rural labour markets have been prompted by the exodus of rural youth, who have frequently left their communities in the search of 'good employment'. This chapter will consider these earlier debates in the light of the new complex dynamics associated with the new immigrant workforce in the Scottish rural labour market. In terms of policy development, it argues for an 'issue approach' to addressing labour market exclusion processes in rural areas, rather than a 'social group approach' confined to the needs of one particular group.

General Employment Patterns in Rural Scotland

Latest data (summer 2007)[8] on economic activity across Scotland show a diverse but apparently positive picture with men in rural areas – based on local government areas – more likely to be in the labour market than nationally (between 72.0 per cent and 85.1 per cent compared with 71.7 per cent). This similarly applies to rural women whose employment rates varied between 59.7 per cent and 76.3 per cent against a Scottish average of 58.7 per cent. Since gaps in labour supply have been recognised as a specifically rural issue (Marsden et al. 2005), the nature of the rural labour market may account for these relatively high rates of employment. However, despite efforts to develop a high-skill high-wage economy in rural areas, evidence points to a substantial and further growing demand for low-skills employment, which has been attributed to the prevalence of small employers offering few 'quality jobs' (Pavis et al. 2000).

There are no readily available data which allow us to assess employment patterns of different ethnic groups in rural and urban areas, although an analysis was conducted for the predominantly rural Highlands and Islands area (excluding Argyll and including Moray) based on the 2001 Census on ethnic economic activity rates. It concluded that there were similar levels of unemployment (around 4 per cent) suffered by 'white' and minority ethnic people. However, minority ethnic group members have often reported that they are overqualified for their employment, and that they are facing a glass ceiling hampering progress in

8   <http://www.keyindicators.org.uk/>, accessed 24 September 2007.

organizations (Crocket and de Lima 2006). More recently, with the arrival of A8 migrant workers, it has been claimed that some employers have given preference to workers from Central and Eastern Europe, for example, as a replacement for Kurdish workers, arguing that the more recent arrivals are more likely to 'fit in' communities (Crocket and de Lima 2006).

Nonetheless, with some of the highest activity rates in Europe, rural Scotland has been facing tightness in labour markets for some time. Unemployment rates are comparable with many other regions in Scotland and the UK and, although no longer an efficient measure of activity, do confirm this general view of an economy operating at close to capacity. Indeed anticipating this, Futureskills Scotland[9] (2006) have been predicting since EU enlargement that 'substantial numbers of incomers will be needed to fill posts in the professional services, health, education and the service sector'; sectors which have employed many migrant workers.

According to a survey conducted in 2003, there were around 240,000 employees in rural Scotland (the Highlands and Islands, Dumfries and Galloway, and the Scottish Borders) who were occupied in about 24,000 workplaces (Futureskills Scotland 2004). These employees were more concentrated in basic skilled occupations compared with the nation as a whole. There are higher proportions of employees in sectors such as agriculture, forestry and fishing, hotels and restaurants (that is the service sector), and lower proportions of employees in financial intermediation, real estate, renting and business activities, health and social work.

Typical of rural regions, the 2002 Scottish Employers Skill Survey showed that, compared with the rest of Scotland, workplaces in rural Scotland are more likely to employ people in jobs which are seasonal or temporary/short term. The structure of jobs is also different with a higher proportion of employees in occupations that typically require lower levels of skills and qualifications, such as elementary, plant, process and machine operatives, personal services, and skilled trades. Conversely, rural Scotland has a lower proportion of employees in jobs at levels such as managerial and senior official, professional, associate professional and technical. Hence, with employment and society becoming increasingly divided, this bifurcation of the labour market suggests that rural Scotland's rising dependence on the secondary labour market – with relatively few primary jobs – will see average GVA (gross value added) and wages per head fall relative to the nation, *ceteris paribus* (Dickens et al. 2003; Newlands et al. 2004; Toynbee 2003).

According to Futureskills Scotland's biennial Employers' Surveys, it is apparent that, typically, wages in rural areas are about 10 per cent lower but workers more qualified than the Scottish average. Geographic location has been identified by rural employers as a key reason to account for low numbers of job applicants, partly explaining why the vacancy rate is higher across rural areas. Other reasons were suggested as not enough people interested in doing the type of job, low numbers of job seekers generally, and long/unsociable hours. Interestingly, rural

---

9   Futureskills Scotland is a governmental organization.

businesses are less likely to recruit employees directly as graduates from further [FE] or higher education [HE] institutions, so that workers are more likely to be attracted from other businesses locally or from outwith the region.

The most common response by rural employers to skill shortages was to use a more extensive range of recruitment channels;[10] elsewhere, training was more extensively used. The skills most often reported as lacking in applicants were technical and practical skills. Over two thirds of rural employers also identified customer handling, problem solving and oral communication skills as lacking in applicants, but problems with literacy and strategic management skills were less of an issue in rural areas than nationally. Consistent with a more highly qualified workforce, skill gaps – where an employee is considered not to be fully proficient in their job – are less prevalent in rural areas but still affected one in four employers across Scotland. As nationally, skill gaps were concentrated in low skilled jobs especially in the largest employment areas, including elementary occupations; plant process and machine operatives; and sales and customer services. The most frequently mentioned deficiencies were in 'soft' skills, such as planning and organizing, problem solving and customer handling. Being able to address such problems appeared to be more difficult in rural areas, with greater distance to training facilities and lower appreciation of what national programmes, such as New Deal, Skillseekers or Training for Work, would offer employers to address skill gaps.

The features of these rural labour markets confirm the pre-conditions since 2004 for attracting significant numbers of migrant workers from outwith Scotland and the UK, and indeed from a reserve army of Polish graduates in particular. As will now be discussed, the fulfillment of the expectations of the latter group has given rise to growing concerns about migrant workers' underemployment in Scotland.

A recent report by the European Foundation for the Improvement of Living and Working Conditions [EFILWC] (2007) observed that overqualification is a common phenomenon for foreign-born workers across the EU countries (as well as for the native born population).[11] However, the phenomenon of migrant workers' overqualification was particularly relevant, for example, for the Mediterranean countries where, to a large extent, migrants are recruited for unskilled jobs. In the UK, almost uniquely, the risk of overqualification appears to be relatively independent from migrant status, as Table 6.1 illustrates.

This may, of course, be different in rural Scotland, especially post-2004 EU enlargement. However, it is still true that overqualification is a wider phenomenon

---

10   Unfortunately there is no comparable information on the use of informal channels although larger establishments, which are less well represented in the critical sectors in rural areas, tend to use a wider range than SMEs.

11   Overqualification is 'measured by the proportion of workers who possess an educational degree of higher level than that required for the job they hold.' (EFILWC 2007, 26).

Table 6.1   Overqualification rates of native and foreign-born population, 2004 (per cent)

	Native-born	Foreign-born
AT	10.3	21.1
BE	15.6	21.6
CZ	5.2	10.0
DE	11.4	20.3
DK	10.4	18.6
EL (Greece)	9.0	39.3
ES	24.2	42.9
FI	14.3	19.2
FR	11.2	15.5
HU	6.3	9.7
IE	15.7	23.8
IT	6.4	23.5
LU	3.4	9.1
NO	8.4	20.3
PT	7.9	16.8
SE	6.5	16.1
UK	15.3	17.8

Source: Table adopted from EFILWC (2007), Table 7, p. 27.

in the UK, and in rural areas – as many rural youngsters who have left their home communities for the lack of 'quality jobs' can testify (Jentsch 2006).

Theoretical Explanations for Migrants' Situation in the Labour Market

Economic migrants have often been viewed as *homos economicus* personified. The neoclassical economic model accounts for migration by workers in terms of differences in wage and unemployment rates between countries. Hence, migrants are seen to be driven first and foremost by labour market mechanisms, so that workers from low wage economies will look for employment in high wage economies. They will carefully calculate the costs and benefits of staying, compare it with those of leaving, and take migration decisions on this basis.[12] Migrant workers are thus seen as rational, amoral agents who operate outwith a social, political and cultural context. Eventually, the laws of supply and demand will result in a situation where wages increase in countries of origin, and decrease in receiving countries, so that international migration will reduce over time (McGovern 2007; *Economist* 2007).

12   See, for example, Hayek, F.A. (1945) and Marshall, A. (1920).

There are, of course, several problems with this model, not least the fact that its analysis does not seem to be able to account for the 97 per cent of people (according to UN estimates) who are not migrating, that is behaving irrationally (McGovern 2007). Perhaps most importantly for our purposes, markets are socially and culturally constructed, and this is particularly obvious when we look at immigrants' positions in the labour market – their relatively low earnings and segregated employment (McGovern 2007; Dustmann et al. 2003). Institutional labour economists have introduced the theory of the dual or segmented labour market with the aim to explain persistent employment divisions, for example, by gender (Piore 1975; Gordon 1982; Danson 1982). On this basis, Piore (1979) attempted to explain empirical findings on immigrants' employment, especially phenomena such as their concentration in low- or semi-skilled jobs with difficult working conditions; in jobs with poor wages which rarely rise; and the reasons why migrants take up these posts (McGovern 2007).

An important aspect of Piore's (1979) analysis was the recognition that work comprises more than certain tasks. It also confers social status to the worker – a reason why native-born workers are disinclined to take menial service sector jobs. After all, there are concerns beyond wages, such as maintaining and enhancing social prestige. At the bottom of the job hierarchy, little status is to be gained. Employers have therefore to rely on those who see low status jobs exclusively as a means to earn money, where the only nexus is cash (Smith 1776). At least at the beginning of their migratory careers, concern with economic survival (rather than social status) will render immigrants inclined to accept such jobs.

In addition, Piore claimed that emigration was not just a function of unemployment or low wages – migration 'push' factors. Rather, advanced industrial societies have an inherent demand for disposable labour. Migrants are filling labour gaps at times of prosperity, when locally established people have the opportunities of accessing higher status jobs. The recruitment of migrant workers then constitutes the cheapest and easiest solution for employers who would need to raise wages to attract locally established employees, but can now offer low-paid employment to immigrants.

While this approach may overly focus on employers' behaviour, McGovern (2007) recommends combining the approach with sociologists' work on processes of occupational segregation on the supply side. Reference is made to Waldinger and Lichter's (2003) qualitative study on why employers hire immigrants, the findings of which demonstrate how the interaction between labour supply and demand feed into processes of labour market segmentation. Key concepts which emerge here as the source of labour market segregation include 'hiring queues', social networks and on the job training. The first, hiring queues, represents a situation where employers rank entire ethnic groups according to arbitrary stereotypes (often focusing on the perceived attitude of workers), and then select from the top rank group first (cf. employability defined by queuing, Hasluck 2001).[13]

Another source of segregation is the common situation where both employers and immigrants find they benefit from hiring through social networks. The former feel they are dealing with a 'known quantity' while the latter can provide job opportunities for friends or acquaintances. However, once this mechanism is used exclusively, employment may be restricted to those ethnic groups established in a firm. This can be further reinforced by the third mechanism of labour segregation – the acquisition of job specific skills or knowledge. Here, workers rely on the assistance of colleagues to share their knowledge and skills, even if there are only routine jobs to be done. Established employees may prefer to work with those with whom they share socio-cultural ties, thereby possibly isolating those from a different ethnic background, and encouraging employers to hire members from particular ethnic groups only (Becker 1975; McGovern 2007).

Interestingly, the influences of such processes may be less pronounced in larger, more structured organizations with formalised selection procedures, where there is a reduced possibility of open conflicts between employers and employees over who should be hired (McGovern 2007). Such businesses are more typical of urban contexts, and the dominance of small and medium-sized enterprises in rural areas is likely to make them particularly open to the influence of the factors mentioned above.

Evidence on Migrants' Situation in Rural and Urban Labour Markets

Migrants' employment rates differ from country to country, or between different models of migration flow. In Scotland, as well as in Ireland and new settlement countries in Southern Europe, migrant workers tend to show high employment rates, but are also likely to be segregated into jobs requiring basic skills only (EFILWC 2007).

There is evidence in the UK to suggest that, during the early months after EU enlargement in 2004, the majority of migrant workers from the A8 states were finding employment in rural areas rather than the traditional migration centres (TUC 2004). Migrants' high representation in rural areas may in part explain why, in Scotland, 69 per cent of EU accession state nationals are known to be employed in mainly low-skilled jobs in hospitality, agriculture and food processing. The UK average (47 per cent) is much lower for these three sectors (Home Office 2005). As with the rest of the UK, the majority of A8 workers in Scotland are employed in the same key sectors. Around two-thirds are engaged in agriculture, food processing, hospitality/catering and administration, business and management, with many of

---

13   One stereotype prevalent in the US being that 'white workers don't want to get their hands dirty' while 'latinos like to work' (Waldinger and Lichter 2003: 176–77 in McGovern 2007).

the latter registered with employment and recruitment agencies and also actually employed in agriculture, food/fish/meat processing industries and in the largest sector overall – hospitality and catering.[14]

From reports of local experiences of recent migrant workers to Scotland, it is apparent that 53 per cent in Lanarkshire had professional qualifications or experience of a trade, 60 per cent of those surveyed in Tayside were university qualified and a further 16 per cent had industry or trade qualifications, and one third of migrants included in a study in the North East of Scotland stated they had formal university/college qualifications.[15] This compares to 29 per cent of people born in Scotland who have higher education qualifications and who are active in the labour market, and much lower proportions amongst disadvantaged groups (Danson 2003).

The data from the WRS (Worker Registration Scheme)[16] returns for Scotland identify A8 migrants as young, without dependants, working on full-time, (mostly) temporary contracts. In the main these workers are low paid: more than four in five migrant workers in Scotland earned between £4.50[17] (the minimum wage in the UK for those over 21) and £5.99 per hour.[18] In a meta-analysis of recent reports on A8 migrants and to particular urban and rural labour market areas within Scotland (Brown and Danson 2008), it has been demonstrated that the majority are being employed in the secondary labour market across rural and urban locations. They fall into the category of 'pragmatists' (those seeking economic opportunities as a primary reason for relocating):

- who relocated for economic/educational purposes;
- whose decision to move to Scotland was secondary in the decision making process;

----

14   Similarly, it should be noted that, for example, many in Eastern England are classified as 'business admin., etc.' when they are in fact in the agriculture and food processing sectors.

15   It should be noted that, in the absence of a reliable sampling framework, many of these local surveys are likely to have been subject to bias having had to use some type of convenience sample. In Tayside, the sample size of employers who provided information was 700 (response rate of 42 per cent), which is reasonable but, for example, the city of Dundee was under represented, and the study focused on specific economic sectors only. By contrast, the Lanarkshire samples were extremely small, with a questionnaire survey that yielded 48 returns from migrants and six returns from employers.

16   Caution is required in any analysis which uses the WRS for examining the impacts of migrant labour on the labour market (see for discussion Brown and Danson 2007). However, the statistics presented here are sufficiently robust and consistent with other data sources that there can be confidence in the conclusions.

17   On 18 December 2008, £4.50 translated as US$ 6.94 and Euro 4.77 (<http://www.xe.com/ucc/convert.cgi,>, accessed 18 December 2008).

18   For more information on the employment status of A8 workers in the UK, see Anderson et al. 2006.

- who had realistic expectations of life in Scotland;
- who faced some barriers in settling in, but these were often not significant;
- who were generally undecided as to whether they would stay on, but were often happy in that current situation.

From this same set of studies, the views of employers were consistent with research conducted elsewhere in predominantly urban areas in the UK (Anderson et al. 2006). Employers in many labour market areas, urban and rural, have identified migrants as an important source of recruitment for hard-to-fill vacancies, that is jobs which are physically demanding, with long unpredictable hours, low pay and status (Anderson et al. 2006). In their reasons for employing A8 migrants, the evidence from the 354 employers consulted in the studies, across a variety of sectors, suggested that they considered that employment of foreign workers ensures the viability and stability of their businesses. Further to this, the introduction of such new labour was considered to have improved business performance and encouraged growth, which, in turn, has led to job creation. As employment has increased in local economies with little evidence of displacement elsewhere, there has been job growth in aggregate. Conversely, employers stated that if job gaps were left unplugged this would lead to a reduction in the quality of products and services. In many cases the need to restructure businesses would be a distinct possibility if foreign workers were not actively recruited.

In summary, the reasons given by employers for recruiting overseas workers were consistently:

- lack of local applicants for job vacancies;
- lack of relevant skills/experience amongst the local workforce;
- better work ethic and more flexibility;
- considerably better attendance records;
- improved loyalty and less social problems; and
- higher productivity.

Unsurprisingly, only in a few occasions was the opportunity to offer lower pay cited as a reason for employing migrant workers. Some recent, new developments have been noted, however, which may render migrant workers' situation in rural labour markets more precarious. First, there are signs that employers in rural and urban areas in the UK may shift increasingly towards the employment of agency workers (mainly migrants) at the expense of 'regular' employees – the latter comprising both locally established people as well as independent migrant workers.

For example, a food processing business in rural England, which made redundant its full time employees (migrants as well as UK workers), replaced them with agency staff only. Most of those new staff were migrant workers, employed on lower rates of pay, less overtime money, fewer holidays and more antisocial shift patterns compared to the previous employees, who themselves had not had a pay rise in three years (Lawrence 2007). The employer argued that wage and shift patterns had to be adapted given that even new investments would not have resulted in the efficiencies required to make the company profitable (Lawrence 2007). While this may appear an isolated case, such developments will be facilitated and are likely to gain strength. This seems to apply even if the UK government implements and enforces the new EU directive, which would give agency workers the same rights as other employees. After all, the current recession means competition and survival strategies are introduced.[19]

Second, it appears that at least newly arrived migrant workers allow employers to sustain employment practices that may create a new bottom segment in the labour market as employers pursue competitiveness almost exclusively based on the minimization of labour costs. A case study of a business in an English town (Mackenzie and Forde 2007), which provided a labour intensive quality control and repackaging service to the glass products industry, and employed large numbers of migrants in low to semi-skilled jobs, made the following observation. As in other studies mentioned above, migrant workers were preferred by employers due to their perceived attitudinal advantage over UK workers. However, as migrants became more embedded in the community, their aspirations tended to change, and they were less likely to work long hours for low levels of pay. Hence, those attributes changed which were most valued by the employers. As a response, employers shifted their recruitment to new arrivals, in this case from migrant workers from Albania to those from Poland and the former Soviet Union. While such examples will exist in both rural and urban areas, it seems that rural businesses in particular are likely to adopt such strategies given their reliance on basic skilled and low paid labour and their potential to isolate each successive immigrant workforce.

Progression Opportunities for Migrant Workers in Scotland

As noted above, several studies have shown that migrants in basic skilled employment frequently have high level qualifications. Often, these qualifications are irrelevant for the industry in which they are employed (Hall Aitken and INI 2007a; Hall Aitken and INI 2007b; de Lima et al. 2005). In the vast majority of cases, migrants would like to use their skills in their employment (SE 2006) although many see barriers to realizing this ambition, including lack of English skills; uncertainty about the recognition of qualifications; lack of confidence; and limited awareness of relevant public agencies which can help them in their

---

19   This Directive 'allows the UK to implement the agreement between CBI and TUC, reached in May 2008, which means that an agency worker is entitled to equal treatment (at least the basic working and employment conditions that would apply to the worker concerned if they had been recruited directly to occupy the same job) after 12 weeks in a given job.' (<http://www.berr.gov.uk/whatwedo/employment/employment-agencies/consultation-2002/page30034.html>)

endeavours. Hence, entry level jobs (for example, in hospitality) provide relatively easy access to employment, and ensure some income and time for orientation when the medium to longer term plan is to look for a more suitable job (Anderson et al. 2006).

Interviews carried out with migrant workers in Glasgow revealed that only a small minority – those with good English language skills – have reported on having had some opportunities to 'climb up the ladder' or to work flexibly in a way which could contribute to career advancement in the medium term. This included cases such as the promotion from a waitress to a shift manager, or an employer accommodating an employee's request to work part time to be able to take a college course (Hall Aitken and INI 2007b).

Training provided by employers for migrants in basic skilled employment has usually been confined to health and safety, and to job specific technical skills. Training which would improve migrants' long-term prospects, and which would confer transferable skills, seems to have hardly ever been on offer in rural Scotland (Sim 2007; Hall Aitken and INI 2007a; de Lima et al. 2005). Employers in the UK have been found to often see the onus of improving standards of English language skills on the employees, regarding them as the main beneficiaries (Learning and Skills Council 2006).

The vast bulk of research which has been carried out in the UK and Scotland to date has focused on workers in the bottom segments of the labour market. This may reflect the fact that such workers are the majority and are particularly vulnerable, and that there is a clear need for (evidence-based) policy and practice development to support this group. However, it also means that we have only limited insights into the situation of migrant workers as a whole, and the different experiences between those in highly skilled or professional employment and those at the bottom of the labour market hierarchy.

Here, the energy sector lends itself to some closer examination. Recent research in Aberdeen – a city which refers to itself as Europe's energy capital – revealed that 67 per cent of businesses in this sector are looking for senior or non-senior engineers or scientists. For operational staff, 57 per cent of employer respondents believed that the most needed skills were in engineering. Reasons for recruitment difficulties included skill shortages, poaching of staff, and unrealistic salary expectations (Farquhar 2007). There is evidence that, at least in this sector, migrants are well represented in management and professional roles. According to a survey, 31 per cent of migrant respondents were mainly managers, 23 per cent senior engineers or scientists and 20 per cent engineers or scientists (Conkerhouse 2007).

Some qualitative evidence is available from a small scale study (Hall Aitken and INI 2007b) in the energy sector in Aberdeen city. Interviews with a range of stakeholders by Jentsch for that research (trade union, business, migrant, local authority and economic development representatives) yielded the following key findings, which were consistent across the representatives:

Where there is an extremely high demand for skilled/professional labour, employers explained that migrant workers had similar opportunities to those enjoyed by UK workers. They also received the required support from the employer (for example, language lessons and training from specialists) to take advantage of those. Especially in large companies, migrant workers enjoyed comprehensive assistance with their relocation, securing accommodation and English language tuition. Given the frequent use of competency assurance courses, and tests of knowledge and skills at the recruitment stage, lengthy qualification recognition processes or challenges with matching foreign with UK qualifications were regarded a minor issue in the industry.

It may, of course, be that migrants are prevented from accessing the labour market, rather than progressing once employment has been gained. Migrant workers may not be at the top of employers' recruitment options. Employers tended to perceive the employment of migrant workers as problematic, given language barriers, issues which arise for health and safety and wider integration concerns, such as sourcing housing (Hall Aitken and INI 2007b).

At the same time, there are still untapped resources in Scotland. The Engineering and Construction Industry Training Board (ECITB) have set themselves targets for the recruitment of women and minority ethnic members for their training opportunities, who so far have remained very much under represented, for a variety of causes on both the supply and demand sides. For example, 25 per cent of the workforce in energy and utility sector consists of women, which compares with 43 per cent of women workers in the wider UK economy.

The situation is even more dramatic in the construction industry, where migrants are often employed in the skilled trades. About 10 per cent of the workforce are women, who work predominantly in professional occupations, such as design and management. However, only approximately one per cent are working in the trades (Scottish Construction Forum 2007). This extreme situation of under-representation has led the Equal Opportunities Commission (2005) to comment on the construction industry as an 'almost no-go area' for women. Efforts have recently been made, for example, by ConstructionSkills to attract women into the industry.

It is particularly surprising that women have remained so underrepresented given that, over the last five years, the industry has experienced a remarkable boom, which has been accompanied by a demand for labour that has highlighted serious skills shortages and gaps in the industry. This has been exacerbated by the fact that the current workforce is ageing. It is understood that a lack of investment into apprenticeships in the past has contributed to labour shortages amongst UK workers in the main trades (de Lima et al. 2007). At the same time, the industry has been highlighted as employing a disproportionate number of migrants in skilled jobs compared with other industries, though evidence on this has been limited to local studies (Boyes 2006).

While the short term nature of contracts in the construction industry may serve workers well in that they can combine a (family) life in their origin country with employment abroad, this may not always be the preferred type of contract. However, the insecurity of moving from project to project in the industry is shared by many construction workers, UK nationals and others.

Initiatives and Policies which Affect Migrants and Rural Communities

Recently, as described in some of the case studies above, support services for migrants have been developed and offered at national and local levels to promote integration and to increase the employability of migrants (for example, language tuition), but problems remain within certain areas, for example the recognition of qualifications from abroad. The Organization for Economic Cooperation and Development [OECD] (2006) has identified different approaches being adopted towards migrant workers across the developed world. They ranged widely, from the pro-active policies to promote integration (that is remove barriers for immigrants to be able to perform as well as native-born workers) of such social democracies as Sweden to the stereotypical 'laissez-faire' attitude towards in-migration by the USA. As is apparent in the UK and Ireland, but also beyond, although national governments have responsibility for immigration policies, many initiatives and strategic support have been introduced at different spatial levels. The importance of players at the local government or regional levels, who adopted policies towards the support of local workers, should not be underestimated.

The OECD has distinguished these different policy approaches towards integrating migrants into two categories (Table 6.2). The less intensive form applies fewer resource activities, with quite minimal intervention and involves basic forms of assisting integration within the local labour market. It has been argued that 'this is akin to the forms of assistance which are currently on offer for migrant workers in Scotland' (Brown and Danson 2008). By contrast, the second category demands high resource activities, and a public policy which adopts a much more interventionist framework, attempting to 'build bridges' pro-actively between the migrant community and employers through, for example, experience programmes and higher-level language training.

It has been considered as critical to the successful and effective introduction of such policies and strategies that they encompass and are inclusive of both host and migrant communities. This should ameliorate any potential negative reactions from the indigenous or the long-established population (that is including both UK citizens and previous migrants) from a targeted policy or 'social group' approach towards assisting migrants. Therefore, an 'issue approach', including better signposting and assistance which is accessible by all should be preferred.

Implications for Rural Areas

For rural businesses facing low demand, high costs and tight labour markets, the opportunities presented by access to new sources of cheap labour appear considerable, apparently offering the very survival of the individual enterprise on occasion. With many remote rural communities confronting the twin demographic challenges of declining and ageing populations, the influx of young, dynamic, motivated and skilled workers promises to address other pressing issues for the locality as well. However, there are dangers in the uncritical acceptance of

Table 6.2   Typology of different policy approaches towards migrant workers

Low Resource Activities	High Resource Activities
• Job search	• Work experience programmes
• Confidence building, help with social networking	• Medium to longer term 'bridging' training in medium-high skills areas
• Understanding cultural differences	
• CV preparation	• Recognition of qualifications gained abroad
	• Assistance for employers in understanding foreign qualifications
• Short-term training to meet specific job vacancies	• Projects to tackle discrimination in recruitment procedures
• Basic language training	• Higher levels of language training, including occupationally specific language use
• Mentoring	

Source: Based on OECD (2006) and Brown and Danson (2008).

such solutions, as they threaten to generate novel ways both of encouraging the 'development of the underdevelopment' of the local economy and of producing new sources of dependency. Hence, unless rural development produces 'quality jobs', immigration to rural areas will remain of a temporary nature at least as concerns well qualified migrants, whilst the employment in the local secondary labour market will suffer downward pressure on wages and skills permanently.

Indeed, accessing the migrant workforce in the current manner will not allow the fundamental restructuring in their labour processes that is necessary to break out of their historic cycles of low investment-low profit-low wages. As secondary employment has a tendency to trap its workers into a dead-end position, there are few positive long term attractions for migrants; without the opportunity to be recruited to positions in better performing sectors there will be few incentives to remain in Scotland. Investment in food processing, tourism and other service sectors is necessary if the industries and the workforce – long-established and migrant – are to improve their prospects and performances in the longer term (Hall Aitken 2006; Danson 2007).

Implications for Immigrants to Rural Areas

Many local authorities covering predominantly rural areas in Scotland seem to have been seriously concerned with their new community members' welfare, as have their urban counterparts. However, as mentioned above, this support has remained at a basic level, and even here, service gaps have remained. For example, the spread of freely available English for Speakers of Other Languages [ESOL] provisions may have helped migrants to acquire language skills needed for some type of career progression, for example, from a basic or semi-skilled occupation to a supervisory post. Some challenges have persisted, such as difficulties with the recruitment of well qualified language tuition providers and providing classes for all levels of ability. Nonetheless, there has been the political will and a good measure of financial commitment to contribute towards meeting migrants' needs over a relatively short period of time (Hall Aitken and INI 2007a).

It is likely that less progress has been made in endeavours to more efficiently match migrants' skills, experiences and qualifications with job opportunities, in part because of the lack of high resource activities by public bodies referred to above. In addition, the particular industries in which migrants are currently employed are unlikely to offer any significant career prospects. As far as migrants with higher education qualifications are concerned, it is very probable that their experiences are similar to those of Scottish graduates from rural areas: there is a dearth of available opportunities, and 'to get on, you have to get out.' (Dey and Jentsch 2000)

In order to further support migrants, it is important for policy makers to identify and acknowledge their diverse needs. No research in Scotland to date has systematically looked at different experiences, for example, of men and women migrants in rural areas. However, there has been some evidence to suggest that when women follow their husbands, they are particularly likely to be employed in menial jobs despite their high levels of qualifications (Hall Aitken and INI 2007a and b). This fits with the wider picture of women (and young people) suffering from disproportionate underemployment in rural areas (Bryden undated). Hence, at least in some cases, gender may be a more significant category for migrants' experiences than nationality, so that a Polish woman in a remote area may have more in common with UK women in that same area than with a Polish man.

Comparisons

There is undoubtedly a tendency in migration studies to focus on one dimension of the population movement – impacts on the host community, experiences of the migrants and their families, less occasionally the implications for the places of origin of the mobile workforce, to the exclusion of an integrated approach. Much less common, and apparently less attractive to academic researchers and other commentators alike, are the comparisons, involving considerations of both similarities and dissimilarities, with other geographical areas. There are of course exceptions, and the conferences on *Celtic Cultures in the Emigrant Context* in 2002 and on *International Migration and Scotland: The Public And Social Policy Agendas* in 2005 at Sabhal Mòr Ostaig, Isle of Skye, are good examples of the integration of local experiences in wider national and international contexts.

The discussion earlier on the flows revealed by the WRS and NINo data, supplemented by the local studies of local and regional labour markets across Scotland, offer some opportunity for assessment and this has been incorporated into the analyses above. However, as has been noted, even though this may allow some comparison of migrant workers in varying rural contexts in different parts of Scotland, extending the evaluations to other countries and to urban contexts in Scotland and in other countries is more problematic. Unfortunately, data limitations preclude much detailed comparative analysis while many studies have been specially commissioned on an *ad hoc* basis with non-transferable or less than robust methodologies. Within the Scottish environment, the statistics do seem to show that the same occupations tend to dominate the employment of migrants, regardless of rural or urban location: between two-thirds and three-quarters of all jobs definitely appear to be in the top ten secondary labour market areas and probably high proportions of the rest are similarly located (Home Office 2007). Information from industries suggests similar distributions of secondary jobs across geographical regions.

These findings contrast with many other studies on mobile labour within the UK, where migration and relocation are often involved with progression up a career ladder. However, secondary labour markets as discussed in this chapter by definition do not offer the context for upward mobility so that movement within this country offers no benefits to the migrant or national worker. Employment in the primary labour market, with its characteristic high and stable wages, career prospects and employment security, though, is concentrated in the cities and metropolitan regions of the UK while higher function positions in such careers tend to be centralised there also. For such escalator regions (Fielding 1991), there is a strong attraction of professional and technical occupations, but as many local economies – urban and rural – are dominated by public and private branch plants there are relatively few high quality employment prospects outwith these favoured areas (Danson 2003).

In terms of international comparisons, it may be particularly fruitful to consider in more detail the situations of Scotland and Ireland, as there have been important similarities. Both countries have recently developed from countries of emigration to immigration, so that their infrastructures had to rapidly adjust to the new community members; the profile of the migrant population looks similar (mainly A8 States, especially Polish; relatively young and well qualified); and while migrants have high rates of employment, they are mainly confined to employment in the secondary labour market – many in rural areas – in both countries (EFILWC 2007).

Conclusions

Limits of Current Research and Policy Implications

While migrant workers from the new accession states who have come to Scotland may often have high qualifications for basic skilled jobs, the reasons for this appear to relate only partly to characteristics often associated with migrants. These include a lack of language skills and foreign qualifications which employers find difficult to match with UK equivalents. The more significant barriers migrants encounter seem to be of a structural nature, and affect also other social groups, including minority ethnic groups and women. It is striking that migrants' employment situation – working conditions, pay and career prospects – are particularly poor in the secondary labour market. However, this tends to be the case also for UK workers in this segment. While migrant workers are disproportionately affected by exploitation due to lack of awareness of rights and support services or limited language skills (a situation which needs to be urgently addressed), a good part of their experiences will be shared with other groups of workers.

Research has not very well succeeded in examining challenges migrants face in the wider context. To what extent are difficulties in finding suitable employment shared by other social groups, and what does this tell us about structural barriers, which are difficult to overcome also by locally established people? What does it tell us about the possible stereotyping of minorities and other groups with a long history of discrimination in the labour market? While it may well be true that employers do not directly replace local labour with migrant workers, it has been argued in this chapter that more subtle processes may be in place. They include employers' ability to sustain working conditions which are incompatible with a life (family) balance; and wages which offer workers little more but social exclusion, and undignified living conditions. There are questions to be asked about untapped human resources – settled minority ethnic group members, disengaged youth, women with caring responsibilities, people with a disability who, for a range of reasons, are not actively seeking employment.

Given the effects labour market structures and processes may have on a wide range of social groups, an issue based approach to research may be more fruitful than one which focuses on the situation and experiences of one group only. Such an approach may also be more promising when our concern is with policy and practice development. Recognizing the root of problems migrants experience is important not least to address such problems at the right level. Structural problems need to be addressed at a structural level, and adding provisions such as ESOL classes will contribute relatively little, unless they are accompanied by structural changes. Again, such changes will help a number of vulnerable groups in the labour market.

Taking an 'issues approach' to policy development (rather than a 'social group approach') has other benefits: it has less scope for causing public controversy which a policy focus on migrants' welfare is sometimes associated with, and it would result in resources being spent equitably and efficiently.

Segmented Labour Market?

Considering research findings in the context of the segmented labour market theory, the assumption that migrants simply fill gaps when there is an economic boom is questionable. Current evidence suggests that, in many cases, the migrant workforce is used by employers to compete on a low skills-low pay basis when their businesses are under particular pressure.

It is also not clear to what extent it is the concern with the 'low status' associated with some occupations which discourages locally established people from seeking available jobs. Their behaviour may to a great part be attributed to the fact that those available employment 'opportunities' preclude a life-work balance. They thus tend to be suitable for those with characteristics often associated with students and migrant workers – young and independent, and possibly intending to stay for a limited time only, so that jobs which can be easily accessed are of particular interest to them. An important characteristic of secondary labour market employment and many of the jobs taken by migrant workers is that they are both easily entered and exited: there are no returns to either party from extended tenure. These are exactly the conditions that make A8 migrants as described here the ideal reserve labour army for the UK economy. Their propensity to return home or move on means that they satisfy the *laissez faire* conditions required by an economy based on low paid low skilled work.

If employers are able to sustain organizational cultures which are detrimental to the employment prospects of more established social groups (migrants who have lived in the UK for some time, and others) it appears that a new bottom segment may be created in the labour market. This segment relies mainly on those migrant workers who have newly arrived, and are not yet embedded in communities where their aspirations could widen beyond immediate economic gains. Their effective exclusion, with both economic and social dimensions, is detrimental to the long run needs and development of rural Scotland, confirming pro-active interventions are essential to break this cycle.

References

Anderson, B., Ruhs, M., Rogaly, B., and Spencer, S. (2006), *Fair enough? Central and East European migrants in low-wage employment in the UK* (COMPAS/ Sussex Centre for Migration Research: University of Oxford/University of Sussex).

Becker, G. (1975), *Human Capital: A Theoretical and Empirical Analysis with Special Reference to Education*, First edition (New York: National Bureau of Economic Research).

Boyes, L. (2006), *Settling in Scotland? A Review of Existing Data on Accession State Migration to Scotland* (Edinburgh: Scottish Council Foundation). <http:// www.scottishcouncilfoundation.org/docs/settling_in_scotland.pdf>, accessed 9 May 2008.

Brown, R. and Danson, M. (2008), 'Fresh talent or cheap labour? Accession State migrant labour in the Scottish Economy', *Scottish Affairs*, 64, 37–52.

Bryden, J., *What are 'healthy' rural communities? How are our rural communities doing in the EU-25 Rural Development in the Enlarged EU?* (Athens Agricultural University Post Graduate Program on Rural Development).

Champion, A. (2006), *Migration and Social Change in Rural England 2006*, <http://www.ncl.ac.uk/curds/publications/pdf/CREmigseminar220306.pdf>.

Conkerhouse (2007), *Energy Research Project. Main report* (Scottish Enterprise: Glasgow).

CoSLA Refugee and Asylum Seekers Consortium (2006), *Briefing paper on the migration of A8 nationals to Scotland* (Edinburgh: CoSLA).

Crocket, B. and de Lima, P. (2006), *Discussion paper: Employment issues – minority ethnic people in rural areas* (Edinburgh: Scottish Government). <http://www. scotland.gov.uk/Topics/People/Equality/18934/employmentissues>, accessed 24 September 2008.

Danson, M. (1982), 'The industrial structure and labour market segmentation: urban and regional implications', *Regional Studies*, 16:4, 255–65.

Danson, M. (2003), *Employability Report to Futureskills Scotland*, mimeo. (Glasgow: FSS).

Danson, M. (2007), 'Fresh or refreshed talent: exploring population change and policy initiatives in Scotland', *International Journal on Multicultural Societies* (UNESCO) 9:1, October.

De Lima P., Jentsch, B. and Whelton, R. (2005), *Migrant Workers in the Highlands and Islands Study 2005*. Research Report. UHI PolicyWeb and INI. <http:// www.hie.co.uk/HIE-economicreports-2005/migrant-workers-in-thehighlands-and-islands-report-2005.pdf, accessed 16 December 2008.

De Lima P., Masud Chaudhry, M., Whelton R. and Arshad R. (2007), *A Study of Migrant Workers in Grampian* (Edinburgh: Communities Scotland).

Dey, I. and Jentsch, B. (2000), 'Rural Youth in Scotland: the policy agenda', *Youth and Policy*, Winter 2000/2001, 11–24.

Dickens, R., Gregg, P. and Wadsworth, J. (2003), *The Labour Market Under New Labour: The State of Working Britain* (Basingstoke: Palgrave Macmillan Publishing).

Economist (2007), 'Hoorah for Shortages', 7 September.

Edwards, R., Reich, M. and Gordon, D. (1975), *Labor Market Segmentation* (Lexington, MA: D.C. Heath).

Equal Opportunities Commission (2005), *Free to choose. Tackling gender barriers to better jobs. GB summary report* (London: EOC).

ETUC (2006), *Temporary agency workers in the European Union* <http://www. etuc.org/a/501>, accessed 9 May 2008.

European Foundation for the Improvement of Living and Working Conditions (EFILWC) (2007), Employment and working conditions of migrant workers. (Dublin: EFILWC).

Farquhar, H. (2007). *Aberdeen City Council Sector Skill Needs Audit*. Draft, Aberdeen City Council, Strategic Leadership: Aberdeen.

Fielding, A. (1991), 'Migration and social mobility: South East England as an escalator region', *Regional Studies*, 26:1, 1–15.

Futureskills Scotland (2004), *Rural Scotland: Key Results from the Employers Skill Survey* (Glasgow: Scottish Enterprise).

Futureskills Scotland (2008), *Labour Market Profile Highland*. <http://www.keyindicators.org.uk/report.aspx?pid=1>, accessed 10 December 2008.

Futureskills Scotland (2006), *The Labour Market in Rural Scotland: An Introduction*, <http://www.futureskillsscotland.org.uk/web/site/home/Reports/NationalReports/Report_The_Labour_Market_in_Rural_Scotland_An_Introduction.asp>, accessed 9 May 2008.

Gordon, D. (1982), *Segmented Work, Divided Workers: The Historical Transformation of Labor in the United States* (Cambridge: Cambridge University Press).

Hall Aitken and INI (2007a), *Migrant Workers in Dumfries and Galloway* (Dumfries: Scottish Enterprise Dumfries and Galloway).

Hall Aitken and INI (2007b), *Research into Migrant Labour and the Economy* (Glasgow: Scottish Enterprise).

Hasluck, C. (2001), 'Lessons from the New Deal: Finding work, promoting employability', *New Economy*, 8:4, 230–34.

Hayek, F.A. (1945), 'The Use of Knowledge in Society', *American Economic Review*, 35: 4, September, 519–30.

Home Office (2007), *Accession Monitoring Report, May 2004–March 2007* (London: Home Office).

Horton, P. (2006), *Health Issues in the Community Evaluation, Lochaber Case Study*, Hall Aitken <http://www.chex.org.uk/uploads/lochaber_case_study_formatted.doc?sess_scdc=92bedb903bac642c8070a6b025f362a5>, accessed 9 May 2008.

Jentsch, B. (2006), 'Youth Migration from Rural Areas: Moral Principles to Support Youth and Rural Communities in Policy Debates', *Sociologia Ruralis*, 46: 3.

Lawrence, F. (2007), 'Poor pay, no rights: UK's new workforce', *The Guardian. International edition*, 1–2, 24 September.

Learning and Skills Council [LSC] (2006), *Employer Perceptions of Migrant Workers Research Report* (Coventry: LSC), December.

McConnachie A (2002), *A History of Immigration to Britain*. <www.sovereignty.org.uk/features/articles/immig.html>, accessed 15 December 2008.

McGovern, P. (2007) 'Immigration, Labour Markets and Employment Relations: Problems and Prospects', *British Journal of Industrial Relations*, 45:2, June.

MacKenzie, R. and Forde, C. (2007), *The 'good worker': the rhetoric of the resource based view of the firm and the reality of disadvantaged migrant workers*. Paper prepared for the Work, Employment and Society 2007 Conference, University of Aberdeen, 12–14 September.

Marsden, T., Franklin, A. and Kitchen, L. (2005), *Rural Labour Markets: Exploring the Mismatches*. Research Report 7 (Cardiff and Aberystwyth: Wales Rural Observatory).

Marshall, A. (1920), *Principles of Economics: An Introductory Volume*, Eighth edition (London: Macmillan).

Newlands, D., Danson, M. and McCarthy, J. (eds) (2004), *Divided Scotland? The Nature, Causes and Consequences of Economic Disparities within Scotland* (Aldershot: Ashgate).

OECD (2006), *From Immigration to Integration: Local Solutions to a Global Challenge* (Paris: OECD).

Pavis, S., Platt, S. and Hubbard, G. (2000), *Social Exclusion and Insertion of Young People in Rural Areas: a Mixed Methods Case Study in Two Contrasting Scottish Regions* (York: Joseph Rowntree Foundation).

Piore, M.J. (1975), 'Notes for a Theory of Labor Market Segmentation', in RC Edwards et al., (eds), *Labour Market Segmentation* (Lexington: D.C. Heath).

Piore, M.J. (1979), *Birds of Passage: Migrant Labor and Industrial Societies* (New York: Cambridge University Press).

Scottish Construction Forum (2007), *Public Consultation on the Refresh of the Industry Plan. Achieving Construction Innovation and Excellence in Scotland* (Glasgow: Scottish Enterprise).

SE (Scottish Enterprise) (2006), *Accession 8 Migrant Labour in Scotland: Review of Existing Evidence and Knowledge Gaps* (Glasgow: Scottish Enterprise).

Scottish Executive (2004), *Analysis of Ethnicity in the 2001 Census. Summary Report* (Edinburgh: Scottish Executive).

Sim, D., Barclay, A. and Anderson, I. (2007), *Achieving a Better Understanding of 'A8' Migrant Labour Needs in Lanarkshire*. Research report to North Lanarkshire Council, Scottish Enterprise Lanarkshire and South Lanarkshire Council.

Smith, A. (1776), *An Inquiry into the Nature and Causes of the Wealth of Nations* [1776], in Campbell, R.H. and Skinner, A.S. (eds) (Oxford: Oxford University Press).

Toynbee, P. (2003), *Hard Work: Life in Low-Pay Britain* (London: Bloomsbury).

Trades Union Congress (TUC) (2004) *Propping Up Rural and Small Town Britain – Migrant Workers from the New Europe* (London: TUC).

Waldinger, R. and Lichter, M. (2003), *How the Other Half Works: Immigration and the Social Organization of Labor* (Berkeley and Los Angeles: University of California Press).

Watt, P. and McGaughey, F. (eds) (2006), *How Public Authorities Provide Services to Minority Ethnic Groups, Northern Ireland, Republic of Ireland, Scotland*. Emerging findings discussion paper. <http://www.nccri.ie/pdf/Service_Provision_Report.pdf>, accessed 9 May 2008.

Wright, Robert E. (2008) *The Economics of New Immigration to Scotland*, David Hume Institute Seminar, Royal Society of Edinburgh, 1 April 2008.

Chapter 7

Immigrants and Receiving Communities in Rural Russia: Experiences from the Central European and the Far East Regions

Irina Ivakhnyuk

Introduction

Since 1992, Russia has been an active participant of international migration flows. After seventy years of tight restrictions on cross-border population movements during the Soviet period, the country was re-opened to international migration. Russia has experienced immigration in its full diversity, including permanent, temporary, regular, irregular, labour, study, circular and transit immigration. The most numerous migration flows have come to Russia from the former Soviet republics which gained sovereignty in 1991. A visa-free entry regime in the Commonwealth of Independent States [CIS] territory[1] has facilitated cross-border population movements. Simultaneously, economic progress in Russia has attracted international migrants from neighbouring states, both for permanent residence and temporary work.

According to United Nations data, Russia ranks second (after the United States of America) among the major immigrant receiving countries, with the total number of immigrants in 2005 amounting to 13.3 million (United Nations 2006). This situation has stimulated numerous studies, surveys and publications on international migration in Russia.[2] A proper understanding of the nature of international migration and a clear interpretation of its reasons and consequences in the post-Soviet context is essential to developing appropriate mechanisms for its management.

---

1 The Commonwealth of Independent States is a regional structure existing since 1993. The CIS member states are: Armenia, Azerbaijan, Belarus, Georgia, Kazakhstan, Kyrgyzstan, Moldova, Russian Federation, Tajikistan, Turkmenistan, Ukraine, and Uzbekistan, i.e. all the post-Soviet states, except the Baltic countries (Latvia, Lithuania and Estonia). In accordance with bilateral agreements, Russia has a visa-free entry regime with all the CIS countries, except Georgia and Turkmenistan.

2 See, for example: Mukomel 2005; Petrov 2004; Ivakhnyuk 2005, 2008; Zaionchkovskaya 2002, 2007; Krasinets et al. 2000; Vitkovskaya and Panarin 2000; Ushkalov and Malakha 1999; Iontsev 1998–2006;

However, so far, Russian migration literature has mainly concentrated on conceptualizing migration flows; attempting to provide generalizable explanations for the phenomenon and applying well-developed Western migration theories to contemporary Russian contexts. Moreover, the role of immigration in demographic developments has been examined, as well as the important issues of irregular migration and ethnic-based intolerance towards migrants. Endeavours have been made to find suitable migration management models for Russia (Iontsev 1999; Mukomel 2005; Ivakhnyuk 2008; Vitkovskaya and Panarin 2000; Petrov 2004).

Concerning the specific topic of immigration to rural areas, this area of research has remained at the periphery of migration studies. This is particularly remarkable given the fact that during the 1990s, net migration from ex-USSR states to Russian rural areas amounted to more than two million (from a total of six million) (Rosstat 2002). The situation can partly be explained with a governmental programme, which allocated refugees to rural areas during that time (Vorobyeva 2001). However, a detailed and comprehensive analysis of migration to rural areas has remained difficult due to a lack of statistical data and rural-focused surveys.

Once empirical evidence has been accumulated, Russian migration academics will inevitably turn to investigate the specific role of immigrants in rural communities in contemporary Russia. After all, rural areas face an even deeper demographic crisis and more difficulties in their transition to the market economy than urban areas. Concerning social and public discourses, immigration is currently an important issue at local level, especially in the most affected Russian provinces. It will also become increasingly important at federal level, particularly as a State Programme on providing support for voluntary resettlement of so-called compatriots[3] to the Russian Federation is being put into practice.

This chapter is a first attempt to describe and analyze the experiences of immigrants, and their possible impacts on the economic, demographic, and social developments of rural areas in Russia. Since Russia is a very extensive and diverse country, it seems useful to examine different geographical areas and rural contexts. For the purpose of this article, two areas, the Central European region and the Far East region, have been selected to study immigrants' and rural communities' experiences. As will be explained in detail below, these areas do not only differ in their geographical, socio-economic and cultural contexts, but also in the characteristics of the immigrants they attract. The regions share the experience that immigration to *rural* communities has been of particular significance. The two study areas can therefore offer different insights into the range and interplay of factors which may facilitate or undermine migrants' integration in rural communities.

---

3   In the Russian legislation, the term *compatriots* is applied to people who originate from Russia or who have Russian ancestors, but who have left the Russian Empire, the Soviet Union, or post-Soviet Russia to live in other countries. All former Soviet citizens constitute *compatriots* (or *former compatriots*) irrespective of current nationality and citizenship.

Methods and Definitions

Data for this research has been drawn, first of all, from official sources, that is publications of the National Statistics Committee of the Russian Federation [Rosstat], the Ministry of Interior and the Federal Migration Service [FMS]. So far, there have been no sociological or economic surveys, which have specifically focused on international migration to rural areas in Russia. However, fragmentary information on migrants to rural areas has appeared in a number of international migration studies (Gelbras 2001; Larin 2003; Petrov 2004) and in the media, and has been reviewed for this chapter

In addition, between March and September 2007, interviews were conducted with experts on international migration in Russia. These experts comprised six academics from Russian research institutions and seven government officers engaged in migration management. Twelve interviews were also carried out with immigrants from Ukraine, Armenia and Italy who have settled in rural Russia, as well as with representatives of Chinese, Uzbek and Kyrgyz diasporas in Moscow and of migrants' associations. The broad subject area discussed with the interviewees consisted of migration and integration of the mentioned ethnic groups.

It is important to note that in the Russian academic literature, the term 'rural area' stands in opposition to that of 'urban area' (see, for example, Glezer and Polian 2005; Nefedova et al. 2001). Administrative and economic roles are thereby referred to as the major criteria for the respective classification. *Rural settlements* are localities where inhabitants are engaged in: (1) agricultural production and processing; (2) forestry and hunting; (3) employment in small-scale mining and manufacturing enterprises; (4) recreational services for the urban population; (5) nature-conservative measures, such as national parks and forest reserves; (6) labour supplies for economic communication networks, namely transmission facilities, oil–and–gas pipelines, railroads, motorways. Rural settlements are classified as agricultural (farms), non-agricultural, and mixed settlements. On this basis, according to the 2002 Population Census (Goskomstat 2004–05) there were 155,289 rural settlements in Russia (including 13,086 depopulated settlements). The total number of the rural population was 38.7 million, that is 26 per cent of the total Russian population.

In this chapter, the term *migration* is applied to the totality of migration flows while *immigration* and *emigration* characterize permanent non-return population movements. Correspondingly, *immigrants* are migrants who come for long-term or permanent residence, in contrast to *labour migrants* or *migrant workers* who stay in their country of destination temporarily. This terminological distinguisher has generally been agreed upon by Russian researchers (Iontsev 1999; Krasinets et al. 2000; Ivakhnyuk 2005). In terms of statistics, classifications are linked to the type of legal document migrants are granted with (temporary stay permit, permanent stay permit, work permit) and their declared purpose of arrival as recorded in their migrant card on crossing the Russian border. However, it is quite clear that categories of migrants are flexible as people can change their temporary status for a permanent one and *vice versa*, for example, after changes in their life circumstances and in their strategies for economic advancement. Hence, the classification stays schematic, but reasonable for analysing purposes.

The term *local people* is used in this paper to distinguish them from migrants, immigrants, newcomers, and non-Russian citizens. It refers to people who have lived in a community for a period of time which preceded the disintegration of the USSR. In most cases, such individuals would regard themselves as forming the core population, both in ethnic and social terms.

The chapter is based on an intra-national analysis of factors which have facilitated or undermined the integration of international migrants to rural areas in two geographical districts of the Russian Federation – the Central European region and the Far East region. Historical, social, demographic, and economic perspectives are applied in order to single out differences and similarities in communities' and immigrants' experiences.

The Central European region of Russia covers the centre of the European part of the Russian Federation. It includes about 30 provinces with a total territory of 1.2 million square km and a total population of 60 million and corresponds to the administrative Central Federal District along the Volga River and the Western part of the Urals Federal District. For the purpose of this chapter, the Far East region is defined as the southern part of the Russian Far East Federal District and the south-eastern part of the Siberian Federal District. These are five Russian provinces neighbouring China, with a total territory of one and a half million square km and total population about 7 million persons (Goskomstat 2004–05).

International Migration to Rural Areas in Russia

Historical Perspective

In contrast to contemporary migration studies in Russia, the migration literature of the nineteenth century provides numerous publications on international migration to rural areas. The subject was thoroughly investigated and conceptualized by statisticians and academics of that time, such as A. Kaufman, A. Vasilchikov, I. Yamzin, and E. Yanson (Moiseenko 2007). The reason for the deep academic interest in this issue was its primary importance for Russia from demographic, economic, and geopolitical perspectives. The number of immigrants, the structure of their families, their demographic characteristics and behaviour, the compatibility of immigrants' lifestyles with local norms and traditions, and their loyalty to local authorities were all prominent themes of surveys and analytical reports (Shpilevskiy 1871; Kaufman 1905; Yamzin and Voshinin 1926).

Immigration was Russia's reality from the mid-eighteenth century when it became the destination for hundreds of thousands of settlers from Western Europe. A major concern of Emperor Peter and later of Empress Catherine was how to inhabit and develop huge fertile lands in the Central European part of the Empire along the Volga River and stimulate agricultural development. In 1763, the specialized State Migration Department – probably the first migration management board in world history – was founded to encourage colonists from Western Europe to move to unsettled areas of rural Russia. Privileges were granted, such as tax relief, freedom of conscience, and exemption from military service. Since then, Russia has had numerous diasporas of Germans and Dutch. The longstanding presence of these diasporas seems to have been an important factor which has contributed to their integration into local communities in Russia's Central European region (Kaufman 1905; Moiseenko 2007). By the end of the nineteenth century, 1.4 million Germans lived in the Russian Empire of whom 77 per cent inhabited rural areas (data of the 1897 Russian Population Census, cited from: Iontsev 1999, 186).

In the geographically distant Russian Far East, immigrants from China and Korea came and settled from the second half of the nineteenth century. In the early twentieth century, the number of Korean and Chinese permanent residents in the Russian Far East Province exceeded 200,000 persons or 15 per cent of the total population of this region, most of them living in rural areas (Kabuzan 1983). They tended to be engaged in agriculture and hunting but also in construction of the Trans-Siberian railroad and the sea port of Vladivostok. Additionally, about 100,000 seasonal workers came annually to the region. Chinese migrants were also very active in commerce: they delivered food and consumer goods from China, such as soy, flour, and cereals. Chinese capital had been invested in 40 per cent of private Far Eastern enterprises in Russia. By 1917, about 60 per cent of the total number of employees in the private and public sector in the Russian Far East comprised Chinese nationals (Kabuzan 1983).

In general, Chinese workers were appreciated by their Russian employers for their perceived discipline, concessive nature, physical endurance, ability and readiness to work long hours, and their low demands for a private life. In addition, such labour was relatively cheap. At the same time, large numbers of Chinese migrants were also of concern to local authorities, particularly in view of of their apparent wide-spread shadow activities, such as gold smuggling, clandestine trade with drugs and fake alcohol, and their operation of opium nests and gambling-dens. Partly as a result of these perceptions, a myth of a 'Chinese threat' arose in Russian political circles and public opinion. However, the main concern of political and academic debates at the beginning of the twentieth century was national security. Anxieties here were related to the mere Chinese presence in the Far East Province. Issues of the impact of Chinese immigrants on local communities and economic development of the region were regarded as of lesser concerns.

In a nutshell, this brief excursion into the historical patterns of international migration to rural areas in Russia is to suggest that communities in particular rural areas have a history in which immigrants have played an important role. Positive or negative, this experience has been passed on from one generation to another. It seems to have formed some kind of 'genetic memory' which appears to have influenced considerably present day attitudes of local people towards newcomers (Larin 2003).

Social and Economic Perspectives

For over 70 years of the Soviet period, Russia was excluded from international migration flows as the USSR was a closed country in terms of the freedom of cross-border population movements. However, since 1992, Russia has become a participant of international migration processes again. Sixteen years is a short period of time, and many problems related to international migration are new for Russia. Challenges have been exacerbated by the fact that the recent international migration inflows have coincided with a very difficult period in contemporary Russian history. Economic decline resulting from a hasty transition to a market economy occurred together with the phenomenon of a social shock. A significant proportion of the population fell into poverty, and the contrast between rich and poor increased dramatically. Simultaneously, there were significant demographic changes, which resulted in a sharply declining population. It is thus not surprising that in the 1990s, uncontrolled and numerous inflows of migrants were adding to the general instability.

Conditions changed in the 2000s, when Russia's need for foreign labour became most obvious. The oil-and-gas sector had fuelled a growth of the Gross Domestic Product [GDP]. Furthermore, the recovery of the manufacturing sector had started, and the construction and service sectors had begun booming as a result of people's growing incomes. Agriculture also demonstrated signs of revitalization (*Ekonomicheski Almanakh* 2007; Zaionchkovskaya 2007).

The migration issue remained an important part of the general political debate on social and economic developments in Russia during the transition period. Since the mid-2000s, it has become a key item of the Russian political agenda. Some officials have tended to blame migrants for labour market imbalances and social tensions while other, more far-sighted politicians realize that migrants, both permanent and temporary, are an integral and important part of Russian society on which the country's future depends, at least economically and demographically (Tishkov et al. 2005; Mukomel and Pain 2006).

Rural areas are usually less attractive for migrants due to lower salaries and reduced economic opportunities. At the same time, the production types in rural areas, first of all agriculture, are usually labour-intensive. This is especially true for Russia, where mechanization and automation in agriculture are lagging behind. It is significant here that rural areas passed through the economic crisis of the 1990s much more painfully than urban areas. Many agricultural enterprises, *kolkhoz* and *sovkhoz* [Soviet-style collective farms] were depressed or ruined. The unemployment rate among the rural population in Russia in the late 1990s (as provided by the International Labour Organization) was over 18 per cent (Ministry of Agriculture and Foodstuffs 2000, 9–11). As a result, many rural people left their villages for cities, where they expected to enjoy better economic prospects. Private commercial farming, which was permitted in the early 1990s, was struggling. New farmers faced financial difficulties and did not receive any governmental support. The former fertile lands went to waste and grasslands remained neglected (Nefedova et al. 2001).

The situation has not been helped by a social infrastructure which has been in decline because of the prolonged economic crisis and a lack of financial resources. Schools, medical facilities, entertainments, as well as transport and communications infrastructures have been in need of investments for renovation and development. The difficult socio-economic conditions in which rural communities have found themselves have clearly affected its people beyond the economic hardship they have suffered: a substantial proportion of the rural population, depressed by unemployment and poverty, have turned to alcoholism and other behavioural patterns which have resulted in their economic and social exclusion. Others have found themselves in a 'poverty trap' where they have neither the means of continuing to live in their rural community, nor of moving away (Glezer and Polian 2005). With many people still choosing the latter option, a large number of villages are likely to join the ranks of depopulated rural settlements in the future. According to projections, between 2006 and 2025, the rural population in Russia will decline by 6 million (16 per cent) as a result of both natural decrease and migration outflow (Vishnevsky et al. 2005).

However, there is also reason for cautious optimism. Since 2002, many Russian provinces have experienced the beginning of a recovery of the agricultural sector. The volume of agricultural production has increased by one and a half times between 2002 and 2006, including a threefold growth in the production of private farms. Rural areas seem to constitute a new and promising sphere for Russian and foreign investors. They gained additional stimuli from a special National Project aimed at developing agriculture, which was launched in 2006 (Amosov 2008). Agricultural recovery requires labour resources. Given the depopulation of rural areas, out-migration and an ageing population, international migrants have become a key development resource for the Russian countryside (Vishnevsky et al. 2005).

In the mid-2000s, only 6 per cent of the labour migrants in Russia were employed in the agricultural sector (Federal Migration Service 2008). However, the number of migrant workers in Russian agriculture seems to be on the rise, and this applies especially to migrants from Central Asian states. This is partly due to the growing demand of the Russian agricultural sector for labour at a time when Russian citizens tend to leave the rural areas in favour of work in urban centres. In addition, it has been observed that there is a growing share of migrants originating from rural areas (Laruelle 2007, 110). In contrast to the 1990s, when migrants were mainly coming from capital cities and other urban area, in the 2000s, rural areas and poorer regions in source countries have become increasingly involved in migration flows. This applies in particular to Tajikistan, Uzbekistan, and Kyrgyzstan, where labour migrants originating from rural areas dominate (Soboleva and Chudaeva 2007). In Kyrgyzstan, almost 90 per cent of the 300,000 migrants (a figure officially cited by the Kyrgyz government) come from the Southern rural areas (Laruelle 2007).

In Uzbekistan, a country in which the agricultural population dominates, migrants come mostly from the Ferghana valley. Though fertile and irrigated, the valley is overpopulated and more than half of its population are unemployed, in particular young people (Sadovskaya 2007).

Where no official statistics are available, the geographical origins of migrants can be traced on the basis of destination areas of migrant remittances: in Tajikistan 70 per cent and in Kyrgyzstan 80 per cent of migrant remittances are addressed to rural areas (Mansoor and Quillin 2006). Migrants' skills in agricultural activities encourage them to seek employment in the agricultural sector when abroad. Thus, close to 70 per cent of agricultural workers in Astrakhan and Volgograd Provinces come from Central Asian states (Zotova 2006).

Demographic Perspective

The demographic crisis in rural areas is deeper than in urban areas in terms of population decline and population structure changes. As in other countries, rural youth in Russia are leaving their villages for cities in search of education, jobs and a more comfortable life. Hence, the share of people at retirement age[4] in the rural population is higher than that of the urban population (21 per cent and 18 per cent respectively in 2002). Over 13,000 Russian villages lost their inhabitants completely, and simply disappeared from the map between the two population censuses of 1989 and 2002. Simultaneously, in the Central European and Southern European regions of the Russian Federation the inflow of migrants from the former USSR republics during the 1990s improved the demographic situation. It indicated that international migration could have much potential.

Immigration to Rural Areas: Russia's Central European and Far East Regions

Russia provides a good example of significant differences amongst rural communities in their reception of migrants. The differences may be explained by the factors outlined above under the different perspectives on immigration. Moreover, migration policies may impact on communities and immigrants in a favourable or disadvantageous way.

In receiving countries, migration policies are usually elaborated and administered at national level. Such policies often fail to take into account regional intra-nation disparities, for example, in terms of place-specific labour demands, and the availability (or not) of a social infrastructure which can accommodate an inflow of new people. Furthermore, it is the local community that receives immigrants, and which is most sensitive to the impact of immigration, rather than the nation as a whole. It is at community level where immigrants and the locally established population will inter-act, and it is first and foremost the community

---

4   According to the Russian Labour Code, the retirement age is 60 years for males and 55 years for females.

members who can welcome and engage with immigrants. They are therefore a very important factor in immigrants' integration process. Let us examine such issues in practice by turning to the experiences of communities and immigrants in two different regions of Russia.

Immigrants in Central European Russia

When in the 1990s refugees from the former Soviet republics rushed to Russia, a number of them settled in rural areas of the Central European region. Many of them were inspired by the *State Programme of Settlement of Refugees and Displaced Persons*, which gave special preferences to migrants settling in rural areas, namely by facilitating access to housing and employment. Immigrants, who had often an urban background, tended to choose in favour of rural communities. This was partly due to the availability of cheaper housing, and a personal plot of land, which could provide sustenance for an immigrant family even when other income sources were insecure. According to official data on permanent migration, every third immigrant who has come to Russia in the 1990s from other former Soviet republics has settled in rural areas (Rosstat 2002).

This immigration inflow gave 'a new breath of life' to many rural communities in Central Russia. In the first half of the 1990s, immigrants were mainly ethnic Russians 'returning' from other former Soviet republics to which they or their ancestors had migrated during the Soviet period. On the whole, the integration process of this group was relatively smooth, aided by the presence of relevant language skills and familiarity with the local culture. After 1997, representatives of titular ethnic groups from Central Asian and Caucasus nations, which were earlier a part of the USSR, joined this inflow. Their adaptation was more difficult but they were still considered by local people and politicians as members of the former 'big family', i.e. the Soviet Union. Moreover, this group consisted mainly of educated people, many of whom had qualifications which were valuable to the receiving communities – school teachers, kindergarten teachers, doctors, physicians, dentists, or agricultural specialists. They therefore tended to enjoy good employment prospects.

For some migrants, the settlement in rural communities was no more than a stopover on their way to Russian cities, but others appreciated the quiet style of life, safety and friendliness of rural people and stayed. Place of origin was a factor here which came into play: Azerbaijani and Armenian migrants have most commonly chosen cities as their destination while immigrants from Kazakhstan, Uzbekistan, Kyrgyzstan and Tajikistan, which are predominantly agrarian countries, have been more likely to settle in rural areas. Many migrants from Belarus have also chosen rural areas. According to estimates, over 45 per cent of Belorussian labour migrants in Russia are employed in agriculture (Nefedova 2004).

Migration to rural areas in the Central European Russia have so far consisted of two major flows: seasonal workers and permanent-type employment-led immigrants. Temporary labour migrants from Central Asian states have come to European Russia in spring; they rent land and grow vegetables, potatoes, rice and other cereals. After the crops have been harvested and sold to wholesalers, the migrants return to their places of permanent residence (Nefedova 2004). Large agricultural enterprises and farmers prefer to hire migrant workers not only because they can pay them less and economize on social expenses. In addition, they regard migrants as hard-working, highly productive, and in general without alcohol-related problems, which many local people are struggling with. At the same time, local people often prefer to seek employment in agro-industrial complexes, or to work for foreign-owned large farms, where salaries are higher (Petrov 2004).

Permanent-type immigrants are often former seasonal workers who after several seasonal stays decide to settle. Koreans from Kazakhstan, Uzbeks and Kyrgyz men frequently come with their families or marry Russian women and work as employers or organize private farms. Sometimes, they prefer to settle in depopulated and empty villages and live as relatively closed communities with minimal contacts with local people. However, more typically, they become part of the local society. Their integration is in to some extent dependent on whether they are interested in being included in the village social structure, but also on the willingness of the receiving communities to accept and engage with their immigrants (Drobizheva 2003). The latter process can be shaped by communities' previous experiences with immigrants and other ethnic groups. It is considered that in multi-ethnic Samarskaya and Ulyanovskaya Provinces, rural societies are much more open to foreigners and migrants feel more comfortable there than in the neighbouring Penzenskaya Province, with its traditional mono-ethnic population structure.[5]

However, such structures can change, and so can attitudes. When recently, the Government of Penzenskaya Province faced a dramatic shortage of medical workers in rural areas, which threatened the public health system, they initiated the recruitment of doctors from Kyrgyzstan and Tajikistan. The Health Ministry reported subsequently that the foreign doctors were initially received with caution, but soon met with kindness by local rural patients (Petelin 2006).

The governments of certain provinces in Central Russia have firmly focused their development programmes on immigrants. For example, the *Plan of top priority measures to improve the demographic situation in the Voronezhskaya Province for 2002–2006* includes a section on encouraging immigration to rural areas of the province as an immediate and strategic target (Mukomel 2005, 174). The reason for a growing interest in immigrants in rural areas of the Central European provinces is primarily related to labour shortages caused by a rapidly declining rural population. According to the 2002 Population Census, 47 per cent of those rural settlements which are entirely depopulated are concentrated in the Central Federal District. Of the total number of rural settlements, 38 per cent have a population of less than ten persons, or no inhabitants at all (Goskomstat 2004–05).

---

5 Author's interview with an expert on immigration to Russia, conducted 1 July 2007.

It is worthwhile drawing out the perceived major advantages of immigrants from other former Soviet republics. The disintegration of the USSR into sovereign states has created a specific situation in post-Soviet Eurasia where international migration flows and immigrants' integration can be facilitated by (1) the absence of language barriers. The Russian language, which was the official language in the USSR, is known to a greater or lesser extent by all the residents of the CIS. (2) Similar norms and values were taught and are relevant in the former common country. (3) There is no problem with the recognition of qualifications and diplomas.[6] It is thus not surprising that politicians have expressed a preference for migrants from the former Soviet republics. For example, comments by Olga Semionova, chief for demographic policy at the State Statistic's Committee, are indicative. She underlined Russia's interest in so-called 'desirable migrants', who share Russian education and mentality. (*ITAR-TASS news agency*, Moscow, 20 October 2000.) On several occasions, President Vladimir Putin cited the importance he places on migrants from the post-soviet republics who share Russian cultural values and have a command of the Russian language. Putin commented that 'attracting people from CIS states is the most natural way to replenish our labour resources … as they can be easily adopted to life in Russia' (Putin 2005).

However, despite these favourable factors, a recent study on ethnic Russian and Russian speaking communities from former Soviet republics to the Russian Federation suggests that some form of integration has remained difficult. While such migrants are keen to re-create a 'home' in a territory largely unknown to them, they encounter numerous obstacles posed by the Russian state and society (Flynn 2007). This is in part due to the lack of an integration policy in Russia for migrants from CIS states. It is simply assumed their integration will occur 'automatically' (Mukomel 2005).

There may be differences in integration prospects between rural and urban areas. It has been argued that rural people have been traditionally tolerant towards newcomers. In villages where every person is in full view of others, people tend to be valued by their deeds. Researchers have commented that rural residents are less influenced by xenophobic slogans of political profiteers than their urban equivalents (Mukomel 2005, 226; Petrov 2004, 110–112).

Russia's transition to a market economy has given rise to business initiatives of both, migrants and Russians. Evidence from different provinces indicate that migrants tend to show more initiative as farmers and business owners in comparison to local villagers. Psychologically, this phenomenon can probably be accounted for by the fact that migrants are ready for radical shifts in their lives. They have already shown initiative by having left their place of origin, in many cases with the purpose of improving their economic circumstances. Much energy will be channelled into achieving this goal.

The mass media have portrayed some immigrants as having come to replace the most enterprising, energetic, and determined rural inhabitants, who had moved

---

6   For more details refer to Ivakhnyuk 2008.

to urban areas in the 1990s since they did not believe in the revival of their village (Avdeeva 2007). It has thus been left to immigrants to revitalize the villages which are their new home. For example, in the Leningradskaya Province, a community of 25 Russian-speaking Koreans from Central Asia[7] has initiated the revival of the Molodezhny *sovkhoz*, near the town of Kirishi. They have rented *sovkhoz* land and attracted over 150 local people to help with the renovation of half-ruined greenhouses. This has resulted in a highly productive and profitable farm supplying close-by and remote urban areas (Saint-Petersburg, Murmansk, Arkhangelsk, and Vologda) with fresh vegetables and pickles. The development of a transportation and communication infrastructure in the region is another side of their activities (Timchenko 2001).

Immigrants come to the rural areas of Central European Russia not only from the former Soviet states but also from other countries, albeit in smaller numbers. These cases may indicate a positive trend of a growing participation by foreign enthusiasts in the recovery and development of the Russian countryside. The database of the Federation of Migrants of Russia[8] is rich with real-life cases of immigrants from remote countries, which are often more economically advanced than Russia, and who have successfully settled in rural areas of the Central European provinces in Russia.

This includes a person who has immigrated from India, and who owns a large pig farm in the Kaluga Province of Central Russia. The man, with an agronomy background, produces pork and has a sausage factory. He arrived in Russia in 1996 as a tourist and stayed on. In 2006, he obtained Russian citizenship and is planning to bring his parents to Russia. He employs two Indian people on the farm, and two in the factory. His remaining staff are Russian. In total, about 200 people are employed on the farm.

Another example consists of a British dairy farm owner in the Vladimir Province. The farm was set up 15 years ago in a depressed *sovkhoz*. The General Manager is American, and lives in Russia together with his family – his wife and 7-year-old daughter. He sold his farm in the USA to move to Russia with the idea of regenerating Russian agriculture. The chief veterinary at the farm is Tajik. The farm has 2,000 thoroughbred cows, imported from Holland and produces milk and dairy products. In contrast to neighbouring farms, the farm employs advanced technologies, which may eventually also be used by neighbours. Beyond the farm business, the farm owner organized a mini-bus to take the farm workers' children to school. He thus contributed to the infrastructure and practically supported local

---

7 Koreans were re-settled to the Soviet Central Asian republics from the Far East region in the late 1930s, under Stalin's ethnic repression campaign.

8 The Federation of Migrants of Russia is a non-government organization dealing with the protection of human rights of migrants from non-former-soviet-states to Russia. It has existed since January 2007. The cases referred to were presented by the President of the Federation of Migrants of Russia in his interview with the author on 29 August 2007.

people. He can be regarded as having given this particular community a breath of new life.

A similar example comprises a man who was born into a family of Russian emigrants in the USA. He owns a large meat and dairy farm in Central Russia. He imported cows from Holland, uses advanced machinery and technologies, and creates jobs for local people. One more example has its origin in an interview[9] with a cheese maker and mandarin farmer of Italian origin, who has lived in Russia since 1993, and is married to a Russian woman. He founded an Italian restaurant in Moscow and moved to the Tver Province a few years later as he was captivated by its natural beauty. He invested in an abandoned former food industry complex. Now he is the owner of a large dairy and cattle farm. He employs 25 workers, five of whom are local Russians, and 20 Uzbek labour migrants. In addition, he owns and operates an Italian restaurant, which specializes on Italian-style cheeses, and which is located close to the highway Moscow–Saint-Petersburg. Lunch at his restaurant and a visit to the farm are an 'agro-touristic' stopover for over 800 tourists every month. The owner hopes that his business will inspire his Russian neighbours to follow suit.

These examples demonstrate that international migrants to rural areas in Central European Russia can be an important resource to develop agriculture and related industries. They often invest in local enterprises; they may help with the development of a social infrastructure; they can be interested in working for the welfare of the area in which they live. Their economic participation assists their integration, and may contribute to a situation where their own (and other local) children will decide to stay in these rural areas rather than to leave for cities. It is also worthwhile highlighting that the persons referred to above can be said to have been successfully integrated in their host communities: they felt comfortable with their environment and were keen to contribute by engaging and working with the locally established population. In most cases, they had knowledge of the Russian language, or were learning it; they had adapted some Russian traditions and values, and had made friends with Russian neighbours. They also participated in the social life of communities (Nefedova 2004). Their presence has changed the life of the communities in which they lived, and generally these changes have been for the better.

Chinese Migrants in the Russian Far East

Turning to the Far East region of the Russian Federation, it is worthwhile reminding ourselves of the area's specific characteristics: rich with natural resources and a strategically important area, the region has always faced a lack of population. In fact, because of its climate, only a rather narrow belt of land along the border with China is suitable for agriculture and living. The Northern territories of the Far East region have a climate of a severity which makes permanent residence a challenge,

---

9   Author's interview conducted 11 June 2007.

and even the southern part of the Far East region is sparsely populated. Less than 7 million people live in the Far East Federal District although its territory roughly equals that of the whole of Western Europe. The situation is in stark contrast to that of the highly populated, neighbouring China to the South. More specifically, the three neighbouring Chinese provinces have a population of over 110 million people. The provinces' population density is a remarkable 30 times higher that of the bordering Russian provinces – Jewish Autonomous Province, Amur Province, Primorskiy Territory and Khabarovsk Territory (Gelbras 2001).

What is even more important, the population size of the Russian Far East region is decreasing (because of the outflow to Central Russia) while the population size of North East China is increasing. Over the period of 1990–2005, the outflow of population from the Russian Far East to the central parts of the country was over one and a half million people, so that every sixth citizen has departed (Ponkratova 2005). Lack of population impedes economic development of the region. It hampers in particular the realization of construction and infrastructure projects within the framework of the *Federal Programme of Development of the Far East Region until 2013*.[10]

In this context, Chinese labour migration to the Russian Far East region bordering China seems an important potential contributor to economic development. At the same time, it is a sensitive security issue. Both Russian and foreign experts discuss the issue of Chinese migration primarily in terms of security threats, and in the context of economic, political, demographic, and territorial integrity (Larin 2005; Wishnik 2005; Alexeev 2002; Gelbras 2001). The issue of Chinese migration to the Russian Far East seems over-politicized in political and social discourses, and in the media. It has been claimed in the media that

> [r]ealistically, there are some 250,000 but at any rate no more than 300,000 Chinese of permanent residence in Russia now. So, in general, this issue is not so acute. It is not so in reality. Objectively, of course, there is a demographic threat of expansion. It is plainly the case, given that there are 270 million Chinese in three provinces in the northeast of China, against five to six million Russians in Siberia and the Far East. For the moment, there is no planned, systematic migration policy on the part of Beijing. God forbid that it should appear. It is for that that we need strategic relations between Beijing and Moscow.[11]

Interestingly, however, there is a difference in attitudes of federal authorities and local administrators towards the challenge of Chinese migration. While the Federal Government tends to voice its concern about Chinese expansion, local governors have a more careful approach. They seem to operate on the understanding that

---

10   Author's interview with an expert on immigration to Russia, conducted 25 April 2007.

11   'Russia-India-China "Triangle" Under Discussion by Pundit on Radio Russia', Radio Russia, Moscow, 30 March 2006.

given their demographic and economic situation, regional economies are likely to degrade without migrants, and neighbouring China has the largest labour migration resource (Larin 2005).

The notion of migrants' integration has played a minor role in Russian political discourse and migration policies. It is partly the neglect of the goal of immigrants' integration which has resulted in wide-spread discrimination practices, affected public opinion negatively and caused damaged social cohesion and ethnic-based tension in certain provinces. This applies in particular to communities with migrants from ethnically and culturally distanced countries, like China.

Chinese migrants to the Russian Far East have come mainly from rural communities in Chinese Northern provinces.[12] Even if they originate not from rural but from urban areas, they are likely to have lived in rural places shortly before their migration. Hence, Chinese migrants often seek employment in the Russian agricultural sector where they can apply their skills. For example, in the Jewish Autonomous Province and in Primorsk Territory, the percentages of Chinese labour migrants engaged in agriculture are over 40 and 17 respectively (Ponkratova 2005, 64).

Chinese labour migrants come to Russia in teams of agricultural employees or as tenant farmers, who rent land from Russian agricultural companies. They produce agricultural crops, vegetables and cereals for local markets. When hired by local employers, they are appreciated as hard-working and assiduous workers. They are usually skilled in market gardening, including greenhouse market gardening, which is most relevant for the short agricultural season in the Far East region.

In addition, there are numerous Chinese circular 'commercial migrants' who come to trade with Chinese consumer goods (textile, clothes, garments, tableware, small wares, tea, rice, etc.). They sell their merchandise in city markets or travel across the region and visit every village with their everyday goods. They are usually welcomed by the local population. (Dyatlov et al. 2007).

A small portion of Chinese migrants tend to settle in Russia permanently, for example, by entering into marriage with Russian women. Immigration by families is exceptional. (Ponkratova 2005). The 2002 Population Census recorded 35,000 Chinese people staying in Russia permanently, of whom 30,000 were Chinese citizens. Among them, 9,700 were registered in the Far East Federal District (The 2002 All-Russia Population Census). However, this number is likely to underestimate the scale of Chinese migration to Russia as many Chinese people come as short-term or unregistered migrants, who have not been included in the census data. Estimates of the number of Chinese labour migrants in the Far East region have ranged from 25,000 to 30,000 (Larin 2003; Ponkratova 2005) to 100,000 (Gelbras 2001). What is clear is that their number is growing: in the Primorsky Territory, the Khabarovsk Territory and in the Amur Province, it increased by 2.1, 4.6 and 12.6 times respectively between 1997 and 2006 (Rosstat

---

12 Author's interview with an expert on immigration to Russia, conducted 15 April 2007.

2007). According to state statistics, Chinese migrants comprise more than 65 per cent of the total percentage of the foreign labour force in the area. Hence two out of every three migrant workers employed in the Far East's agricultural sector are of Chinese nationality (Rosstat 2007).

The Chinese migration issue to Russia in general, and to the Russian Far East region in particular, is to some extent affected by the negative perceptions of the past. Such negative perceptions have been fuelled by some politicians. The hundred-year-old myth of an alleged 'Chinese threat' or 'yellow peril' has been revived by political extremists and also been taken up by the mass media to evoke images of a 'dangerous neighbourhood' (Gelbras 2001).

A prominent example of the negative role played by the mass media consists of the so called 'cucumber affair', which was reported in June 2006 in the surroundings of the city of Abakan (the capital of the Republic of Khakassia)[13] (Stateinov 2007). Local newspapers published a number of articles about Chinese farmers who cultivate cucumbers for local markets, and suggested that the fertilizers they used had a double purpose: to increase their crops, but also to poison local people. It was alleged that 'China has a strategic long-term plan to conquer the Russian territories', and that poisoning the Russian population was part of that plan (Dyatlov et al. 2007, 208). Permanent confrontations between Chinese cucumber growers and local authorities lasted for two summer months, followed by repeated scientific tests, and emotional comments by locally established people in newspapers and on television. As a result, Chinese greenhouses in the Rastsvet village[14] were destroyed and all the Chinese workers' documents, such as their visas, medical certificates and work permits were copiously checked. Some of these workers were expelled from Russia for the alleged violation of migration regulations. A headline which could be found in the local newspaper seems to capture the tenor of the conflict: 'Stop the invasion of Chinese vegetable growers!'[15] The 'cucumber affair' was commented upon even in the federal Russian press (Stateinov 2007). Local government officials issued categorical statements, such as 'Chinese citizens do not exert any positive cultural influence on the life of the region' (quoted from: Larin 2005, 57).

With such a politically sensitive background, the integration of Chinese migrants, whether entrepreneurs or seasonal workers, can hardly have gone smoothly. Rather, the contributions made by Chinese migrants to agricultural production and consumer goods supplies for the population of the Far East provinces have often remained under-appreciated by locally established people, in part due to the political and historical myths stirred up by the media. However,

---

13   The Republic of Khakassia is not a part of the Russian Far East Federal District, but Southern Siberia. However, the two regions share similar problems.

14   The village of Rastsvet is located 20 km from the city of Abakan. Close to the village, there is a settlement of Chinese migrants engaged in vegetables growing.

15   *Vecherniye Novosti* [Evening News], (30 August 2006), in Nota Bene, Ust-Abakan.

attitudes by people in the Far East to the Chinese neighbours are likely to also have been influenced by their own experiences. Many people in the region have had contacts with Chinese migrants and may also have travelled to China. Border-cross rules for citizens of the border provinces have been eased, and the Border Service has registered annually over half a million visitors of the citizens of the Amur Province, Primorsky Territory and Khabarovsk Territory to China for business, private purposes or tourism. The economic progress of Chinese cities is impressive.

Concerning Russian people's attitude to Chinese migrants in the Far East, there is the widespread view that Chinese migrants do not usually take an interest in acquiring the Russian language, perhaps with the exception of those who must have a minimum knowledge to succeed in their business, such as travelling traders. Even in cases where immigrants have long-term plans in Russia, they may not have well developed inter-actions with their hosts, and prefer to employ Chinese migrants. They may show little involvement in the local social life, and not be too concerned about the development of the village in which they live (Dyatlov et al. 2007, 71; Ponkratova 2005, 80–81).

It could be that there is a certain relationship between some Chinese migrants' reluctance to get immersed in the Russian culture and the fact that the Russian interpretation of history differs from the official Chinese view. The latter treats the Russian Empire as an invader of Chinese territories. In Chinese school-books, the Chinese–Russian border runs much further to the North than is the case in the commonly recognized global political maps (Gelbras 2001).

There is also the more general issue of Chinese diasporas and their common traits. Such diasporas can, of course, be found all over the world. They are usually characterised by close links to mainland China. Notwithstanding the diversity of these Chinese communities, for example, in terms of social class, regional and political differences, Chinese expatriates tend to manifest an extremely strong sense of a shared identity, and a powerful attachment to China. The country's increasing integration into the global economy, coupled with its 'peaceful rise' as a centre of global power is understandably a cause of pride for many overseas Chinese (Jacques 2008).

This shared identity can also appear to have exclusive characteristics. For example, in Moscow, Chinese people have created their own oasis of Chinese culture with its own closed infrastructure. There is evidence of the existence of semi-legal Chinese restaurants without any sign-posts which would inform the wider public about their existence.[16]

Hence, from the perspectives of both, Chinese and Russians, the issue of integration has been affected by a complex set of historical and political factors. Moreover, there is the common phenomenon of seasonal workers, who only stay in Russia for a number of months, who understandably manifest little interest in

---

16 Author's interview with an expert on immigration to Russia, conducted 25 June 2007.

engaging with local communities, or in the economic and social progress of the areas of their short-term stay. Sometimes, their focus on short-term gains may have long-term consequences. For example, the plots rented by some Chinese vegetables growers for a season often stay non-productive for several years because of over-use of growth-stimulating chemicals (Stateinov 2007).

There is the wide-spread perception that a lack of integration is the most serious challenge of Chinese migration to the Russian Far East region. It is especially topical in the context of a projected growth in numbers of Chinese labour migrants. In the Amur Province, the Primorsky Territory and the Khabarovsk Territory, the numbers are estimated to increase from 27,000 in 2006 up to between 120,000 and 180,000 by the year 2012, according to most cautious regional labour market forecasts (Ponkratov 2007, 132).

Revisiting Migration Policies: Focus on Rural Areas

In 2006–2007 migration policies in the Russian Federation were revisited and dramatically revised.[17] The new Federal Laws on migration management put in force in January 2007 reflect a fundamentally new approach to migration policies: the aim is to encourage regular migration to Russia. Clear and easy-to-follow procedures are proposed for the purpose of entry into the country, obtaining residence permit and work permission for citizens of the former Soviet states. The migration legislation reform is aimed at attracting both permanent immigrants and temporary labour migrants from CIS countries.

With these new laws, the process of hiring CIS citizen has become simpler for both employee and employer. There are now far fewer requirements for the temporary employment of people coming from the CIS countries with which Russia has visa-free arrangements. People from these countries are now able to receive a work permit without prior recommendation or job offer from a Russian employer. The permit should be issued within 10 days (as opposed to 25–31 days prior to the law change). The only documents required consist of an identity document, an immigration card, and an HIV test result. The payment of a state fee (Euro 30) is also required. A work permit for one year allows holders to change their employer during their stay in Russia within the administrative unit (province) where it has been issued. The stay can also be prolonged for another year.

The latest amendments aim at helping foreigners to come out of the shadows and receive legal status. In 2007, over 1.2 million work permits were granted to

---

17   The new stage of migration policy in Russia is reflected in: the *Federal Law on Registering foreign citizens and persons without citizenship in the Russian Federation* (put in force on 15.01.2007); the *Federal Law on Amendments to the Federal Law on legal status of foreign citizens in the Russian Federation* (put in force on 15.01.2007); *the 2006–12 State Programme on providing support for voluntary resettlement of compatriots to the Russian Federation* (adopted by President Decree 22.06.2006).

migrant workers from CIS countries. The number thus doubled compared with 2006, and trebled compared with 2005. However, by mid-2008, it became clear that the new laws, which have been welcomed by migrants, conflicted with unreasonably small foreign workers quotas. The process of legalization of labour migration to Russia, which started in 2007, experienced a setback. With no reliable methods for calculating the demand for foreign labour (i.e. no efficient interaction schemes between different state authorities, and no data collection and submission programmes), quotas became the stumbling block for the new liberal model of labour migration management. Notwithstanding, the 'philosophy' of the recent labour migration management reform suggests new attitudes of the Russian State towards migrants from the former Soviet states by giving them preferences in terms of stay and employment legalization in Russia. This can be regarded as the major value of the reform. An attempt to make Russia a welcoming country will have an impact on the volume of immigration and can consequently contribute to its demographic and economic interests.

Russia's new approach to migration policies may have a considerable impact on international migration to rural areas. This applies in particular to the *2006–12 State Programme on providing support for the voluntary resettlement of compatriots to the Russian Federation* (Federal Migration Service 2006), which gives new incentives to compatriots who live in other countries and have a desire to return to Russia. The Programme is guided by the emerging idea of attracting people with some link to Russia who, for various reasons, are living outside the country. It is thereby assumed that the Programme would be attracting people whose integration is likely to be least problematic. The participants of the Programme are released from the compulsory conditions for obtaining Russian citizenship as postulated by the 2002 Russian Federal Law On Citizenship, which includes a five-year uninterrupted stay in Russia, a legal source of income and knowledge of the Russian language.[18]

The Programme aims to attract immigrants and facilitate their integration through the following means: compatriots and their family members who would like to move to Russia for permanent residence are provided with State guarantees and social support, including refund of travel expenses and transportation of their paraphernalia; indemnities of the State duty for the paper work to regularize their status in the territory of the Russian Federation; a one-off grant (travelling allowance); in the absence of an income from labour or business activities, a monthly allowance is provided up to the point at which Russian citizenship is granted, albeit for no longer than six months; a 'compensation packet', including free access to pre-school institutions, secondary education, vocational training, social welfare, health care, and assistance in job seeking; and a simplified scheme of getting Russian citizenship within six months (instead of the usual five years period).

The Programme could serve the pragmatic purposes of alleviating the demographic crisis and labour shortages in particular regions of Russia. The latter

18 See http://www.regnum.ru/news/1063651.html.

is aided by the fact that preference is given to those compatriots who are willing to move to areas where the economic and demographic situation needs urgent human inflow. This includes, of course, the rural areas of the Central European and the Far East regions of Russia.

At the initial stage of the Programme, twelve 'pilot' provinces of the Russian Federation are participating in absorbing migrants who come to Russia as participants of the Programme. For example, the Tambov Province will accept over 20,000 immigrants, mainly from the CIS states, who authorities prefer to settle in rural areas. Over the past years, the rural population of the Province has decreased annually because of natural decrease and the outflow of the population to bigger economic centers – Moscow and Saint-Petersburg. The village named *Novy* [New] for the settlement of 200 families of the *Doukhobor*[19] from Georgia is under construction in the Tambov Province. Moreover, houses specifically constructed for immigrants will include social infrastructure objects like food stores, first-aid posts and geriatric social homes.

Later on, all interested provinces can benefit from the State-supported immigrant inflow. In total, over one million persons are expected to re-settle to Russia as participants of the Programme within five years.[20] If successful, realization of the Programme can contribute to the revival of the Russian countryside, at least in some areas. Supported by the State, immigrants could contribute to the development of the areas in which they settle. Immigration could thus become of even greater significance to rural than to urban areas.

However, three years of the realization period have had disappointing results. During 2007, when 50,000 re-settlers were expected to come to Russia, the actual number of newcomers arriving through the Programme was less than 400 persons[21] while the total number of people who came to Russia for permanent residence in 2007 was 286,900 (Rosstat 2008). The reasons for low levels of effectiveness of the Programme are mainly of legal and organizational nature. Major legal obstacles include the requirement to hold Russian citizenship only, without the possibility of dual citizenship. Moreover, a 30 per cent income tax rate is levied during the initial six months of stay in Russia compared to a 13 per cent income tax rate applied to Russian citizens. A lack of housing of appropriate quality, high

---

19   A religious sect which traditionally lives separate from other religions in close communities, and that decided to resettle in Russia as an entire community. In all other cases of the Resettlement Programme, compact settlement has not been witnessed.

20   The Programme is to be realized in three stages: *the first stage* (2006): development of legislation assigned to provide the legal base for the realization of the Programme; assessment of demand for human resources by the administrative units (republics, provinces, and territories) of the Russian Federation; information campaign; *the second stage* (2007–8): resettlement of the Programme participants; integration of compatriots; evaluation of the results; if necessary, modification of further regional projects of immigration encouragement; *the third stage* (2009–12): further realization of resettlement regional projects; evaluation of the results of the Programme; if necessary, shaping of a new Programme.

21   See http://globalrus.blogspot.com/2007_12_01_archive.html.

prices for dwellings, the inaccessibility of mortgages for re-settlers and limited temporary accommodation impede re-settlement processes. While rural areas may suffer in particular from any such problem, their difficult situation is further exacerbated by a lack of jobs. This can be demonstrated with the Kaluga Province, which has called for Programme participants to settle in rural areas: almost 90 per cent of the total number of 768 newcomers who arrived between September 2007 and October 2008 have chosen an urban residence, primarily because of wider job opportunities.[22] Simultaneously, according to Valeri Loginov, the Deputy Governor of Kaluga Province, about 40 per cent of potential immigrants would like to live in rural areas (Filippova 2007, 21).

In 2008, the realization of the Programme gained speed. Measures to stimulate the re-resettlement of compatriots at federal level[23] were accompanied by initiatives of local authorities at province level. Access to housing for Programme participants was especially facilitated. For example, the Tambov Province governor decreed the possibility for re-settlers to participate in the provincial programme '*Social Development of Rural Areas up to 2010*'.[24] This will open for them the possibility of moving into newly built dwellings on an equal footing with local villagers.

Conclusion

What can be gleaned from having looked at the two Russian regions, and their experiences with immigrants to rural areas? Some of the experiences in the central European region have demonstrated that, of course, historical, socio-economic and demographic factors can all contribute to the nature of immigrants' reception by their host communities. If communities have a long-standing experience with immigration, and have seen this phenomenon to improve their living standard, they are likely to welcome immigrants; if there is a labour demand which immigrants can help to meet, they are likely to be regarded as a useful resource; if rural communities would disappear off the map unless they can attract new community members, immigrants are likely to be seen as a possible solution to demographic challenges.

In addition, examples of immigrants' experiences and contributions have shown that individual motivation is also an important factor to both, communities' economic and social development, and the extent to which immigrants are likely to see their abode as a permanent 'home'. Similarly, migrants' status, for example, whether seasonal or permanent, can indirectly affect the kind of reception from the receiving communities. The latter may be perceived as having more of an interest in the social and economic development of a community, especially if

---

22　See http://www.regnum.ru/news/1070054.html.

23　http://www.regnum.ru/news/1000051.html.

24　http://www.regnum.ru/news/1046111.html.

such immigrants have arrived as families. Such observations seem particularly useful when we consider the situation in Russia's Far East.

Here, policy makers have focused on 'compatriots' in their strategy to encourage migration to rural areas. The assumption is that if a language, educational system, culture and history are shared to a great extent, this will facilitate 'integration'. However, it appears that while such shared experiences and knowledge may well help migrants to be socially and economically active, this is neither sufficient, nor necessarily required for a satisfactory life in rural communities. The latter point has been demonstrated by those immigrants to Central European Russia who had no prior link to Russia at all, but who appear to be regarded even by Russian officials as 'model immigrants' in terms of the contributions they have made to their communities. The former point has been proven by the fact that a number of 'compatriots' have attempted but failed to make rural Russia their home.

Clearly, for some immigrants, rural communities will always be no more than a stepping stone on their way to cities, while others will appreciate the kind of life rural communities can offer, and will settle there. Hence, policies which focus on certain ethnic or national groups of immigrants (rather than on all immigrants who would like to live and work in rural communities) seem too narrow to reap the best possible success for rural communities.

The fact that the Far East currently benefits in particular from Chinese migrants can further underline this point, and is another aspect which policies should consider. Immigration from China is bound to continue, given the demographic imbalances in the Far East region. In view of the concerns about the integration of Chinese people into Russian (rural) communities, ignoring the issue by focusing on an entirely different group of immigrants will not solve the perceived challenge Chinese migrants pose. Rather, such policies are likely to have the difficult effect of discrimination and exclusion of 'non-compatriot' potential and actual immigrants; they may also perpetuate prejudice and negative attitudes towards 'non-compatriot', new community members, thereby encouraging social tensions.

There are also issues which need to be addressed at community level. Rural people have the reputation of being traditionally tolerant of newcomers. However, when rural communities are affected by negative historical experiences, or by the perception that immigrants are reluctant to engage with them, they can ostracize 'undesirable' neighbours, and even encourage them to leave. Given this situation, local decision-makers need to be sensitive to their community members' historical experiences, and possibly address myths and prejudices which are rooted in the past, and which negatively affect immigrants today.

Another particularly rural aspect of immigration to Russia is the fact that land is obviously of special value for rural people. Maintaining the fertility of soil is clearly of vital importance for the sustainability of agricultural areas. A situation has arisen where seasonal workers from Central Asian states, who repeatedly come to the Central European region of Russia to grow vegetables, fruit or cereals, are appreciated for their reasonable land treatment. By contrast, some Chinese seasonal migrants in the Far East territories, who apply soil-exhausting technologies, have attracted negative attention from some local agrarians. Policies need to be developed here which help to protect the land through control of its use, resulting in the prevention of negative impacts. This will not only help all agrarians, but will also change the currently negative image of some immigrants.

The labour-intensive nature of some types of agricultural production and the high demand for seasonal workers make international migrants an important element of rural development, especially in areas where there is a high demand for labour. The countryside may discourage employment-led migrants by the fact that wages tend to be lower. However, rural areas also have clear advantages, including some of a material nature. Migrants are driven to rural areas by cheaper housing and access to a piece of land if they intend to become permanent residents. Temporary and seasonal workers can access a familiar type of job if they originate from rural areas in their home countries, and immigrants who act as rural entrepreneurs can have easy access to business facilities as local villagers seem less businesslike. Due to these reasons, rural destinations are chosen especially by immigrants from underdeveloped rural regions in source countries. If the material incentives can be provided in the future, this trend is likely to continue.

Though international migration to rural areas is still at the margins of the academic debate, it has gained importance in public debates at local level, especially in those areas in which rural migrants are already the reality. In many cases, the numbers of migrants to (rural) Russia are likely to grow as a result of the imbalance between demographic decline and economic progress. The experiences of communities differ for historical, socio-economic, demographic and contemporary political reasons, which in turn partly shape the experiences of contemporary immigrants.

A lesson to draw from this study is that processes of integration are two-dimensional as they involve both, the receiving community as well as immigrants themselves. On part of the host community, tolerance and openness, the willingness to welcome immigrants, an understanding of the advantages of additional human resource and the readiness for inter-cultural dialogue are important factors in the integration process. The type of status of the migrant, i. e. permanent, temporary, seasonal, or undocumented, their ethnic background, their future migration plans and strategies are significant on part of international migrants. Those who come to rural areas with their families, especially with children, and intend to stay there long-term, are more likely to be welcomed and invited to participate in rural development, economically, socially and culturally.

Further in-depth studies of rural social structures and immigrants' integration experiences and strategies could generate better insights into effective migration policies and support mechanisms which 'fit' specific areas. Such policies and mechanisms should assist established and new community members to jointly shape the economic, social and cultural future of their area. While the main action needs to be at local level, the role of the Federal Government will be to introduce relevant policies, and to provide associated legal and financial support.

References

Alexeev, M. (2002), 'Migration in the Russian Far East: Security Threats and Incentives for Cooperation in Primorsky Krai', in Judith Thornton and Charles E. Ziegel (eds), *Russia's Far East: A Region at Risk* (Seattle: University of Washington Press), 319–47.

Amosov, A. (2008), O strategii razvitiya agrarnoi sferi [On Agriculture Development Strategy] In: *Economist*, N:9, 48–53 [in Russian].

Avdeeva, S. (2007), Pereselentsi delayut vibor [Re-settlers Make Their Choice] In: *Zemlyaki* [Compatriots], N:11, November, 21–24 [in Russian].

Ekonomicheski Almanakh (2007), [Economic Digest 2007] Annual edition of the Faculty of Economics of the Moscow State Lomonosov University [in Russian].

Federal Migration Service (2006), *Gosudarstvennaya Programma sodeystviya dobrovolnomu pereseleniyu sootechestvennikov v Rossiyu na 2006–2012 gody* [The 2006–2012 State Programme on providing support for voluntary resettlement of compatriots to the Russian Federation] <http://www.fms.gov.ru/programs/list.php>, accessed 21 April 2008. [in Russian].

Federal Migration Service (2008), *Monitoring legalnoi (zakonnoi) vneshnei trudovoi migratsii v Rossii za 2006–2007 godi* [Monitoring of regular international labour migration in Russia in 2006–2007] (Moscow: Federal Migration Service) [in Russian].

Gelbras, V. (2001), *Kitaiskaya Realnost Rossii* [The Chinese Reality of Russia]. (Moscow: Muravey Publishing House) [in Russian].

Glezer, O. and Polian, P. (eds) (2005), *Rossia i yeye regiony v XX veke: terrotiria-rasseleniye-migratsii* [Russia and its Regions in the XX century: Territory-Population-Migrations] (Moscow: OGI) [in Russian].

Goskomstat (State Committee on Statistics of the Russian Federation) (2004–2005), *All-Russian Population Census, 2002.*

Filippova, O. (2007), Nevelikoye pereselenie [Smallish Re-settlement]. *Migratsia* [Migration], N:4, December, 20–21 [in Russian].

Iontsev, V. (1998), 'Kratkii istoricheskii ocherk immigratsii v Rossiyu i emigratsii iz Rossii' [Brief Historical Overview of Immigration to Russia and Emigration from Russia], in *Naseleniye i krizisi* [Population and Crises]. Scientific series, vol. 4 (Moscow: Dialog-MGU, 54–77) [in Russian].

—— (1999), 'Mezhdunarodnaya migratsiya naseleniya: teoriya I istoriya izucheniya' [International Migration of Population: Theories and History of Studies]. Scientific series *International Migration of Population: Russia and the Contemporary World*, vol. 3 (Moscow: Dialog-MGU) [in Russian].

—— and Ivakhnyuk, I. (2002), 'Russia in the World Migration Flows: Trends of the Last Decade (1992–2001)', in *World in the Mirror of International Migration.* Iontsev, V. (ed.), Scientific series *International Migration of Population: Russia and the Contemporary World*, vol. 10 (Moscow: MAX Press), 34–78.

Ivakhnyuk, I. (2005), *Mezhdunarodnaya trudovaya migratsiya* [International Labour Migration]. (Moscow: TEIS) [in Russian].

—— (2008), *Yevraziyskaya migratsionnaya systema: teoriya i politika* [Eurasian Migration System: Theories and Politics]. (Moscow: MAX Press) [in Russian].

Jacques, M. (2008), 'As China's power grows, the diaspora starts to flex its worldwide muscle', *The Guardian*, 11 June 2008 <http://www.guardian.co.uk/commentisfree/2008/jun/11/china.comment>, accessed 1 July 2008.

Kabuzan, V. (1983), *Kak zaselyalsya Dalniy Vostok* [How the Russian Far East was populated]. (Khabarovsk) [in Russian].

Kaufman A.A. (1905), *Pereseleniye I kolonizatsiya* [Resettlements and Colonization] (Saint Petersburg) [in Russian].

Krasinets, E., Kubishin Y. and Tiuriukanova Y. (2000), *Nelegalnaya migratsiya v Rossii* [Illegal migration in Russia]. (Moscow: Academia) [in Russian].

Larin, V. (2003), *Kitaitsy v Rossii vchera i segodnya* [The Chinese people in Russia yesterday and today] (Moscow: Muravey Publishing House) [in Russian].

—— (2005), 'Chinese in the Russian Far East: Regional Views', in Akaha, T. and Vassilieva, A. (eds), *Crossing National Borders: Human Migration Issues in Northeast Asia* (Tokyo – New York – Paris: United Nations University Press), 47–67.

Laruelle, M. (2007), 'Central Asian Labor Migrants in Russia', *The China and Eurasia Forum Quarterly*. August, 5:3, 102–120.

Drobizheva, L. (2003), *Sotsialniye problemi mezhnatsionalnikh otnosheniy v postsovetskoy Rossii* [Social Problems of Interethnic Relations in Post-Soviet Russia] (Moscow: Centre for Common Human Values) [in Russian].

Dyatlov, V., Abdulova I., Kovalskaya M., Okhotnikov A., Pinigina Yu, and Ryzhova N. (eds) (2007), *Migranty i diaspory na Vostoke Rossii: praktiki vzaimodeistviya s obshestvom i gosudarstvom* [Migrants and diasporas in the Russian East: practices of interrelations with the society and the State]. (Moscow-Irkutsk: Natalis) [in Russian].

Flynn, M. (2007), 'Reconstructing 'Home/lands' in the Russian Federation: Migrant-Centred Perspectives of Displacement and Resettlement', *Journal of Ethnic and Migration Studies*, Vol 33, Issue 3, April.

Iontsev, V. (ed.) (1998–2006), *International Migration of Population: Russia and Contemporary World* (Moscow: MAX Press). <http://www.demostudy.ru/menu.htm>, accessed 21 April 2008.

Mansoor, A. and Quillin, B. (eds) (2006), *Migration and Remittances. Eastern Europe and the Former Soviet Union* (Washington DC: World Bank).

Ministry of Agriculture and Foodstuffs (2000), *Ezhegodny doklad po resultatam monitoringa* [Annual Report on Monitoring Results]. (Moscow: VNII selskogo hozyaistva) [in Russian].

Moiseenko, V. (2007), 'Izucheniye migratsii v Rossii vo vtoroi polovine XIX – nachale XX veka' [Migration Studies in Russia in the second half of the 19th – the beginning of the 20th centuries], in Iontsev, V. (ed.) (2007),

Proceedings of the International Conference 'Migration and Development' (Fifth Valenteevskiye Chteniya) 13–15 September 2007, Moscow, Russia, vol. 2, 557–63, (Moscow: Moscow University Press, SP Mysl') [in Russian].

Mukomel, V. (2005), *Migratsionnaya politika v Rossii: postsovetskiye konteksty* [Migration policies of Russia: post-Soviet contexts]. (Moscow: Institute for Sociology of the Russian Academy of Sciences, Dipol) [in Russian].

Mukomel, V. and Pain, E. (2006), *Nuzhni li migranti Rossiiskomu obshestvu?* [Does Russian Society Need Migrants?]. (Moscow: Liberal Mission Foundation) [in Russian].

Nefedova, T. (2004), 'Nerusskoye selskoye khozyaistvo' [Non-Russian agriculture], *Demoscope Weekly*, no. 179 [in Russian]. <http://demoscope.ru/weekly/2004/0179/analit06.php>, accessed 21 April 2008.

Nefedova T., Polian P. and Treiwish, A. (eds), (2001), *Gorod i derevnia v evropeiskoy Rossii: sto let peremen* [City and Village in European Russia: Hundred Years of Changes] (Moscow: OGI) [in Russian].

Petelin, G. (2006), 'Gastarbaitery v belykh halatakh' [Guest workers in doctor's smocks], in *Russkiy Kurier* [Russian Courier] 35(567), [in Russian]. <www.ruscourier.ru/archive.php?id=1745>, accessed 21 April 2008,

Petrov, V. (2004), *Migratsiya naseleniya i etnicheskiye migranty v sovremennoi Rossii* [Migration of Population and Ethnic Migrants in Contemporary Russia]. (Krasnodar: Kuban State University) [in Russian].

Ponkratov, R. (2007), *Mezhdunarodnaya trudovaia migratsiia na Dalnem Vostoke Rossii* [International Labour Migration in the Russian Far East]. Unpublished PhD thesis. Moscow State Lomonosov University [in Russian].

Ponkratova, L. (2005), 'International labour migration in the Far East of Russia: realities and prospects', in Iontsev, V. (ed.), *Labour Migration. Management Issues and Migrant Workers Rights' Protection in Russia*. Scientific series 'International Migration of Population: Russia and the Contemporary World', vol. 14 (Moscow: TEIS), 62–72.

Putin V. (2005), Speech at the Security Council meting of the Russian Federation on 17 March 2005 [in Russian]: <http://www.kremlin.ru/text/appears/2005/03/85300/shtml>.

Rosstat (2002), *The Statistical Yearbook of Russia* (Moscow: The National Statistics Committee of the Russian Federation).

Rosstat (2007), *Trud i zanyatost v Rossii* [Labour and Employment in Russia] Statistical Bulletin. (Moscow: The National Statistics Committee of the Russian Federation)[in Russian].

Rosstat (2008), *Rossia v tsifrakh* [Russia in Numbers]. Statistical Bulletin. Moscow [in Russian].

Shpilevskiy M.M. (1871), *Politika narodonaseleniya v tsarstvovaniye Ekaterini II* [Population Policies during the Reign of Catherine II] (Odessa) [in Russian].

Sadovskaya, Y. (2007), 'International Labour Migration, Remittances and Development in Central Asia: Towards Regionalization or Globalization?', in Iontsev. V. (ed.), *Migration and Development*. Scientific Series 'International

Migration of Population: Russia and the Contemporary World', Vol. 20 (Moscow), 163–184.

Soboleva S. and Chudaeva, O. (2007), 'Chelovecheskii capital trudovoi migratsii' [Human capita of labour migration], in *Proceedings of the International Conference Migration and Development (Fifth Valenteevskiye Chteniya)* 13–15 September (Moscow, Russia), 103–118 [in Russian].

Stateinov, A. (2007), 'Kitaiskiy biznes: mertviy pomidor' [Chinese Business: A Dead Tomato], in *Zemlyaki* [Compatriots]. Information and Analytical Journal of the Federal Migration Service of Russia 7: 73–6 (Moscow). [in Russian].

Timchenko, S. (2001), 'Vyzhivaniye v teplichnikh usloviyah' [Survival in greenhouses], in *Nezavisimaya Gazeta*, 133 (2443) [in Russian].

Tishkov V., Zaionchkovskaya, Zh. and Vitkovskaya, G. (2005), *Migrations in the Countries of the Former Soviet Union* (Global Commission on International Migration).

United Nations (2006), *International Migration 2005*. (New York).

Ushkalov, I. and Malakha I. (1999), *Utechka umov: masshtaby, prichini i posledstviya* [Brain Drain: Scales, Reasons, and Effects]. (Moscow: Editorial URSS) [in Russian].

Verlin, Y. (2002), 'Cherniy nal i zheltaya ugroza' ['Black Cash' and Yellow Danger], in *Expert* 11, [in Russian].

Vishnevsky A., Kvasha Y., Kharkova T. and Sherbakova Y. (2005), 'Rossiyskoye selo v demograficheskom izmerenii' [Rural Russia in demographic dimension], in *Demoscope Weekly*, 253–4 [in Russian]. <http://demoscope. ru/weekly/2006/0253/tema01.php>, accessed 21 April 2008.

Vitkovskaya, G. and Panarin S. (eds) (2000), *Migratsiya i bezopasnost v Rossii* [Migration and Security in Russia]. (Moscow: The Carnegie Endowment, Interdialect) [in Russian].

Vorobyeva, O. (2001), *Migratsionnaya politika* [Migration Policies], in Scientific Series 'Migration of Population'. Supplement to the Journal *Migration in Russia* [in Russian].

Wishnick, E. (2005), 'Migration and Economic Security: Chinese Labour Migrants in the Russian Far East', in Akaha, T. and Vassilieva, A. (eds), *Crossing National Borders: Human Migration Issues in Northeast Asia* (Tokyo – New York – Paris: United Nations University Press), 68–92.

Yamzin, I.L. and Voshinin, V.P. (1926), *Ucheniye o kolonizatsii i pereseleniyakh* [Studies on Colonization and Resettlements] (Moscow) [in Russian].

Zaionchkovskaya, Zh (2002), 'Desyat let SNG – desyat let migratsiy mezhdu stranami-uchastnikami' [Ten years of the CIS – ten years of migrations between the participating states], in *Naseleniye i obshestvo* [Population and Society] 62 [in Russian].

—— (2007), 'Pochemu Rossii neobkhodima immigratsionnaya politika?' [Why Russia needs immigration policy?], in Zaionchkovskaya Zh., Molodikova I. and Mukomel V. (eds), *Metodologiya i metody izucheniya migratsionnykh protsessov* [Methodology and Methods to Study Migration Processes] 114–41, (Moscow: Center for Migration Studies) [in Russian].

Zotova, N. (2007), Pochti sem'desiat protsentov sel'khozkul'tur Astrakhanskoi i Volgogradskoi oblastei vyrashchivaetsia migrantami iz Srednei Azii," [Close to 70 per cent of agriculture in Astrakhan and Volgograd is cultivated by Central Asian migrants], Ferghana.ru, 13 September 2006, <http://www.ferghana.ru/article.php?id=4590> [in Russian].

Chapter 8

Conclusion: Comparative Perspectives on Rural Immigrants' Integration

Birgit Jentsch and Myriam Simard

What insights can be gained into rural immigration on the basis of the experiences in the different countries and the case studies covered in this book? In general, recent migration flows have been very complex. Across the developed world, they have been characterised by increasing seasonal, temporary and circular migration, in rural areas benefiting especially (but not exclusively) the labour intensive and seasonal agricultural sector. Some important differences have been noticeable. For example, educational levels of rural immigrants in Northern Europe are predominantly high, mixed in Southern Europe and Canada, and predominantly low in the USA, with some immigrants being highly skilled. Despite their different backgrounds, rural immigrants tend to be in poorly paid jobs with difficult working conditions. In fact, a striking observation has been the many shared experiences across the countries which have occurred even with the different contexts and characteristics of rural immigration.

One common experience amongst the countries and regions included in this book consists of the fact that immigrants have made significant contributions to addressing important challenges in rural areas. Economically, they have been seen, and have acted, as a solution to skills and labour shortages. From immigrants' perspective, as mentioned above, a frequently shared experience seems to be their either temporary or continuous vulnerable position in the labour market, often independent of their qualifications and skills. Even those immigrants who have been successful in the labour market, and who are able to practice their profession, are likely to have gone through a phase in which they found themselves at the bottom of the employment hierarchy. Let us look in more detail at the factors which shape immigrants' employment, social and community life experiences.

Immigrants in Basic Skilled Jobs

The industries in which immigrants in basic skilled jobs are particularly likely to be employed tend to be similar across several countries studied here. In Ireland, Scotland, Southern Europe and in North America, immigrants to rural areas are well represented in agriculture (a sector in which they can also often be found in Russia), construction, the social services, food processing and the service sector.

Several chapters referred to the secondary labour market in relation to immigrants' employment. Segmented labour market theorists have attempted to understand the position of immigrant and locally established workers in the labour market. At the risk of oversimplifying their deliberations, one focus has been on the fact that employment confers social status. Low status jobs are shunned by the locally established population, making space for those whose main motif for employment is financial, rather than status related. Hence, especially newly arrived immigrants tend to be inclined to accept jobs at the bottom of the employment hierarchy. This process may be reinforced by employers' stereotypical assumptions about ethnic groups' work ability, as well as immigrants' and employers' reliance on their personal networks for accessing jobs.

Social status concerns were highlighted in the Greek studies in different ways. Immigrants often assumed symbolic roles to demonstrate the social prestige of a new 'farmer-boss'. At least in the first few years of the arrival of immigrants, locally established farmers attempted to prove their social and economic position in local society by avoiding manual work themselves, and employing migrant labour instead. Status concerns are also part of the reason for the low employment participation rates of locally established young people in rural Greece (and, indeed, elsewhere in rural Southern Europe). Local youth aim to gain the highest possible employment status by delaying labour market entry, usually by studying, until a desirable position has been found. They will prefer employment in urban rather than in rural areas, since jobs available in the latter will rarely satisfy their aspirations. In part due to these status concerns, and despite relatively high levels of unemployment in Greece, young immigrants are able to find low quality employment if they accept the poor working conditions which the locally established population reject. For young male immigrants to rural communities, this applies especially to jobs in agriculture, and the heavy industry. For women, the main activities seem to be caring for the elderly, and domestic work (Baldwin-Edwards 2002a).

In other countries, social status issues appeared to be less pronounced. In rural Ireland and Scotland, immigrants have predominantly been seen as an important source for hard to fill jobs. In contrast to Greece, this has occurred in the context of tight labour markets with low rates of unemployment. The main problem with available jobs here may not be the low status associated with them. Rather, these jobs tend to be physically demanding, and have unpredictable hours, thus making an employment-life balance difficult. They also yield low pay. Employment of this kind is particularly difficult to accept for those locally established people who are interested in social participation and maintaining their social networks, or who have family obligations.[1] Such employment may, however, be of interest to

---

1   Today's young people in particular are interested in a life which balances their professional, family and personal aspirations. They are often aiming at a good quality life concerning their working hours and their time to pursue leisure activities. See, for example, Desjardins, B. and Simard, M. (2008), *Motifs de migration, besoins et insertion*

newly arrived immigrants, who are prepared to live temporarily in overcrowded (and therefore affordable) accommodation, and who are attracted by earnings which are much higher than what could be achieved in their countries of origin. However, as has been found in the UK, once immigrants' aspirations may include becoming socially, culturally, as well as economically established, such jobs will become increasingly unsuitable for them. Employers would thus have to rely on a continuous inflow of new immigrants.

However, at least in the context of the EU15,[2] for economic and demographic reasons, the high immigration levels post-2004 from the accession states (commented upon in the Scottish and Irish chapters) will not be sustainable in the long-run. The new EU member states have experienced strong economic growth, which has improved employment opportunities and increased wage levels. In many cases, depending on the geographical area and a person's skills and qualifications, it has now become an attractive option for immigrants to return, and incentives to emigrate have been reduced. Demographically, most accession states have rapidly ageing and eventually shrinking populations. They do not have the potential for continued, large scale immigration (Jentsch and MacDonald 2007).

Highly Qualified Immigrants and Professional Jobs

Immigrants in most countries covered in this book have predominantly been found in low or semi-skilled jobs, and in low paid employment. While the Canadian chapter focused on general practitioners working in their profession in remote rural areas in Quebec, even here, many of the immigrant physicians had experienced an extended period of employment in poor jobs (for example, in the service industry) while waiting for the recognition of their qualifications. This drawn out process took on average eight years. Similar experiences of highly qualified and skilled immigrants working in basic skilled jobs have been observed in Ireland and Scotland, which could also partly be attributed to difficulties with the recognition of qualifications in these two countries. Additional factors seem to distinguish the situation of immigrants there from the position of the physicians in Quebec. In this Canadian province, the following three conditions were in place, which are currently missing in the Scottish and Irish case: first, since the early 1990s, immigration to rural areas has been actively promoted by a government policy and

---

des jeunes néo-ruraux dans Brome-Missisquoi ainsi qu'une synthèse comparative avec les jeunes néo-Arthabaskiens, Rapport de recherche de l'INRS-UCS. Montréal, octobre 2008, 83 p. Available on line (French language only) www.ucs.inrs.ca/default.asp?p=rr, accessed 19 January 2009.

    2   EU15 refers to the member countries in the European Union prior 1 May 2004, comprising the following 15 countries: Austria, Belgium, Denmark, Finland, France, Germany, Greece, Ireland, Italy, Luxembourg, Netherlands, Portugal, Spain, Sweden, United Kingdom.

action plan. Second, the need for physicians in rural areas had been established and immigrants been identified as a possible solution to the problem. Third, since the early 1980s, a specific programme has existed to encourage immigrant physicians with credentials from outside Canada and the United States to formally commit themselves to practice in rural and remote areas for a certain period of time. It has been discussed in the Canadian chapter that despite support measures in place, immigrant physicians' retention has proven sometimes difficult due to professional, social and familial factors. Especially the latter draws our attention to the importance of meeting the needs of immigrants, as well as their families. Included here are educational opportunities for children, professional opportunities for spouses, and the quality of community life and community relationships.

The key aspects of some of the measures adopted in Quebec seem worthwhile considering also in other national or sub-national contexts. This includes exploring the need for (certain types) of professionals in the first place. While in countries such as Ireland and Scotland, the lack of progression opportunities for immigrants has been deplored, little has been done to establish exactly what type of higher qualifications immigrants have, how to accelerate their recognition, to what extent there is a need for them in rural (and indeed urban) areas, and how to attract immigrant professionals to, and retain them in, rural areas.

In fact, if we wanted to single out one factor, receiving countries have often neglected the issue of the recognition of professional qualifications obtained abroad. Professional equivalencies can be difficult to obtain, and institutionalized barriers such as protectionism of professional associations tend to restrict access to licenses which allow professionals to practice. This has resulted in a waste of human resources and expertise, as well as professional deskilling among immigrants, particularly for those of non-European origin, with knock-on effects on their chances for social and professional integration. This situation is particularly deplorable when it occurs in geographical areas, such as rural communities, where there is a shortage of certain professional skills. It is clear that rural areas will not be able to retain highly skilled immigrants unless quality employment is available which allows immigrants to benefit from their educational level and competences, and to develop them further. It is thus an urgent requirement for all countries to strengthen and accelerate their recognition processes of qualifications, and to reduce the common, long delays during which immigrants can only access basic skilled employment. Any improvements here can in return have positive impacts on immigrants' integration processes, and their staying or leaving decisions. The gains of providing professional spaces for immigrants as their qualifications are recognised, and the integration of highly qualified immigrants in the labour market should therefore be important issues to consider especially in the context of rural immigration and rural development.

Research in both provinces, Quebec (Canada) and the Penzenskaya Province (Russia) has examined immigrant physicians' role in rural communities. In the latter region, doctors from Kyrgystan and Tajikistan were first cautiously and then kindly received by the locally established and mono-ethnic rural patients. This could reflect the desperate need for medical personnel, as well as the recognition of the valuable contributions made by immigrants. The focus on immigrants as a solution to shortages of General Practitioners in Quebec seems to support this idea to some extent. At least for those immigrants (and subsidy recipients) who stayed beyond their first contract, there had been reports of respect and social recognition by the community for the contribution they had made as both physicians and citizens. However, it is also clear that even where there had been a need for physicians, some communities were not able to welcome their new General Practitioners, and to engage with them socially and culturally. This led GPs to leave sooner than would have been the case had their community experiences been more positive. It can be concluded that an approach which sees immigrants from a merely instrumental perspective, i.e. first and foremost as required labour force, is likely to be insufficient if the goal is to attract and retain immigrants long-term. Even if immigrants' economic needs are met, many other factors will contribute to their general well-being, and will influence their staying or leaving decisions. These issues are pursued further below when the concept of integration and its wider context are considered.

Structural Factors Shaping Employment Opportunities: Beyond Segmented Labour Market Theory

Immigrants' different employment opportunities and experiences are a particular stark reminder of the fact that this group is, of course, far from homogeneous. Their opportunities are shaped by a wide range of factors, pertaining to the labour market but also to other structural and non-structural factors. This can demonstrate some limits of the segmented labour market theory and its explanation of immigrants' employment positions, which appears to neglect the effects of important influences beyond labour market processes. For example, it has been demonstrated in the chapter on Greece that differences in employment opportunities for immigrants can sometimes be linked to their legal status. Although Romania and Bulgaria joined the EU in January 2007, citizens of these countries are not legally able to gain employment in Greece. However, they still work seasonally, providing the cheap and unauthorised labour that keeps production costs low. Their earnings and living conditions are poor.

This illustrates that immigration controls can construct certain types of workers, and facilitate particular types of employment relations (Anderson et al. 2006). Even where immigrants have work permits, they may regard themselves as being 'tied' to an employer, and 'accept' any working conditions for fear of losing their employment and in some case their immigration status. Concrete examples include temporary migrant farm workers in Canada who must return to their countries of origin once their contracts end. This category of flexible and isolated workers has increased continuously and is exposed to rights violations and the arbitrary power of their employers. In rural areas, if immigrants were in principle free to change employers, there may be practical difficulties, such as a lack of alternative employment options. Hence, in reality, many immigrants may indeed be completely dependent on an employer even if immigration policies granted them flexibility.

We are reminded that geographical locations and their related working conditions and quality of life will also shape immigrants' experiences. The US chapter in particular demonstrated the importance of analysing the rural-urban dimension. While rural immigrants are more likely than their urban counterparts to be employed in the US, they are also more likely to be underemployed. Moreover, almost half of the immigrants living in rural areas have been found to live in poverty, suggesting that many rural immigrants are amongst the working poor whose earnings are insufficient for affording a decent living. This reality raises the question how immigrants can be attracted to rural areas and encouraged to stay on a long-term basis if decision makers and employers are not determined to work towards the provision of acceptable living conditions, and a decent quality of life for this group. The link to poverty is crucial here, as it helps us to understand one of the factors which clearly limits rural immigration and integration.[3] If immigrants and their families are not convinced that they can live well in rural areas with regard to all aspects of their lives – whether economic, cultural, social, and political – they will not want to stay. Their marginalization will encourage them to leave again. It is therefore necessary to move beyond the view of immigrants as a 'reserve army of labour' in rural areas for jobs which are not valued and poorly paid. In all countries, immigrants' living and working conditions need to be urgently improved if it is considered desirable that immigrants settle and contribute to the socio-economic development of rural areas in the long-term. The quality of life, the richness of the social and community life, the diversity of skills and services feature as crucial factors which attract immigrants, alongside economic factors which are linked especially to the local system of production (Lollier et al. 2005)

The extent to which labour markets are regulated is clearly another factor which determines immigrants' position in the labour market and which can account for national differences of immigrants' experiences. Neoliberal ideologies (including ideas that productive enterprises should be privatised and that welfare provisions should be minimised if not eliminated), which gained prominence in a great number of countries in the 1980s, have resulted in sharply widened inequalities and poorer living conditions for many people globally, as well as within countries. In terms of the labour market, neoliberal influence has allowed employment conditions to become increasingly polarised between stable and well-paid jobs

---

3   See in particular a document by the International Labour Office which well demonstrates the relationship between agriculture, rural livelihoods and poverty (ILO 2003). It defines four pillars of decent work: 1) fundamental rights for workers in agriculture; 2) employment and increases of incomes for women and men in agriculture: 3) social protection; 4) social dialogue.

and precarious and poorly remunerated work (Wallerstein 2008; Tremblay 1994; Rosenberg 1989; Lebaube 1988).

The mid-1990s saw a reversal of some of those developments, for example, with labour movements in general, and organisations of rural workers in particular, demanding government protectionist policies (Wallerstein 2008). However, many labour markets have remained poorly regulated, or, are characterised by, minimum standards which are not well enforced. Employers can therefore offer poor working conditions and wages to immigrants. This situation was addressed in Ireland following the large inflow of A8 immigrant workers. It was argued that if the rights of all workers were better protected, that is, the employment conditions for immigrant and Irish workers improved, this would also result in a decreased demand for immigrant labour. Hence, the number of labour inspectors were tripled under the 2006 Social Partnership Agreement. This point can be further supported by the fact that following EU enlargement in 2004, the UK and Ireland have experienced much higher levels of immigration than Sweden, although all three countries offered A8 immigrants unrestricted access to their labour markets. It has been suggested that this can partly be attributed to the highly regulated labour market in Sweden, where all employees' working conditions are protected by collective agreements, which are also effectively enforced. Hence, employers' demand has remained relatively low (Ruhs 2006).

While Greece has also a well regulated labour market, deficiencies have remained with the enforcement of labour laws, and the informal economy has thrived with the incorporation of illegal immigrants. The advantages employers may perceive with the employment of illegal immigrants (for example, avoiding social security payments, and ignoring health and safety requirements), combined with the structural importance and social acceptance of the informal economy suggest that this sector will remain relatively strong (Baldwin-Edwards 2002a). The Greek chapter commented on the contradictory effects of the continuous regularization programmes. On the one hand, they have created a more secure environment for immigrants. On the other hand, the continuous arrivals of new waves of immigrants have put pressure upon wage-levels in the formal and informal economy. The replacement of rural 'traditional/old immigrants' with 'newcomers' has often been linked with state/institutional and employers' attempts to restrict collective action and collective bargaining for higher wages and better working conditions, which were sought by those 'traditional/old immigrants'.

Even if the informal economy in Northern Europe and North America is not comparable to that found in Southern Europe, employers' motivations for the recruitment or immigrants are likely to be similar. Opportunities of accessing cheap labour can sometimes allow rural businesses to survive. In the long-term, this represents neither a basis on which immigrants can build their lives, nor can it help rural communities. As the Scottish chapter concluded, the continuation of businesses based on poorly paid, poorly skilled employment can lead to the 'development of underdevelopment' of the local economy. Immigrant labour can thus be regarded as supporting businesses and sectors which may otherwise be economically unviable. Trapped in jobs in the secondary labour market, immigrants are likely to leave when an opportunity presents itself elsewhere. Hence, rural development which produces 'quality jobs' becomes a precondition for the retention of immigrants and locally established people, especially youth, in rural areas.

In short, an important structural factor particularly relevant for the employment opportunities of immigrants comprises national immigration controls. This factor interplays with (generally national) labour market regulations and their (lack of) enforcement, as well as the particular local labour market conditions in which immigrants find themselves. Rural labour markets tend thereby to be associated with limited employment options especially in the context of globalization. These factors cannot only contribute to explaining immigrants' position in the labour market *vis-à-vis* national citizens, but they can also account for cross-national differences in immigrants' employment and wider welfare situations. Further research could usefully focus on these structural factors, their impact on rural immigrants, and their implications for endeavours to encourage a more balanced geographical distribution of immigrants.

Immigrants Posing Challenges to Rural Areas

The US and Russia chapters highlighted that communities do not exist in a vacuum, but will be affected by policy decisions at higher levels. So far, national level decision makers have rarely been attentive to the actual and potential impacts of immigration policies on localities. The contradiction has been referred to that immigration policies are designed and administered at national level, but the impacts of immigration are most intensely felt at regional and local level. Rural areas in particular can struggle with a rapid increase in the immigrant population that in urban areas may hardly be noticeable. Public services (such as housing and health care) which are often already under pressure can find themselves more burdened as the number of users rises, usually without the concomitant increase in resources. Social tensions associated with linguistic, religious, and other cultural differences are also often magnified in smaller communities, especially if they have a largely mono-ethnic history.

However, there could also be advantages for immigrants in rural areas. Effective inter-agency cooperation in small towns and rural areas may be facilitated by officials who know each other well, and work together. Integration opportunities arising through informal social networking and other channels (for example, faith-based communities and dynamic civil society actors) can promote integration, even if such support may be less structured than in urban areas. As the case study in North Cork, Ireland, has illustrated, while such support can be very important, it cannot replace mainstreamed statutory services and provisions, which recognise the fact that diverse communities have distinct needs. Moreover, in most cases, communities will need to be actively supported to become welcoming, and to offer informal support. Some Canadian initiatives may be of interest here. Different strategies of mobilization and inter-cultural familiarisation of the local community as well as participation and common planning with different governmental levels have been implemented, following measures which promoted regional and rural immigration in different provinces. The rationale has been that the true impact of immigration outside metropolitan areas must include dialogue and the active collaboration of the different governmental levels (federal, provincial, regional and municipal). Similarly, there needs to be the wish at local level to welcome and integrate the new residents. Several analysts have considered all these issues to be the *sine qua non* for the success of a more balanced regional and rural distribution of immigrants. The Canadian initiatives have been carefully developed according to original and flexible formula, which were adapted to the priorities and particularities of the receiving communities.

The Irish chapter reflected on challenges posed by recent immigration inflows, which will often be shared by other new settlement countries. Because of the organised and pre-approved nature of arrivals in the past and, importantly, the relatively limited numbers involved, it was possible for Irish planners to implement a managerial approach based on advance planning. Earlier immigrant groups had therefore a minimal impact on the service provisions of the host society. By contrast, Irish planners have been shown to be unprepared for the larger numbers who have been arriving in the last 10 years, and Ireland's immigration policies and practices have been overburdened. While individual targeted initiatives have been common, and indeed highly successful on occasion, there has been a lack of strategic planning, a shortfall in funding and insufficient reliable evidence upon which to base future approaches. The situation has been similar in Scotland. The large inflow of immigrants post-2004 was unexpected in its size, but also welcome, at least by policy makers and employers. Some activities have been undertaken to establish the needs of the new immigrants, as well as their social and economic impacts, with almost all local authorities and a number of development agencies having commissioned research on these topics. While efforts have tended to be *ad hoc* and have lacked co-ordination, many public bodies (and private organisations) have demonstrated their eagerness to support immigrants. The challenge of having to develop quickly an infrastructure to meet the new diverse needs will take some time to address.

The Scottish chapter touched briefly on the issue of racism and discrimination. With the arrival of EU Accession State immigrants, it has been claimed that some employers have given preference to migrants from Central and Eastern Europe, for example, as a replacement for Kurdish workers. Employers have argued that the more recent arrivals are more likely to 'fit in' communities. Similarly, it has been discussed in the Southern European context that despite a general acknowledgement of migrants' positive contribution by locally established people in rural areas, negative stereotypes have been maintained, and cultural differences often not accepted. This raises the question of the role and impact of differentiation and discrimination in small communities.

Analyst Pugh (2007) has observed complex interactions between local dynamics and communities mirroring the reactions and responses to minority groups of society at large. While rural life may present a greater potential for oppression since being different in the countryside implies an exposed situation, personal accounts show that responses to difference are not necessarily negative. Difference can in some cases be appreciated and be a source of local pride. However, the potential threat of racism always exists, and is more difficult to escape in rural than in urban areas. According to this author, more research is required to understand better the many dimensions of social location and difference, the latter including personal traits such as age, gender, occupation, as well as ethnicity, which will all shape individuals' relationships with other community members and groups. Returning to the Scottish and the Irish cases, the issue of whether minority ethnic groups who are visibly different from the majority are discriminated against in favour of immigrants from EU member states ought to be further explored. The discrimination of visible minorities in general seems a research topic worthwhile investigating in more depth in all countries.

Further studies on difference and discrimination in rural communities should also take account of the changed circumstances which have occurred in rural communities. This includes the contemporary transformation of the countryside, and the resulting new socio-demographic profile of rural communities in western countries (Luginbühl 2007; Leader magazine 2000; Kayser 1990). Rural societies, which for a long time remained homogeneous, mono-ethnic and centred on agricultural production, have become more diversified and complex in their economic activities and in their populations. The dominance of agricultural activities in rural areas is no more, and the countryside has become increasingly characterised by its multifunctionality[4] (Perrier-Cornet 2002). The new rural inhabitants, who have settled in rural areas, include immigrants, internal life-style migrants (who left major conurbations to enjoy a better quality of life), artists, different types of entrepreneurs and self-employed people who can work from a distance using new information technology.

The question is how to support diverse populations with different interests and values, which can divide them and lead to conflicts. One of the principal challenges consists of finding strategies which promote the social and cultural mix of these diverse populations, so that altogether (immigrants and non-immigrants, long established and new community member) they can construct the rural community of tomorrow: a dynamic, heterogeneous, welcoming and open society (Simard 2007). Clearly, one would expect such communities to successfully integrate immigrants (and other groups). We will now turn to consider the concept of integration drawing on the relevant discussions in the different national and sub-national contexts.

---

4   Multifunctional uses of the countryside are of productive, residential, recreational and protective nature (Perrier-Cornet 2002).

The Concept of Integration and its Wider Context

The Introduction referred to some of the problems associated with the concept of integration. These included the fact that it tends to be used in a vague and flexible manner, with different analysts focusing on various possible aspects of 'integration'. The economic dimension of integration tends thereby to be prioritised over other possible dimensions, such as social, political, cultural and legal. This section will look at the variable uses of the term in the chapters in this book, relating to different geographical, socio-economic, cultural and political contexts. Important aspects of integration are to be identified and analysed, with some consideration given to how the concept relates especially to rural areas. We do not consider this a complete account of the concept, but are aiming to tie together some of the chapters' findings relating to it, with a particular emphasis on a cross-national perspective. This should result in a discussion with some useful, new ideas on which future research can build.

What have we learnt from reviewing the experiences of different countries *vis-à-vis* rural immigrants' integration? A number of dimensions of integration processes and outcomes have been referred to in the different chapters. An understandable key concern apparent in all countries was that of economic and professional integration, which relates not only to immigrants' access to jobs, but to employment which is commensurate with immigrants' skills, experiences and qualifications. As with the well-established population, if immigrants (including both spouses, where relevant) do not have access to jobs related to their skills and to a source of adequate income, this economic hardship will also detrimentally affect, for example, their social, cultural and political participation.

If the successful retention of immigrants can be regarded as a likely indicator of some level of economic and professional integration, experiences of immigrant physicians in rural Quebec have highlighted the importance of good working conditions, including a reasonable workload and a positive team spirit amongst colleagues. It was found here that these immigrants' priorities regarding their professional choices were often dependent on the different phases of life. Immigrants' wishes and priorities for particular types of integration may then differ over time, in some cases similar to the situation of internal, 'life-style' migrants. Young families have often moved to rural areas because they prioritised a better quality of life (such as community neighbourliness and trust) over higher salaries and career progression (Mauthner et al. 2001).

Where professional integration is the primary goal, there are clear links with issues of education. The US chapter showed that with regard to educational attainment, immigrants in rural areas are at a distinctive disadvantage compared with their urban counterparts. Given that educational attainment will impact at least to some extent on labour market opportunities, it seems advisable to consider immigrants' economic and professional integration together with their educational integration. Accounts of immigrants' experiences in rural Cork demonstrated the importance of adult education, both in terms of language training (with lack of proficiency in English constituting an important barrier in the labour market), but also in acquiring further and higher educational qualifications. A number of structural factors were identified which impeded access to provisions, including oversubscribed and under-funded services. Access difficulties due to distance were also mentioned, which can be regarded as particularly relevant for immigrants in rural areas. In terms of compulsory education for children as set out in law, fewer problems were identified for immigrant children, with some language support having been provided.

In terms of immigrants' social integration, education is one of the key social provisions made available by the state (and usually to a lesser extent by private providers). Other state provisions which can affect immigrants' social integration tend to include housing and health care. The housing sector usually consists of predominantly private provision out sizing a relatively small level of state provision. The Irish chapter referred to immigrants' experiences in North Cork, who tended to live in privately rented accommodation. They were usually unable to compete for social housing with locally established people, and did not have the financial means to buy a home. While in general, findings suggested that the housing situation in North Cork was satisfactory, there existed some evidence of overcrowding in North Cork, and reference was made to findings of poor accommodation standards in Ireland.

Beyond the mere quality of accommodation, there are issues of spatial integration. The US chapter referred to research conducted during the 1990s, which found that there was decreasing integration between Hispanics and whites (measured at the sub-county level). So while Hispanics are diffusing to rural counties, they are clustering spatially within them. Interestingly, this can be interpreted in two ways. While such form of segregation may suggest a lack of inter-action with the majority ethnic group of the host society, at the same time, it may represent integration at ethnic community level, as these immigrants all share a common culture and a non-English language. It may also refer to structural factors of exclusion of the minority group, the rich and white suburbs being prohibitively expensive for many immigrants.

Other important aspects of integration have been referred to on the basis of immigrant physicians' experiences in Quebec. This is again provided that we view the successful retention of immigrants as one indicator of a level of integration. Social, cultural and community experiences were ranked highly by these immigrants, and seemed to influence their own and their families' staying or leaving decision. Perceptions, such as the welcome received by the host community, available opportunities of participating in community life, and recognition for contributions made by immigrants, are highly relevant here. By contrast, hostile or indifferent attitudes towards immigrants and their families manifested by other community members resulted in a lack of involvement in community life and meant that immigrants and their families did not feel a sense of belonging. They were likely to leave again. Missing socio-cultural and community engagement may be a response to unhelpful behaviour by other community members, but can conceivably also have structural causes (for example, racist inter-institutional arrangements and discriminatory interactions in the social and cultural sphere).

In order to promote the various types of integration identified here (economic and professional integration; social integration, including education, health care, housing, and related spatial integration; socio-cultural and community integration[5]), there are clearly different implications and priorities for distinct groups of immigrants, depending not least on their legal status, skills, qualifications, and their actual and potential position in the labour market. For example, let us consider undocumented immigrant workers for whom regularization and the acquisition of employment rights would be a step towards economic (and other forms of) integration. Their situation is obviously very different from that of immigrant health professionals in jobs which do not use their qualifications and skills, who are waiting for the recognition of their qualifications to move towards professional integration. Both situations also differ from basic skilled immigrants who may perceive themselves successfully integrated economically, but whose lack of skills in the language of the host society has impeded social integration.

The examples also highlight that integration may have aspects we may refer to as objective (i.e. tangible and measurable), and others we may consider to be more subjective (i.e. less tangible, and difficult to measure). Both are equally important. For example, we could reasonably conclude that qualification-employment discrepancies indicate immigrants' lack of economic and professional integration. There may be concrete data or information available to support conclusions – as demonstrated with the US chapter's references to research and census data. Such conclusions would be more difficult to draw for immigrants' socio-cultural and community integration, and general feelings of well-being. Here, immigrants' perceptions would be the key indicators. The qualitative approach chosen to investigate retention factors for immigrant physicians in Quebec underscores this point. Neglecting subjective views of employment and community life will compromise the aim of many rural communities to retain immigrants long-term.

More than this, immigrants' own views of integration priorities can help to re-evaluate the norms and interests associated with the receiving society's concept of integration, which is usually dominant. Rather than working towards the achievement of goals associated entirely with the behaviour of the majority, we could develop a more nuanced approach to integration which is also grounded in immigrants' ideas of what is worthwhile to be integrated in, and at what time in their life cycles. This might also help the receiving society to understand, accept and support immigrants' wishes and conduct.

---

5   Other dimensions of integration sometimes referred to, such as political, (IOM 2006), are clearly also important, but did not explicitly feature in the empirical findings of the different studies included in this book. Perhaps following some 'hierarchy of needs', they may be regarded by immigrants who are still in the process of getting established as issues to address at a later point.

At national level, the implications and priorities for the promotion of different types of integration will also differ, in part related to the dominant characteristics of their immigrants, and in part linked to important structural factors relevant for each country. The definition of 'integration' provided in the chapter on Southern Europe is instructive here. It referred to economic integration as 'the acquisition of access to the right to work with all the accompanying formal labour rights.' (Kasimis) This definition may partly have been shaped by a particular concern with the relatively large group of undocumented immigrants in Southern European countries, for whom the acquisition of rights and opportunities, which are comparable with the long established population, will be most difficult to achieve. There is a special rural dimension to this issue due to the high demand for immigrant workers in the labour-intensive and still very important agricultural sector in Southern Europe. In Greece in particular, the restructuring of agriculture has favoured labour intensive cultivations, and resulted in the continuous hiring of new, often undocumented, agricultural immigrant workers.

If legal integration is high on the agenda in Greece, in Scotland, the focus has recently been more on professional integration. The Scottish chapter highlighted the situation of well qualified immigrant workers from the A8 states in dead-end jobs in the secondary labour market, where their expertise and skills remain underutilized. Some attempts have been made by different agencies to address the situation and promote professional integration, driven by the main twin aims to fill jobs which require high levels of qualifications (mainly in urban areas), and to retain immigrants. In the Russian case, the focus has been on encouraging 'compatriots' to immigrate with the belief that due to a shared language, shared educational qualifications and similar cultural backgrounds, their integration would occur automatically. Hence, integration issues remained off the agenda.

Countries' integration priorities will differ also for political and ideological reasons, including citizenship conceptions. The most obvious example here seems to be immigrants' social integration in the sense of access to social services, and (briefly mentioned only in the Irish chapter) to cash benefits – a controversial area. The two extreme positions here are first, the exclusion of immigrants from access to citizen-based provisions, and second, immigrants' inclusion, on the basis of their internationalised human rights. While in many countries, welfare approaches towards immigrants will lie somewhere in-between these positions (possibly closely linked with their immigration regimes), we can assume a divide between the USA and other countries covered in this book. Certainly, the non-federal welfare system of the USA is very different from the well developed welfare systems of most EU countries and Canada, which we would expect to meet immigrants' needs to a greater extent (Baldwin-Edwards 2002b).

The notion of different integration priorities, which was discussed above, can also be extended to other sub-levels, which impact on integration, for example, individual and hosting community. For most of these levels, facilitating factors for and barriers to integration in a rural context have been identified in the different chapters. These included for individual immigrants the (lack of) interest in acquiring the language of the host country, and in inter-acting with other community members; for hosting communities, historically rooted views of groups of immigrants, and positive or negative approaches to cultural differences.

As a corollary, it has become clear that immigrants' integration processes are shaped by a range of complex and interactive factors. We have identified a number of dimensions of integration in rural areas, and have commented that a wide range of factors will determine immigrants' and host societies' integration priorities. A case was made that a concept of integration should take into account immigrants' views on their own integration priorities at different times in their lives. These considerations may indicate that one of the theoretical problems with the concept of integration –its vagueness and flexibility- could also be its strength in practice. Insights gained through the different national and sub-national studies have demonstrated that concepts of integration and related policies and aims are context dependent: they will in part reflect different perceived priorities at various geographical and political levels, as well as the main characteristics of the immigrant population. Integration priorities may therefore range widely, and may in part be politically or ideologically driven. In practice, this will result in different agendas for different countries, regions or communities.

It is clear that integration process will be complex and long, and may often only fully be realised with the second (or even third) generation. New research could usefully explore the experiences over time of rural immigrant youth who migrated with their parents. The process of integration refers then to several generations. Other new areas for research would focus on particular sub-categories of .immigrants (for example, economic migrants, immigrant families, and refugees) and examine if and how those categories affect integration processes in rural communities. Does the integration process of 'visible minorities' differ from immigrants who are not so easily discernable as such? Comparative studies could also consider immigrants' integration in rural compared to small, medium or large urban contexts, or in remote compared to accessible rural areas.

In addition, it seems that integration debates need to open up and consider wider inequality issues. The Introduction referred to the fact that integration is frequently seen as a two-way process between the individual immigrant and receiving communities, requiring changes from both. Reflecting on the experiences of the different countries, this appears a limited, and in some ways unfair, view of requirements. We have noted that immigrants and communities operate in a wider context and within structural constraints. These shape immigrants' capacity to embrace a new environment and established community members' ability to interact positively with new members. This wider context includes globalisation and also a range of policies (such as immigration, social, and economic policies) developed at levels well above community level. Such policies are often insensitive to the needs and abilities of communities, and indeed immigrants.

Concerning rural areas, we must recognise that these are, of course, heterogeneous. Differences include their economic performance, with accessible rural areas usually performing better than remote places. However, despite these differences, a particular structural factor impacting on integration processes which has been highlighted in several chapters is the predominant low skills – low pay labour market. It tends to neither adequately provide for the employment needs of locally established people, nor for immigrants, with the latter often being used as a reserve army of labour filling jobs locally considered undesirable. In terms of economic integration alone, the prevalence of jobs in the secondary labour market presents a significant barrier. The prevalent poor working conditions in the agricultural sector merit particular attention here.

Finally, there is obviously a place for an extensive exchange on the questions of what immigrants' integration means and should mean, how it can be supported, and what factors may undermine it, and how to address these. However, it is important to recognise that integration would most usefully be discussed in a context which recognises wider inequalities and aims to support all vulnerable groups in a society. Here, we can recognise the general relevance of the conclusions drawn in the Scottish chapter: by addressing first of all a particular challenge, for example unemployment, and then second, considering the different implications for different social groups, we would adopt an equitable and more comprehensive approach.

The Future

The global financial crisis, which began in September 2008, provides a new prism through which to reconsider the trends identified in the case studies within this book. The crisis has challenged existing budgetary assumptions, not least tax revenues, employment and economic growth – constraining room to manoeuvre and causing all governments to reconsider and reprioritise public and social policy initiatives, particularly those that involve heavy spending.

What will be then the current impact of the crisis on rural immigration, and what might the longer term consequences be? In all countries, the financial crisis has resulted in falls in employment, and reduced job opportunities for immigrants. This will have different implications for different groups of immigrants. Where immigrants qualify for welfare state benefits (such as the EU accession state members to Ireland and Scotland), they may decide to stay and wait for an upturn in the economy. It is likely that many immigrants will return, mainly those who have skills now needed in certain industries in their countries of origin. This includes industries in Central and Eastern Europe which are supported by public funding, such as EU regional funds, and are therefore less affected by the financial crisis. It remains to be seen if workers' mobility in the EU gains in vigour and flexibility resembling North America, where workers move between states in search for better jobs.

While it is clear that some immigrants will be in difficult socio-economic situations in their host country, we must be mindful that this is also the case for those locally established people who tend to be most vulnerable in the labour market. Many basic skilled and poorly educated citizens of immigrants' host countries may now see themselves competing for jobs with much better qualified, young and flexible immigrant workers. Such a situation could contribute to fuelling anti-immigrant sentiments. This reinforces the point raised above that any policy initiatives which are to promote employment opportunities must cater for all social groups, with the focus being on addressing inequality (Phillips 2008). Additional conditions need to be in place to prevent anti-immigrant attitudes amongst the wider public. This includes politicians taking seriously the responsibility to avoid situations where immigration issues become politicised for perceived short term political gains. Journalists, too, have a role to play here by covering immigration issues fairly. The task of the research community is to continue documenting immigrants' experiences and situations in cities as well in rural areas to challenge any public misperceptions on immigration.

Concerning rural areas in particular, relevant stakeholders will have to urgently consider the future development of rural economies, so that there will be decent employment prospects for immigrants and locally established people alike. This means recognising the heterogeneity of rural regions, and developing flexible policies and programmes which are appropriate for the different needs and opportunities of rural places. Successful, integrated rural development policies will be a crucial precondition for immigrants' economic, professional, social and cultural integration. They will also help established community members to feel that they can and should be welcoming to new members on whom the sustainability of many communities may well depend in the years to come.

References

Anderson, B., Ruhs, M., Rogaly, B., and Spencer, S. (2006), *Fair enough? Central and East European migrants in low-wage employment in the UK* (COMPAS/ Sussex Centre for Migration Research: University of Oxford/University of Sussex).

Baldwin-Edwards, M. (2002a), 'Southern European Labour Markets and Immigration: A structural and Functional Analysis', *Mediterranean Migration Observatory* [Working Paper No. 5].

Baldwin-Edwards, M. (2002b), 'Immigration and the Welfare State: A European Challenge to US Mythology', *Mediterranean Migration Observatory* [Working Paper No. 4].

International Labour Office (ILO). (2003), *Decent work in agriculture*, Background paper, International Workers' Symposium on Decent Work in Agriculture, International Labour Organization, Bureau for Workers' Activities, Geneva, September. 15–18.

IOM. (2006), *IOM Policy Brief. Integration in Today's World.* IOM: Geneva. <http://www.iom.ch/jahia/webdav/site/myjahiasite/shared/shared/mainsite/

policy_and_research/policy_documents/policy_brief_1.pdf>,   accessed   9
   February 2009.
Jentsch, B. and MacDonald, B. (2007), *Future Migration Flows from the European
   Union Accession States to Scotland and Ireland: Economic, Demographic and
   Social Factors.* Paper presented at the conference 'Demography and Economic
   Change: The Cases of Ireland and Scotland', Glasgow, 19–20 September
   2007.
Kayser, B. (1990), *La renaissance rurale. Sociologie des campagnes du monde
   occidental* (Paris: Armand Colin), 316.
Leader magazine (2000), 'The (Re)population of Rural Areas', *European
   Observatory*, No. 22, Spring.
Lebaube, Alain (1988), *L'emploi en miettes*, Hachette, 258 p. (coll. 'Mutations').
Lollier J-C., Prigent L., Thouément H (dir) (2005), *Les nouveaux facteurs
   d'attractivité dans le jeu de la mondialisation* (Presses Universitaires de
   Rennes).
Luginbühl, Y. (dir.) (2007), *Nouvelles urbanités, nouvelles ruralités en Europe*
   (Bruxelles: P.I.E. Peter Lang).
Mauthner, N., McKee, L. and Strell, M. (2001), *Work and Family Life in Rural
   Communities* (York: Joseph Rowntree Foundation).
Perrier-Cornet, P. (dir.) (2002), *Repenser les campagnes* (Éditions de l'Aube et
   Datar).
Phillips, T. (2008), Speech at the Confederation of British Industry (CBI) Migration
   Summit, London, 28 October 2008. <http://www.equalityhumanrights.com/
   en/newsandcomment/speeches/Pages/CBIMigrationSummit.aspx> accessed
   21 January 2009.
Pugh, R. (2007), *New Migrants and Minorities: Understanding Difference and
   Discrimination in Rural Areas.* Paper distributed at the conference 'International
   Migration and Rural Areas: Global Perspectives', 11–12 October 2007, Isle of
   Skye, Scotland.
Rosenberg, S. (1989), 'De la segmentation à la flexibilité', *Travail et société* 14:4,
   387–438.
Ruhs, M. (2006), 'Greasing the wheels of the flexible labour market: East European
   labour immigration in the UK', (COMPAS: Oxford), Working Paper 06-38.
Simard, M. (2007), 'Nouvelles populations rurales et conflits au Québec: regards
   croisés avec la France et le Royaume-Uni', *Géographie, Économie, Société*
   numéro spécial sur Conflits d'usages et dynamiques spatiales: les antagonismes
   dans l'occupation des espaces périurbains et ruraux (dir. T.Kirat et A.Torre,
   CNRS et INRA), 9:2, 18–213.
Tremblay, D. (1994), 'Chômage, flexibilité et précarité d'emploi: aspects sociaux',
   *Traité des problèmes sociaux, Québec, Institut Québécois de Recherche sur la
   Culture*, 623–52.
Wallerstein, I. (2008), 'The Demise of Neoliberal Globalization', *Yale Global
   Online*, <http://yaleglobal.yale.edu/display.article?id=10299>, accessed 20
   January 2009.

Index